WITHDRAWN

Resolution Family Law Handbook

SECOND EDITION

The College of Law
of England and Wales

LIBRARY SERVICES

The College of Law, 14 Store Street, Bloomsbury, London WC1E 7DE
Telephone: 01483 216387   E-mail: bloomsbury-library@lawcol.co.uk

Birmingham • Chester • Guildford • London • Manchester • York

Related titles from Law Society Publishing:

Ancillary Relief
Andrew Newbury, Shona Alexander and Ann Corrigan

Child Law Handbook
Liz Goldthorpe with Pat Monro

Civil Partnership: Law and Practice
Andrea Woelke

Domestic Abuse (forthcoming)
Jane Wilson

Health and Social Care Handbook
Caroline Bielanska with Fiona Scolding

Mental Capacity (2nd edn)
Nicola Greaney, Fenella Morris, Beverley Taylor

Pensions and Family Breakdown (2nd edn)
David Davidson

Resolution Family Disputes Handbook (forthcoming)
General Editor: Andrew Greensmith

Titles from Law Society Publishing can be ordered from all good bookshops or direct (telephone 0870 850 1422, email **lawsociety@prolog.uk.com** or visit our online shop at **www.lawsociety.org.uk/bookshop**).

RESOLUTION FAMILY LAW HANDBOOK

SECOND EDITION

General Editor: Andrew Greensmith

The Law Society

ISBN–13: 978-1-85328-893-7

First edition published in 2007

This second edition published in 2010 by the Law Society
113 Chancery Lane, London WC2A 1PL

Typeset by IDSUK (DataConnection) Ltd
Printed by TJ International Ltd, Padstow, Cornwall

FSC

Mixed Sources

Product group from well-managed
forests and other controlled sources

Cert no. SGS-COC-2482
www.fsc.org
© 1996 Forest Stewardship Council

The paper used for the text pages of this book is FSC certified. FSC (the Forest Stewardship Council) is an international network to promote responsible management of the world's forests.

Contents

Foreword to the first edition

Resolution, in its previous incarnation the Solicitors Family Law Association, has a distinguished history. It has achieved many things of which it must be proud, but for me its most significant contribution has been to change the attitude, creed and working practice of its members.

Once, long ago, it was acceptable for specialists to be in it for themselves or in it to gladiate for the passing client and to hell with the consequences. Today Resolution encourages its members to be specialist professionals who, whilst dedicated to serve the passing client, put high the interests of society as a whole. Essential qualities in a Resolution member are, therefore, expertise, the ability to learn from experience, integrity, insight and responsibility. A case well settled is always a greater achievement than a case well fought.

The *Resolution Family Law Handbook* is another demonstration of the leadership and commitment of the association. It will, I am sure, provide a valuable tool, especially for the young entry, not least because it is permeated by the values for which Resolution stands.

The Right Honourable Lord Justice Thorpe
Royal Courts of Justice
14 February 2007

Preface

This book is a perfect example of collaboration between lawyers, for the common good. All the authors of this book have given their time to pass on their specialist knowledge of family law in a way that will promote good practice.

I hope that the second edition of this book will be regarded as continuing to assist those new to family law and those requiring a refresher in particular areas to approach the subject area in a way that is consistent with the Resolution Code of Practice.

On behalf of Resolution, I would like to thank all those who have been engaged in the production of this book. The professional colleagues and families of the authors deserve special appreciation for allowing the authors to give a considerable amount of time to the writing process.

Especially, I would like to thank Janet Noble for her tireless efforts in helping to put the team together and then working closely with each of the authors, encouraging each of us to meet deadlines. At times this must have been akin to herding cats but, as I trust the reader will agree, a very worthwhile project.

Finally, I would like to express my respect to all members of Resolution who have the vision constantly to develop and improve standards in family law and who make the production of this book possible and worthwhile.

Andrew Greensmith
February 2010

About the editor and contributors

GENERAL EDITOR

Andrew Greensmith was admitted as a solicitor in 1986, and after a period in general litigation practice, he has specialised in family law for the past 15 years. Andrew is head of family law at Dickson Haslam in Preston where he is committed to adopting a non-confrontational approach to family law which includes promoting alternative dispute resolution (ADR) as an integral part of his practice. He has developed a busy collaborative law practice and is a member of the Chartered Institute of Arbitrators. He sits as a deputy district judge on the Northern Circuit.

Andrew was elected national chair of Resolution in 2006 and spent his year in office facing the challenges of the reform of the legal aid system, Child Support Agency (CSA) and helping position the association as a major representative body in the context of a changing legal landscape following the Clementi review.

Having always taken an interest in his profession, Andrew has sat on the Council Membership Committee of the Law Society and is a member of the Consumer Panel of the regulatory board of the Bar Council.

CONTRIBUTORS

Noel Arnold is a solicitor at Philcox Gray & Co in London. He read law at King's College London, and worked at a London law centre before joining a leading rights-based firm in London as a trainee solicitor. Noel specialises in private and public law Children Act cases and has a particular interest in local authority duties and obligations to children and the public law aspects of children law.

Noel has written for the Law Society previously and has published several articles on the law relating to children. He is a member of the Law Society's children law sub-committee and writes the children law update for the *Solicitor's Journal*. Noel has provided training on his area of expertise and was seconded to the Ministry of Justice's Care Proceedings Programme in 2008.

Charlotte Bradley is a partner at Kingsley Napley Solicitors and is highly recommended in the legal directories. She specialises in all aspects of family law with a particular interest in cases involving foreign jurisdictions, both the financial and children aspects. As such, she chaired Resolution's international committee 2003–06. Charlotte is a mediator and collaborative family lawyer, having been one of the founding members of the collaborative family law model in the UK. Charlotte writes regular articles and other publications.

Sue Brookes read law at St John's College, Oxford. She is a senior solicitor in the Manchester office of Mills & Reeve.

Sue has specialised in family law since 2004. Her particular interest is high value ancillary relief cases involving businesses and trusts. She is a member of Resolution and a committee member for the Manchester Area Association of Women Solicitors.

Emma Collins is a partner at Mace & Jones where she heads the Knutsford family team. Recognised in *Legal 500*, Emma specialises in all aspects of family law, in particular high value/complex financial issues for both married and unmarried couples, with a particular interest in cohabitation law and Inheritance Act claims.

She is a Resolution accredited family law specialist (Advance Financial Provision II and Cohabitation) and is trained and active as a collaborative lawyer. Emma is a member and former chair of the Resolution publications committee (responsible for the production of various precedent books including *Consent Order Precedents*). She is also a member of the Resolution cohabitation working party and treasurer of the Manchester region committee.

Emma is a contributor to *Kelly's Draftsman*.

Punam Denley is a solicitor, mediator, collaborative lawyer and a partner at International Family Law Group (iFLG). She specialises in all aspects of family law, especially those with international financial and/or children issues arising from the breakdown of a relationship. Punam is an elected member of Resolution's London region committee. Her past memberships include legal aid, procedure, children and child support committees. She is a member of Lawyers for Liberty, the International Academy of Collaborative Professionals and the European Women Lawyers Association.

Punam writes and lectures regularly on family law matters, and is author of a book on divorce and separation published by Lawpack (2010).

Emma Harte has been a specialist family law practitioner and member of Resolution since qualification in 1993. She became a partner at Alexiou Fisher Philipps in 2001.

She is a fellow of the International Academy of Matrimonial Lawyers (IAML), a Resolution accredited mediator and trained collaborative lawyer, and is chair of Resolution's alternative dispute resolution committee and a member of the International Academy of Collaborative Professionals (IACP).

Emma is recommended in Chambers Directory as a leading specialist family lawyer and recognised as a 'senior figure in the ADR community'. The *Legal 500* also recognises her focus on mediation and collaborative law.

She is committed to trying to resolve family disputes in a pragmatic and constructive way, and as well as assisting married couples, she also helps to resolve cohabitation disputes and civil partnership disputes. Many of her cases involve an international element and complex financial issues. A number of her cases have been reported.

Jacqui Jackson is Director of Standards at Resolution and a deputy district judge on the Midland circuit. She has written and lectured extensively on cohabitation and co-wrote *Living Together Precedents* (Sweet & Maxwell), *You, Your Partner and the Law* (Century) and wrote *Splitting Up Precedents* (Sweet & Maxwell). She also contributed to Resolution's *Precedents for Cohabitation Agreements*.

As Director of Standards Jacqui is responsible for the Resolution specialist accreditation scheme, she supports the standards committee in safeguarding and promoting the Code of Practice and guides to good practice, she deals with complaints against members of Resolution and works on policy and responses to consultation papers. Prior to joining Resolution she worked as a family law solicitor in private practice for 20 years.

Stephen Lawson was admitted as a solicitor in 1984 and now heads the civil litigation department at Forshaws Davies Ridgway.

Stephen has substantial experience in high value personal injury claims, fatal accident claims, inheritance disputes, and professional negligence cases. Stephen has also gained a national reputation for his work with the CSA/Child Maintenance and Enforcement Commission (CMEC) claims.

Stephen is national secretary of the Association of Personal Injury Lawyers (APIL) and sits on the Resolution national committee for CSA and maintenance.

Vicky Ling is an independent management consultant. She is a founding member of the Law Consultancy Network, comprising some of the UK's most highly regarded law firm management consultants.

Vicky has worked in the voluntary sector, for local government and the Legal Aid Board. She has specialised in legal practice for over 15 years and has worked with over 200 firms in private practice. She has worked with Resolution for five years, as a trainer and author of its *Legal Aid e-news*. She is co-author (with Simon Pugh) of *Making Legal Aid Work*, which was published by Legal Action Group in 2009.

Andrew Newbury is a partner with Pannone LLP, Manchester. He contributes to various family law textbooks and lectures frequently on family law matters. Andrew appears regularly on national television, radio and in the press commenting upon topical family law issues. He is also trained as a collaborative lawyer.

Andrew is a fellow of the International Academy of Matrimonial Lawyers. He sits on the Resolution training committee and for many years chaired the committee as well as being chair of Resolution Manchester region.

Andrew specialises in ancillary relief work and particularly those cases which involve family businesses, trusts or an international element. He is rated as a leader in his field by Chambers & Partners.

James Pirrie is a partner at London-based Family Law in Partnership (FLiP).

James has long been an elected member of Resolution's national, CSA and ADR committees, having also been involved in its legal aid, pensions and procedure committees and is a member of the US-led National Child Support Enforcement Association.

He was instrumental in the arrival of collaborative practice in Europe during 2003 and in 2005 was voted on to the board of the International Academy of Collaborative Professionals. He is an accredited mediator, a Resolution accredited specialist and sets the 'Finance for Children' paper. He contributes to Resolution's *Precedents for Consent Orders* and contributed to Sweet & Maxwell's *Cohabitation: Law and Precedents* publications. He co-wrote Resolution's *Claims under Schedule 1 to the Children Act 1989* and has contributed to its forthcoming *Emergencies Handbook and the Resolution Family Disputes Handbook* (Law Society Publishing). He has the Financial Planning Certificate and G10 qualifications of the Chartered Insurance Institute.

Nigel Shepherd is a partner in Mills & Reeve LLP and heads the family law team at the firm's Manchester office. He is a former national chair of Resolution and is a current member of Resolution's national and executive committees and its media team. He is a former chair of Resolution's national mediation committee and of Resolution in the north west. He is Resolution's lead spokesman on divorce reform.

Nigel is a fellow of the International Academy of Matrimonial Lawyers. He lectures for both Resolution and commercial organisations. He was one of the Judicial Studies Board team responsible for training the judiciary on the issue of pension sharing on divorce. Nigel specialises in the more complex financial aspects of relationship breakdown, but his reputation extends to dealing sensitively with private Children Act work.

Nigel is a regular contributor to the print and broadcast media.

Lucy Thomas is a senior solicitor at Kingsley Napley. She qualified in Manchester in 1999 before moving to London in 2004. Lucy specialises in all aspects of family law including complex financial matters arising from divorce, cohabitation disputes and all issues relating to children. Lucy is also a Resolution trained mediator, practising sole and co-mediation.

Jane Wilson is senior partner at Hall Smith Whittingham LLP of Crewe and Nantwich. She qualified as a solicitor in 1980 and is a higher court advocate (Civil Proceedings) and a Resolution accredited specialist (Domestic Abuse and Advocacy – Children (Private Law)). She is chair of the Resolution domestic abuse committee and a member of the Cheshire Domestic Abuse Partnership Strategic Management Group.

Andrea Woelke is principal of Alternative Family Law. He is a Resolution accredited specialist in family law with particular expertise in international family law, child abduction and cohabitation. He is also a mediator and collaborative family lawyer.

Andrea regularly writes and lectures on family law in England as well as in Germany. He is an authority on civil partnership and the author of *Civil Partnership* (Law Society Publishing), one of the leading textbooks on this subject. He is also a co-author of *Model Letters for Family Lawyers* (Jordans) and *International Aspects of Family Law* (Resolution) and has contributed to many other publications.

Andrea is a member and past chairman of the Resolution international committee, a member of the German Bar Association and chair of the Lesbian and Gay Lawyers Association (LAGLA). Andrea is fluent in German and speaks several other languages. Many of his cases have a German or other international aspect.

David Woodward is a solicitor and partner of TLT Solicitors in Bristol and head of the private business group. He was admitted in 1975 and has been in practice as a specialist family lawyer since 1981.

He is noted as a 'leader in his field' in *Chambers UK* and *Legal 500* with a specialism in high value financial relief cases. He is an accredited specialist and accreditation examiner. David is the former chair of Bristol Resolution, secretary of Resolution, chair of the Resolution standards committee and a member of the Law Society's family law committee.

He trained as a mediator in 1991 and is chair of Bristol Family Mediators Association and contributed to *Family Mediation: Past, Present and Future*.

David is to be found in Debrett's (2009) *People of Today*.

Table of cases

Table of statutes

Table of statutory instruments

Table of European legislation

Abbreviations

ACTAPS	Association of Contentious Trust and Probate Specialists
ADR	alternative dispute resolution
CA 1989	Children Act 1989
CAFCASS	Children and Family Court Advisory Support Service
CLS	Community Legal Service
CMC	case management conference
CMEC	Child Maintenance and Enforcement Commission
CAC	contact activity conditions
CAD	contact activity direction
CPA 2004	Civil Partnership Act 2004
CPC	child protection conference
CPP	child protection plan
CPR 1998	Civil Procedure Rules 1998
CPRC	child protection review conference
CSA	Child Support Agency
DEO	deduction from earnings order
EPO	emergency protection order
FDR	financial dispute resolution
FLA 1996	Family Law Act 1996
FPR 1991	Family Proceedings Rules 1991
HFEA 2008	Human Fertilisation and Embryology Act 2008
IACP	International Academy of Collaborative Practitioners
IPFDA 1975	Inheritance (Provision for Family and Dependants) Act 1975
LLP	limited liability partnership
KPI	key performance indicator
LSC	Legal Services Commission
MCA 1973	Matrimonial Causes Act 1973
NRP	non-resident parent
PHA 1997	Protection from Harassment Act 1997
PWC	parent with care
SGO	special guardianship order
SQM	Specialist Quality Mark
TLATA 1996	Trusts of Land and Appointment of Trustees Act 1996

CHAPTER 1

Introduction

Andrew Greensmith

1.1 THE CHALLENGE OF FAMILY LAW

It is not so long ago that the divorce caseload of a firm was given to the more junior (often female) members of staff. Family law was traditionally regarded as a part of the litigation function of solicitors and divorce practitioners were usually considered to be a part of the litigation departments of firms. For example, I recently saw an organisational chart for a firm of solicitors which had the family law partner answerable to the litigation partner. The firm was divided into contentious and non-contentious departments and family law fell into the contentious side.

Fortunately this out-moded approach to family law has, in the main, gone and family lawyers see themselves as private client solicitors offering a particular service dealing with issues unique to their chosen area of practice.

Family law is perhaps the most fascinating area of law but it is arguable that it is also the most difficult discipline of all in which to choose to practise. Why is this?

The first answer is the most obvious. Family lawyers act for individuals at the times when they are at their most vulnerable: the young child; the abused spouse; spouses who have dedicated their entire adult lives to bringing up a family only to find themselves rejected by their partner in whom they have placed a lifetime of trust; spouses who have built up a personal financial empire only to face the prospect of having to start all over again. Dealing with the emotional spectrum of these challenges effectively and professionally takes a special type of practitioner.

The second answer is less obvious. In a legal world of increasing technicality, family lawyers have had to find a way of practising in a highly uncertain area – indeed, it is arguable that family lawyers have developed their own jurisprudence. Family lawyers have to work with nebulous concepts. They advise on statutes which are based on concepts such as 'fairness' with no definitive answer as to what that means. They have to deal with presumptions, such as 'the best interests of the child' where there are often competing and compelling views as to what a particular child's best interests are.

The courts have a fundamental role to play in both the interpretation and the development (some would say the creation) of family law. It is the role of the courts to interpret outdated statutes. Judges are faced with the task of having to reflect what they believe a modern society needs. In endeavouring to achieve this, judges often 'impute' words and phrases into the statutes they are trying to adapt.

A layman reading the judgment in *Miller* v. *Miller* and *McFarlane* v. *McFarlane* [2006] UKHL 24 would be forgiven for thinking that the words 'acquest', 'compensation' and 'sharing' feature in s.25 of the Matrimonial Causes Act 1973 (MCA 1973), which of course they do not. But that does not make these words irrelevant. It is just an example of the courts trying to make up for the inadequacy of a statute which was enacted over 30 years ago so that it can be applied to a world where social values have radically changed.

1.2 THE ROLE OF THE FAMILY LAWYER

The most important function of the family lawyer is to manage the client's expectations. In order to do this effectively, it is insufficient for the family lawyer to have an understanding of where the law is currently. Instead, it is absolutely essential that he or she has a 'sense' or 'feeling' of where the law is 'going'.

This applies as much in the management of expectations in financial matters as it does in matters relating to children. For example, when a client says he or she wants to achieve joint residence of a child, the lawyer has to be aware of the current thinking on joint residence and the 'way it is going', bearing in mind that if an application were to be issued, it might take the best part of 12 months to reach a final hearing and by then there might have been several reported cases on the very point on which the lawyer was expected to advise a year previously.

In financial matters, lawyers have to anticipate how nebulous concepts such as 'needs' will be interpreted in the unfortunate event that an application ever reaches trial. And in addition to trying to second guess the judges and managing the process, the family lawyer has to deal with the extreme and often volatile emotions caused by the breakdown of a relationship and even the potential loss of contact with a child.

1.3 RESOLUTION

Each contributor to this book is a member of Resolution. Resolution was founded as the Solicitors Family Law Association (SFLA) in 1982 by John Cornwell, a solicitor practising in London who had a vision that family law was more than simply litigation. John, and a handful of like-minded lawyers, recognised that the traditional litigation model of family law practice was failing those who needed to resort to the law to resolve their disputes. They understood that simply battling issues out was not in the best interests of their clients. Whilst some lawyers may have felt comfortable applying a wholly adversarial approach to family law, this meant that their clients, and more often than not their clients' children, were suffering as a result. The Solicitors Family Law Association was formed and it continued to grow under that guise for 20 years.

In recognition that the association's membership no longer comprised exclusively solicitors and in an attempt to dispel the public's perception of the association as a private members' club, the association was renamed 'Resolution' in 2005.

Resolution's 5,000 members are family lawyers committed to the non-adversarial resolution of family disputes. The majority of members are solicitors, although this has recently been extended to include other practitioners in the family law arena. Resolution members abide by a Code of Practice which emphasises a constructive approach to family problems and encourages solutions that take into account the needs of the whole family, and the best interests of any children, in particular (see **Appendix 1**).

Resolution as an organisation is committed to developing and promoting best standards in the practice of family law among both its members and family lawyers in general. Resolution explores and promotes other means of resolving family disputes, such as mediation and collaborative law, so that couples can negotiate solutions without using the courts. Many Resolution members also practise as mediators and collaborative lawyers and many are accredited by the organisation as specialists in particular aspects of family law, such as contact cases or financial aspects of separation.

Resolution publishes various guides to improve standards of practice and provides training in law and in the skills and understanding that family lawyers need to help their clients face the most difficult of times. The association also campaigns for better laws and better support and facilities for families and children undergoing family change.

As Resolution has developed, its standards and approach have become the norm in the practice of family law rather than the exception. The ethos of the association has provided the catalyst of change which has stimulated significant and permanent progress. The Resolution Code of Practice has been incorporated into best practice and has been included in the *Family Law Protocol*, 2nd edn (Law Society, 2006) and as such is a mandatory practice standard.

1.4 BEST PRACTICE THROUGH ALTERNATIVE DISPUTE RESOLUTION

Never has dispute resolution (often referred to as alternative dispute resolution, or ADR), which has been pioneered by members of Resolution, been more relevant than it is at present. While the courts do their best to tell us

3

what we need, more and more clients want to order their future by achieving what they want. It is the lawyer's job to assist clients to achieve their objectives while being in a position to manage their expectations. The court process is increasingly being seen as the default provision.

This is a tall order, especially for the recently qualified, or the practitioner from another field who has started to practise family law.

It is the family lawyer's duty to be familiar with the various methods of resolving family disputes. Mediation, collaborative law and arbitration offer modern, relevant and highly effective ways of achieving our overall aim of representing our clients to the best of our ability. The methods of ADR are set out in **Chapter 13** and the principles outlined there will apply across the entire family law spectrum.

This development in family law is the most significant improvement in the discipline over the last 10 years. Whilst these 'alternative' methods of dispute resolution are still labelled as such, in practice they are rapidly becoming the usual method of approaching family law problems and are regarded by many as the 'primary' method of resolving a dispute, rather than an alternative method.

1.5 SKILLS NEEDED BY FAMILY LAWYERS

What are the qualities that the modern family lawyer needs? To a great extent family lawyers need the same qualities as practitioners in other fields. They must have both a sound legal knowledge and the skills to be able to explain the law to others, and it is these additional skills which set family lawyers apart and which add to the notion that family law has developed into a highly specialised field of practice.

For many years, Resolution has recognised that family lawyers need very specific skills. The association has a section which concentrates on educating its membership in personal and interpersonal skills. The importance of developing these for the family lawyer cannot be overstated.

Family lawyers deal with the law at times when their clients are at their most vulnerable. People's lives are suddenly, often without warning, thrown into turmoil. It might be that a father of three children comes home to find a note on the kitchen table that his wife of 15 years' standing has left him and their children; or a mother might be met at the door on her return from a night out by a social worker telling her that her two children have been taken into the care of the local authority because of allegations of sexual assault being made against her husband, the children's father.

If the family solicitor is to provide a full service to these people he or she has to deal with the client's emotions while remaining objective in order to advise clearly and to represent effectively.

People's personalities and emotions are what set them apart from each other. Social mores encourage relationships to be formalised in the context of marriage yet individuals enter marriage often not realising that they are creating legal relations with each other. The House of Lords has stated that couples who marry form a legal 'partnership of equals' (see Baroness Hale in *Miller* v. *Miller* and *McFarlane* v. *McFarlane* [2006] UKHL 24).

It is not surprising, therefore, that when marriages break down, it is inevitable that lawyers become involved. These lawyers, and particularly solicitors, have to recognise that clients who at first welcome their involvement may later start to resent it as the lawyers become the focus of the clients' confused emotions.

During long and complex family proceedings, clients' personalities can change. These changes can sometimes be so significant that they might even develop personality disorders. They can become emotionally attached to their lawyer, transferring their emotional attachment from their partner to the lawyer. Typically, this might happen where the client is leaving a relationship which has been fraught by a high level of interpersonal conflict. If this transfer is not recognised and effectively managed by the solicitor, it could lead to the development of an inappropriate relationship between solicitor and client. The client will be unable to distinguish between the lawyer as an objective professional adviser and the lawyer as a friend, and this unhealthy progression to attachment will militate against the client's best interests.

Resolution has published an excellent DVD to assist solicitors in recognising and dealing with these issues and this should, in my view, be compulsory viewing for all family lawyers (to contact Resolution see **Appendix 2**).

1.6 STRUCTURE OF THE BOOK

This book concentrates on the 'nuts and bolts' of family law. It is intended to give an overview to the practitioner who is new to the subject, or who needs a refresher, but it does not purport to present an in-depth analysis of the subjects it covers. It is written by eminent and experienced practitioners who want to share with the readers their experiences of putting family law into practice. In compiling this book, those involved have endeavoured to explain the essential topics and the tools which form the backbone of the discipline of family law.

It is hoped that those who advise clients in family law matters will be able to refer to this book and be confident that it will provide the basic knowledge that they will need to provide a professional service.

Those who advise clients on a daily basis will, I am sure, agree that their clients are best served by constantly being reminded what stage they have reached in the process. It is essential that clients see the 'big picture' as this helps them to focus on the relevant issues. Family lawyers have to recognise that they are usually dealing with clients who have had no legal experience and who may quickly become lost in the matrix of family courts and the law.

Clients need constantly to be reminded of 'where they are' and what the next step is, how long it is expected to take, how much it will cost and what the range of outcomes may be. Those experienced in the field do this all the time, but those less experienced often have difficulty in understanding just how confused their clients can become.

However, in order to explain the big picture, you must be able to see it yourself. The aim of this book is to help family lawyers to see the big picture so that they can feel confident passing that information on to their clients.

1.7 STAND-ALONE CHAPTERS

Efforts have been made to ensure that each chapter stands alone. The layout will hopefully mean that topics can be quickly located and worthwhile use can be made of the contents.

While this book is predominately designed to be an accessible reference book, there is much to be gained by reading the book from cover to cover. As any family law practitioner will confirm, all areas of family law overlap. It is impossible to understand properly any one area of family law without a grasp of the whole subject. It is part of the constantly developing nature of family law that in order to advise in one area, it is often necessary to have a 'feeling' of where another area is heading.

For example, it is impossible for a lawyer to advise a client as to whether mediation or collaborative law ought to be considered without having a competent grasp of what might happen if an application were to be made to court in the conventional way. Similarly, it is often impossible for lawyers to advise clients whether joint residence of children should be considered as an option until they are able to advise on the potential financial outcome of the case.

1.8 PRESENT CHALLENGES

Family lawyers are accustomed to change, but there are two particular areas which have to be acknowledged as challenges which are shaping the way in which family law will be practised in the future. These are funding and the delivery of service.

1.8.1 Provision of legal services

The Legal Services Act 2007 received Royal Assent on 30 October of that year. When fully implemented, the Act will reform the way legal services in England and Wales are regulated and aims to put consumer interest at the heart of the regulatory framework. The Act sets out a framework for reform, which includes setting up a Legal Services Board and an Office for Legal

Complaints, and enabling legal services to be provided under new business structures. There is no doubt that the Act will cause changes to the way legal services are delivered to clients. The biggest impact on family law will be the ability for lawyers to be employed by non-lawyers to provide advice and services to an unconnected client. This has colloquially been called 'Tesco Law'. Whether the major providers such as supermarkets and car breakdown companies will be able to commoditise family law sufficiently to be able to sell it from their shelves has yet to be seen, but family lawyers are not necessarily exempt from reform in this area and need to be aware of opportunities in the future.

It is often said 'He who pays the piper, calls the tune'. In the event that family lawyers find themselves in a position that they must administer their skills for their clients while effectively working for anonymous shareholders, who are motivated only by profit, they must somehow remain true to their ideals and not lose sight of the interests of those whom they really serve.

These developments might be what 'the consumer' wants. It is doubtful, though that these are changes that the same consumers would want if they were suddenly to find themselves in the position of being 'the client'.

1.8.2　The future: one law for the rich – no law for the poor?

If family lawyers are to be true to their calling, they will have to adapt to this changing legal landscape. In order to practise family law to the exacting standards they have set themselves over the last two decades, family lawyers will have to find ways of dealing with these obstacles. If they are unable to do so, and anecdotally, this will happen in many cases, professional administration of family law will become the preserve of the rich.

The development of family law, particularly in financial matters, has already become the responsibility of the rich, those who are able to fund hugely expensive litigation without which our Law Lords would not have the opportunity of expressing their opinion of the law and thereby shaping it.

It would be morally wrong if justice in all family law matters, particularly those involving cases where the state intervenes in the lives of children, also fell to those who could afford it. It would be a travesty if this were to happen, but I fear it is inevitable if those who pass legislation never visualise themselves as being in the position of those who need the law to protect their families.

1.8.3　Transparency/media access to the courts

Following two consultation papers, the government has opened up the family courts at all levels to the media to give the impression that the public interest is protected by allowing the press to observe the courts' proceedings. Reporting restrictions are governed by s.12 of the Administration of Justice

Act 1960, s.11 of the Contempt of Court Act 1981 and s.97 of the Children Act 1989 as interpreted by the case *Clayton* v. *Clayton* [2006] EWCA Civ 878. The rights of the press to attend courts have been expanded by two President's Practice Directions dated 20 April 2009 – one governing the county court and the other the Family Proceedings Court. The basic position now is that the press can attend any proceedings, unless excluded by the judge, but cannot report on the detail of the case – only the substance. It is likely that the law will change to enable the press to report on the substance, provided children are not identified. This change could have a dramatic effect on the administration of justice in family proceedings which have hitherto been essentially 'private' in nature.

1.9 THE QUALITIES OF THE FAMILY LAWYER

A good family lawyer is one who listens, empathises, manages and most of all helps clients to achieve their reasonable expectations in the least acrimonious way possible.

The fact that a family lawyer has an excellent understanding of the law is of little use to clients unless that lawyer has the requisite skills to be able to put this knowledge into practice.

I sincerely hope that this book will help you to acquire the knowledge and understanding of family law needed to attain those goals.

CHAPTER 2

Marriage

Charlotte Bradley and Lucy Thomas

2.1 INTRODUCTION

> Marriage, as understood in Christendom, may for this purpose be defined as the voluntary union for life of one man and one woman, to the exclusion of all others.

> *Hyde* v. *Hyde and Woodmansee* (1886) LR1 P&D 130

In England and Wales, marriage creates an altered legal status which is imposed by law once couples have agreed voluntarily to marry and have complied with the required statutory requirements. Those requirements are set out in the Marriage Act 1949 (as amended). Whilst sometimes described as a contract, marriage is more than merely an agreement between parties, it is a status conferred by law. Its definition is therefore reliant, largely, on compliance with legal regulations.

Although a cohabitee is often referred to as a 'common law spouse', this phrase does not have any meaning in law, nor does it have any legal recognition.

The legal position of cohabitees may change in the near future as the Cohabitation Bill is currently at Committee Stage. If passed, the legal and financial position of cohabitees will be significantly altered. Details of the progress of the Bill can be found at **www.lawcom.gov.uk/docs/lc307.pdf**

The formalities (sometimes called solemnisation) of marriage can be either religious (but subject to legal requirements) or civil. These points are dealt with at **2.3.3** below.

It should be noted that a civil partnership (as defined by the Civil Partnership Act 2004 (CPA 2004)) creates a legal union between two people of the same sex and is therefore distinct from marriage. Many people say that the introduction of CPA 2004 has in essence created 'gay marriage', albeit that technically this description does not exist in law. CPA 2004 came into force on 5 December 2005, and as a result, same-sex couples can now obtain recognition of their relationship by registering their civil partnership, thus obtaining a new legal status. The purpose of CPA 2004 was, in many respects, to achieve parity of treatment for same-sex couples as compared to married couples. The legal rights which a civil partnership confers mirror many of the rights given to married couples, for example in relation to tax (in particular inheritance tax), rules of intestacy, protection from domestic violence, etc. Furthermore, specific procedures are required in order to dissolve a civil partnership, akin to the process of divorce.

The definition and understanding of marriage differs between legal jurisdictions, religions and cultures, and the formalities required to create a marriage also differ widely. This chapter deals with marriages created and celebrated in England and Wales where marriages are defined in part by civil requirement and also by religious tradition; in addition, it also touches upon the validity and recognition in England and Wales) of foreign marriages.

2.2 REQUIREMENTS FOR A VALID MARRIAGE

If a marriage is defective (i.e. if it does not comply with the requirements of validity set out below) then it can be either void (void ipso jure) or voidable.

2.2.1 Void marriages

Under the Matrimonial Causes Act 1973 (MCA 1973), s.11, any marriage created after 31 July 1971 will be void (invalid) if any of the following apply.

Parties are within the prohibited degrees of relationship

Marriage between persons who are closely related (known as 'prohibited degrees' of relationship) are void. The categories of prohibited persons are set out in the Marriage Act 1949, Sched.1 (as amended) and the Marriage (Prohibited Degrees of Relationship) Act 1986. They include child, grandparent, grandchild, parent, parent's sibling, adoptive child and adoptive parent, sibling and sibling's child. The prohibited degrees relate to ties of consanguinity and affinity. In short, they refer to the closeness of the relationship. In broad terms they prevent marriage between blood relatives and step relatives. Nevertheless, first cousins may marry and a man can marry his divorced wife's sister.

Either party is under the age of 16

The statutory minimum age at which people can enter into a marriage is 16. Any marriage entered into with a person who is aged less than 16 is void. If one of the parties to a marriage is aged between 16 and 18, certain consents are required pursuant to the Marriage Act 1949 as follows:

(a) consent of each parent who has parental responsibility and the consent of each guardian, where applicable;

(b) if there is a residence order in force, then the person in whose favour the order has been made must give consent in place of those at (a) above;

(c) if there is a care order in place, then in addition to the consent of those at (a) and (b) above, the local authority referred to in the order must also consent;

(d) if (b) and (c) do not apply (i.e. there is no existing residence or care order in place) but there was a residence order in force just prior to one of the parties to the marriage turning 16, then the person in whose favour that order was made is required to give consent in place of those at (a) above.

If the consent of any of the persons detailed at (a) to (d) above cannot be obtained, then a superintendent registrar of births, deaths and marriages can dispense with the need for consent or the court can give consent. In those circumstances, the application can be heard by the High Court or by the county court and, unless the court directs, the application would be heard in chambers. If a request for consent has been made to the relevant persons detailed at (a) to (d) above but is refused, then the relevant persons must be joined to the application.

The consent required where one of the parties to a marriage is aged between 16 and 18 does not have to be given in a requisite form. It can be implied although the superintendent registrar or the court may require written confirmation.

If a party to the marriage (who is aged over 16 but under 18) is a ward of court, then the consent of the High Court is required. (It should be noted that similar requirements apply where someone aged between 16 and 18 intends to enter a civil partnership.)

Statutory requirements concerning notice and solemnisation have not been complied with

The statutory requirements concerning notice and solemnisation are dealt with in more detail at **2.3**.

At the time of the marriage either party was already married

If there is an existing valid marriage, any later marriage will be bigamous. Bigamy is a civil and criminal offence under English law and an existing marriage renders any subsequent marriage void. This relates to the definition of marriage, namely the voluntary union of one man and one woman to the exclusion of all others. English law therefore adopts a monogamous concept of marriage.

Parties are not respectively male and female

In England and Wales, parties to a marriage must be male and female. Only persons of the opposite sex can marry and their sex, prior to the introduction of the Gender Recognition Act 2004, was determined as at birth and based on biological factors (*Corbett* v. *Corbett (otherwise Ashley)* [1970] 2 All ER 33). Prior to the introduction of the Gender Recognition Act in 2004, gender reassignment was not recognised by the courts in terms of altering gender and the courts continued to make decisions based on the gender of a person at birth, despite the fact that in 2002 the European Court of Human Rights had found that this approach was incompatible with Arts.8 and 12 of the European Convention for Protection of Human Rights and Fundamental Freedoms (the Convention on Human Rights).

The Gender Recognition Act 2004 came into force on 6 April 2005. As a result, a person who undergoes gender reassignment may apply for a full gender recognition certificate and be treated, as from the date of any such certificate, as being of the gender on the certificate rather than the gender recorded on the original birth certificate.

If the person is married, an interim certificate will be issued initially. Under MCA 1973 (as amended), the existence of such an interim certificate is now a ground to render the marriage voidable. One of the parties to the marriage may apply for a decree of nullity within six weeks of the interim certificate being issued (and may make an application for financial provision, as with divorce proceedings).

It should also be noted that once a full certificate has been issued the person in receipt would then be free to marry on the basis of that person's acquired gender. It should further be noted that, if the other party to the marriage did not know that one or other party had changed gender, that would also be a ground to render the marriage voidable.

If a decree of nullity is made absolute on the ground that an interim gender recognition certificate has been issued to a party to the marriage then the court which makes that decree must, on doing so, issue a full gender recognition certificate to that party and send a copy to the Secretary of State (Gender Recognition Act 2004, s.5(1)). If an interim gender recognition certificate has been issued to a person and that person's marriage is subsequently dissolved or annulled (otherwise than on the ground that an interim recognition certificate has been issued) within six months of the interim certificate being issued, or the spouse dies within that period, then that person may make an application for a full gender recognition certificate within six months beginning with the day on which the marriage is dissolved or annulled or the death occurs. (Such an application would be made to a Gender Recognition Panel.)

In the case of a polygamous marriage entered into outside England and Wales either party was at the time of the marriage domiciled in England or Wales

The Matrimonial Causes Act 1973 originally stated that any polygamous or 'potentially' polygamous marriage (i.e. a marriage entered into outside

England and Wales under laws that permit polygamy) which was celebrated outside England and Wales after 31 July 1971 would be considered void if, at the time of the marriage, either of the parties were domiciled in England and Wales. The position has changed slightly as a result of the Private International Law (Miscellaneous Provisions) Act 1995. Accordingly, MCA 1973, s.11(d) will only apply where an actual rather than a 'potentially' polygamous marriage is celebrated outside England and Wales and one of the parties at the time of the marriage was domiciled in England and Wales. In those circumstances that marriage will be void, but it is no longer the case that such a marriage will automatically be void where the marriage which is celebrated outside the jurisdiction is 'potentially' polygamous (see above). The section therefore now only applies to those marriages which are actually polygamous at that point.

2.2.2 Voidable marriages

Under MCA 1973, s.12, any marriage created after 31 July 1971 will be voidable (capable of being annulled) if any of the following apply.

Incapacity of either party to the marriage to consummate it

Lack of physical capacity to consummate a marriage (capacity to have sexual intercourse) could render a marriage voidable. Technically a marriage does not have to be consummated in order to be valid. Nevertheless, if it is shown that one party lacks the capacity to consummate the marriage or has wilfully refused to consummate a marriage, then those matters could render the marriage voidable. It should also be noted that the relevant issue is an incapacity or inability to consummate, rather than a capacity to conceive. Issues of sexual satisfaction are also irrelevant: the question is whether one party is able to consummate a marriage by way of complete sexual intercourse. (Where the said incapacity stems from impotence then that could lead to lack of capacity unless the impotence was known about at the time of the marriage.)

Wilful refusal to consummate a marriage may also render it voidable, albeit that the person refusing to consummate cannot petition for a decree of nullity.

Lack of consent

Section 12 states that a marriage is voidable on the grounds that either party to the marriage did not validly consent to it, whether in consequence of duress, mistake, unsoundness of mind or otherwise.

Marriage must be entered into voluntarily and knowingly (i.e. with capacity). If a marriage is entered into as a result of threats or duress then it is potentially voidable, provided that the threat/pressure exerted is sufficient to destroy the reality of consent and to overpower free will. When considering whether a marriage has been rendered voidable, the court will look at the impact that the threat or the duress has had on the recipient. It will look for a genuine and reasonably held fear of some form of immediate danger to life, limb or liberty (*McLaron* v. *McLaron* [1986] 112 Sol J 0419).

Even where a marriage has been consummated, one or either party could still claim that it is voidable as a result of duress. It should also be noted that an arranged marriage is not automatically voidable, unless there has been a degree of threat or duress (*Hirani* v. *Hirani* (1983) 4 FLR 232). It is important to distinguish between an arranged marriage and a forced marriage (*NS* v. *MI* [2007] 1 FLR 444).

Marriages of convenience would also be valid, unless there is an element of duress. A marriage simply requires consent and knowledge; motive is irrelevant. The fact that the immigration authorities may not recognise the marriage for immigration purposes is an entirely separate matter.

If either party was mistaken as to the identity of the other party, or was mistaken as to the nature of the ceremony then this would remove consent and therefore render the marriage voidable. In addition, a mock marriage would also be voidable for lack of consent. On the question of mistake, being mistaken about somebody's character, wealth, circumstance or 'condition' is not sufficient to render a marriage voidable. The categories of 'acceptable mistake' are limited.

One party was suffering from a mental disorder and was unfit to enter into a marriage

If it is shown that one party to a marriage lacks mental capacity (sometimes referred to as soundness of mind), then this could lead to a finding that the party was unable to give full and voluntary consent to the marriage, as is required under MCA 1973. The court would have to be satisfied that the party was capable of understanding the nature of the contract being entered into and the responsibilities attached to it. Mental incapacity can relate to a specific mental disorder and could potentially render a marriage voidable. A party to a marriage must have mental capacity at the time the party enters into the marriage. The state of mind prior to or subsequent to a marriage is irrelevant. Mental disorders for these purposes are defined by the Mental Health Act 1983 but, in addition, a court would have to be satisfied that any such mental disorder (as defined by the Act) meant that the person concerned was unable to live in a married state or to carry out the duties associated with marriage. In other words, it is a twofold test. It is not enough to establish that there is a mental disorder; rather a court would have to be satisfied that that mental disorder rendered the party concerned mentally unable to appreciate and to live within the bounds of marriage.

If a party to the marriage is intoxicated or under the influence of drugs at the time of the marriage, this could potentially render that person unable to give consent to the marriage (*Ford* v. *Stier* [1896] P 1 and *Mehta (otherwise Kohn)* v. *Mehta* [1945] 2 All ER 690).

Issues of intoxication and drug use would fall into the category defined as 'or otherwise' (MCA 1973, s.12).

Suffering from a venereal disease in a communicable form at the time of the marriage

The discovery that one or either party is suffering from a venereal disease could render a marriage voidable.

Pregnancy by another person

If the parties discover that the woman is pregnant by another man at the time of the marriage, then this could lead to a decree of nullity.

Provisions under the Gender Recognition Act 2004

See **2.2.1** above. If an interim certificate is issued after the date of the marriage, that could render the marriage voidable, as could discovery, following the marriage, that one party acquired his or her gender under the Gender Recognition Act 2004.

2.3 PROCEDURAL REQUIREMENTS

For a marriage to be valid in England and Wales, the parties must comply with prescribed procedural forms and ceremonies. A large body of legislation and case law exists governing the procedural requirements connected to marriage. The Marriage Act 1949 consolidated previous legislation in this area. It came into force on 1 January 1950 and affects all marriages from that date onwards (it does not cover Northern Ireland or Scotland). Since then, various other Acts have been passed which deal with ceremonial requirements for marriage in England and Wales. They include the Marriage (Secretaries of Synagogues) Act 1959, the Marriage (Registration of Buildings) Act 1990, the Marriage Ceremony (Prescribed Words) Act 1996 and the Marriage (Wales) Act 1986.

The procedural requirements relating to marriage can be divided into a number of categories, namely church weddings in a Church of England or Church of Wales church, civil marriages, marriages for Quakers and Jews, and other religious ceremonies. The procedural requirements differ for each category, although there are similarities.

In broad terms there are two procedural requirements in relation to marriage: any person seeking to be married in England and Wales must give notice in the requisite form; and the marriage must then be solemnised.

2.3.1 Notice of the marriage

Section 50 of the Marriage Act 1949 sets out the requirements for 'delivery' of the certificate of notice. Put simply, the certificate, confirming that the relevant notice has been given (as discussed above), must be passed to the relevant person as it is that document which gives that person authority to solemnise the marriage. By way of example, if a marriage takes place in a registered building in the presence of a registrar, the certificate must be passed to the registrar. If the marriage takes place in a registered building in the absence of a registrar, the certificate must be passed to the authorised person. The authorised person, as defined under the Marriage Act 1949, is somebody who has been appointed/authorised to carry out solemnisation of marriages in the absence of a registrar and is certified to do so. For Quakers (the Society of Friends) and for Jewish marriages, there will be a designated appointed officer authorised to carry out this task. The certificate of notice must be passed to them.

For a valid marriage to take place in the Church of England or Church of Wales the party must make public the banns, obtain a common licence, obtain a special licence or obtain a superintendent registrar's certificate.

Church marriages

The publication of banns relates specifically to marriages which take place in the Church of England or Church of Wales. Historically they were designed to warn parents and guardians of a child's intention to marry. Today, they are simply a way of announcing an intention to marry. Specifically the banns must be read aloud on three successive Sundays prior to the ceremony. A fundamental part of the banns is that they are made public in this way so that, potentially, members of the congregation can register any objections to the marriage. If couples live in different parishes then the banns must be publicised in both parishes and a certificate must be obtained from the church in which the marriage is not going to take place and provided to the vicar in the church where the marriage is to take place. Once the banns have been read the parties must marry within three months.

As an alternative to publishing banns, parties to a marriage can obtain a common licence if they are temporarily resident in a different parish. The application for such a licence must be approved by the Bishop of the parish where the marriage is due to take place. In addition, they must have been resident in the parish for 15 days leading up to the application for the licence and one of the parties must have been baptised. The parties must then marry within three months of the licence being granted. Common licences are generally only awarded where there are good reasons, for example if either party has moved overseas.

A further alternative is to obtain a special licence, albeit that this is quite unusual. Such a licence is discretionary and is granted by the Archbishop of

Canterbury. It means that the marriage can take place at any time and at any place within a period of three months. One of the parties to the marriage must have been baptised. There is no residency requirement. Special licences are only issued in special circumstances where, for example, a marriage is due to take place in hospital. Interestingly, members of the Royal Family have to apply for a special licence to marry at St Paul's Cathedral, which is not a registered location.

The church where the marriage is due to take place must be in the same registration district; the party must have been resident in the district for seven days prior to giving notice and must remain there for 21 days after giving notice. They are awarded a certificate within seven days and must marry within 12 months.

Civil marriages

For civil marriages, one of the parties has to be resident in the relevant district for seven days prior to giving notice. Both parties must attend the registry office to give notice in person to the superintendent registrar. If the parties live in separate districts then they must attend and give notice in separate districts. Once notice has been given there is a waiting period of 16 days before the parties can marry. A civil ceremony cannot involve any religious aspects.

Giving notice of marriage in this way has to be done in a prescribed form, which includes details of the parties' names, surnames, marital status, occupation, place of residence, nationality, place of marriage and how long they have resided in the district.

Specific procedures for notice re different faiths

Certain specific procedures and requirements for giving notice relate to specific circumstances as follows:

(a) those marrying within the Society of Friends (commonly known as Quakers);
(b) those marrying in the Roman Catholic faith;
(c) those marrying according to Jewish law;
(d) where a party resides in Scotland or where the marriage is to be solemnised in Scotland;
(e) where one party resides in Northern Ireland;
(f) where one party resides outside the UK; and
(g) Islamic marriage.

The Marriage Act 1949 allows Jews and Quakers to marry, provided they have given the requisite notice and obtained a certificate or licence, in accordance with their own traditions, referred to as 'usages'.

17

THE SOCIETY OF FRIENDS (QUAKERS)

In broad terms the regulations applying to marriages according to the Society of Friends are the same as for civil marriages generally save that there are two key additional requirements as follows.

1. The parties must apply to the registering officer (at the society) at one of the monthly meetings, they must make a declaration (in writing or verbally) that they are either both members of the society or where one of them is a non-member, they must confirm that they are in sympathy with the practices and understanding of marriage exercised by the society and a non-member must also produce letters of recommendation from two other members.
2. The registering officer at the Society of Friends must produce a form confirming that the formalities have been complied with and the form must then be forwarded to the registrar when the parties give notice.

JEWISH MARRIAGE

For Jewish marriages a secretary of a synagogue may keep marriage register books and become an authorised person to keep the registers. If the secretary of a synagogue is not authorised to carry out marriages the registrar will be required. (It should be noted that Jewish marriages must comply with not only civil requirements but also Jewish law.)

ROMAN CATHOLIC CHURCH

The legal requirements for marrying within the Roman Catholic church are as for a civil marriage save that, if one party of the marriage is of the Roman Catholic faith then the publication of banns is not required. Instead, that person's priest must give permission for the marriage.

WHERE ONE PARTY RESIDES IN SCOTLAND

If one party of the marriage lives in Scotland, that party must give notice of the marriage in Scotland and the person living in England can give notice in England. Under Scottish law, once notice is given, a certificate confirming capacity to marry will be issued in accordance with the Marriage (Scotland) Act 1977. This has the same force as if a certificate of notice had been issued by a superintendent registrar in England. When notice is given in Scotland it is deemed to be given in England.

WHERE ONE PARTY RESIDES IN NORTHERN IRELAND

The party who lives in Northern Ireland can give notice in the relevant district provided that he or she has lived there for not less than seven days before the notice is given. Notice must be given in accordance with Northern Ireland law. Once notice has been provided, the registrar in England can generate a certificate within 15 days thereafter.

ISLAMIC MARRIAGE

A mosque can be registered for the solemnisation of marriage. If it is not registered, the parties will have to attend a separate civil marriage ceremony. All other requirements for a civil marriage must be complied with. Notice should be given to the superintendent registrar. If the building is in a different registration district from where the parties live they will have to show that it is their usual place of worship.

2.3.2   Registration of marriages

Marriages, like births and deaths, have been registered in England and Wales since 1837. Each local register will have a record of all marriages which have taken place within that district, whether at the local registry office or at approved premises. As with giving notice, the law requires that a marriage must also be registered – either by the registrar (if the marriage is solemnised in his presence) or by the relevant authorised person (it should be noted that the authorised person cannot register a marriage to which they are a party or a witness). The Registrar General will provide marriage register books so that the marriage can be registered and certified copies of the register can be produced. A marriage must be registered immediately following solemnisation, in duplicate. The entry must be made in two books in the prescribed form. The marriage must be registered in the same building as the ceremony, and in the presence of the parties and two witnesses. The entry must be signed by the parties, their witnesses and the authorised person.

(A registrar can charge for allowing a marriage to be carried out in his presence. The charge is £40 if the marriage takes place in a registered office and £47 if it takes place in a registered building.)

There are statutory rules governing the keeping of marriage register books: for example they are retained by the registrar, authorised person, secretary of the synagogue or registering officer of the Society of Friends. Certified copies of all of the entries must be submitted by those persons to the superintendent registrar on a quarterly basis. There are very specific provisions for the keeping of the marriage books, including the fact that they must be retained within a fireproof box.

The specific provisions dealing with the registration of marriages, the keeping of marriage books and certificates generally are set out at ss.53–57 of the Marriage Act 1949 (as amended). The law provides that the marriage books, whether held by a registrar or by the authorised persons detailed above, must be available for inspection and for searches to be carried out. Certified copies of a marriage certificate can normally be obtained from the authorised person (i.e. from the place at which the marriage took place) as the authorised person will be able to provide a certified copy of the entry from the marriage book. Alternatively, Indices are kept by the Registrar General.

The registrar or the authorised person may produce a copy of the marriage certificate at the time of the ceremony for £3.50 (SI 2002/3076). The cost of a certified copy thereafter is £7.

The Central Index is retained by the Registrar General and searches can be carried out in respect of marriages that took place from 1900 onwards, albeit that marriages which have taken place in the previous 18 months may not have been submitted on to the Indices and a search should therefore be carried out at the place of marriage in the first instance. Copy marriage certificates can be obtained from the Central Index of the General Register at PO Box 2, Southport, Merseyside PR18 2JD or online at **www.gro.gov.uk**.

2.3.3   Solemnisation

There are various other statutory requirements which must be complied with and which relate to the solemnisation of marriage (the ceremonial element which follows the giving of notice and precedes the registration of a marriage).

A marriage cannot be solemnised until a certificate of a superintendent registrar has been given, i.e. requisite notice and the solemnisation must take place within the applicable period (as detailed at **2.3.1** above).

A marriage ceremony must take place either at a registry office or on approved premises (unless it is a Jewish marriage or Quaker marriage). The approved premises must be certified. The central registry office keeps a full index of all approved premises and a list can be obtained from it directly. The doors of the premises must remain open (unlocked) during the ceremony.

Marriages must take place between 6 am and 6 pm (Jewish and Quaker marriages are excluded from this). They can technically take place on Sundays and during public and bank holidays. With that said, some churches will not allow marriages during Lent or Advent or indeed on Sundays. This is within the discretion of each individual church.

Declaration in the prescribed form

For marriages other than those taking place in a Church of England church, a Jewish or Quaker marriage, the parties in all of the circumstances must at some stage of the ceremony make a solemn declaration in the prescribed form. The words are referred to within the Marriage Ceremony (Prescribed Words) Act 1996, s.1 (inserted into the Marriage Act 1949, s.44). The words include a declaration and then an element of contract. The parties to the marriage can either say 'I do solemnly declare that I know not of any lawful impediment why I, X, may not be joined in matrimony to Y' (this is the declaration). The contracting words are 'I call upon these persons here present to witness that I, X, do take thee, Y, to be my lawful wedded wife/husband'. Since February 1997, the parties can use an alternative form of wording namely 'I declare that I know of no legal reason why I, X, may not be joined in marriage to Y' or by replying 'I am' to the question 'Are you, X, free lawfully to marry, Y?'. The alternative contracting words are 'I, X, take you, Y, to be my wedded husband/wife' or 'I, X, take thee, Y, to be my wedded wife/ husband'. The registrar or religious celebrant will discuss the choice of words in advance.

Approved premises

Since 1995, civil marriage ceremonies can take place on approved premises, i.e. at places other than registry offices. The relevant statutory provisions are now the Marriages and Civil Partnerships (Approved Premises) Regulations 2005, SI 2005/3168. An application to approve a particular premises must be made by its owner or trustee. The application must be made in writing and must include a plan of the premises and identify the rooms in which it is envisaged the marriages will take place. The local authority must, following receipt of the application, make arrangements to inspect the premises. There must also be a period of public notice of the application so that the plan and application are available for inspection. The application must also be advertised in a local newspaper. There are various criteria which are applied by the local authority in determining whether or not premises are 'suitable' for marriages. The criteria are set out in the 2005 Regulations above but include:

- the venue must be a 'seemly and dignified venue' for the 'solemnisation of marriages';
- the venue must be available for public use, and have relevant fire precautions; and
- the venue must only be used for civil marriages and, as mentioned earlier, civil marriages may not contain any religious content.

If approval is granted then 'standard conditions' as defined under the regulations, must be attached to the approval. These include:

- the premises must always be available at reasonable times for inspection;
- somebody must be appointed by the holder of the approval (known as the responsible person) to ensure compliance with the conditions, and the responsible person must be available on the premises for an hour prior to the ceremony and throughout each ceremony;

- notice that the premises have been approved must be displayed at the entrance for at least one hour prior to the ceremony and throughout the ceremony;
- no food or drink may be sold or consumed in the room in which the ceremony is to take place for one hour prior to the ceremony or during the ceremony;
- the arrangements for and content of each marriage ceremony must meet with the prior approval of the registrar of the relevant district;
- any reading, music, words or performance which form part of the ceremony must be secular in nature.

This list is not exhaustive. The authority may attach additional conditions in certain circumstances.

The approval of a premises is valid for a period of three years and can be transferred from owner to owner. An application for renewal must be made not less than six months and not more than 12 months before it is due to expire.

Approval of a premises can be revoked if the conditions attached to the approval are not complied with or if the use of the premises is altered so that it is no longer suitable for the solemnisation of marriages. Before revoking any approval, the authority must give notice to the holder of the approval in advance.

Any marriage which takes place on approved premises must take place in the presence of two witnesses, both parties and a registrar or other authorised person. As mentioned previously, a prescribed declaration and contracting words are required.

Registrar General's licence

As mentioned above, in certain limited circumstances a marriage may be solemnised by Registrar General's licence. This normally applies where one of the persons to be married is seriously ill and cannot be moved to a place where the marriage could take place in other circumstances. Notice must be given in the prescribed form to the superintendent registrar of the relevant district in which it is intended that the marriage will take place. The Registrar General may require evidence that there is no lawful impediment to the marriage, that consents are in place and that there is good reason why the licence should be granted. Further, the Registrar General must be satisfied that one of the persons to be married is seriously ill and not expected to recover and cannot be moved to a place at which the marriage could normally be solemnised. These requirements are set out in the Marriage (Registrar General's Licence) Act 1970. The Registrar General must also be satisfied that the person who is ill can and does understand the nature of the marriage ceremony.

Once the certificate is issued the marriage may be solemnised any time within one month of the day on which the notice was entered into the marriage notice book. If the marriage is not solemnised within that period the notice and the Registrar General's licence are void. The marriage must be solemnised at the place stated in the notice of marriage and with the requisite ceremonial requirements. It must not comply with the rights and ceremonies of the Church of England or the Church of Wales, the Jewish, Roman Catholic or Quaker traditions. Provided the marriage is not solemnised according to the usages of the Society of Friends or the usages of the Jewish faith, it must be in the presence of a registrar (if it is a purely civil ceremony the superintendent registrar and the local registrar must attend) with two witnesses and the appropriate declaration.

2.4 NULLITY PROCEEDINGS

If a marriage can be shown to be invalid, nullity proceedings may be applied for. A decree of nullity, pronounced by the court, is a declaration that the marriage is void (that it never existed) or that it was voidable (that it is treated as valid until the date of the decree). It should be noted that a civil decree of nullity is quite distinct from a declaration of nullity by the Roman Catholic church which of itself has no civil or legal implications and no impact in relation to children, property rights, etc.

If a marriage is void then it has never existed and technically there does not need to be a decree of nullity. Nevertheless, for financial reasons, such a decree is sometimes useful as it empowers the court to make financial provision, as is available for divorcing spouses such as maintenance pending suit payments. If a marriage is voidable, it remains valid until a court annuls it by way of a decree of nullity. Such a decree must be pronounced during the party's lifetime. The marriage is treated as existing and as valid up to the date of any decree.

The procedure to secure a decree of nullity is similar to that for divorce proceedings. As with divorce, a decree nisi will be pronounced in the first instance and a decree absolute of nullity can be made not sooner than six weeks later (unless ordered by the court to be made earlier). A petition of nullity must be produced and an acknowledgement of service filed. The petitioner then files an affidavit in support of the petition of nullity together with a request for directions for trial. In most circumstances there may need to be a hearing in open court before the court will agree to pronounce a decree nisi of nullity.

As with divorce and judicial separation proceedings, the petitioner must also file a statement of arrangements for children form so that the court can satisfy itself that suitable arrangements are in place for any relevant children.

The 'one-year rule' does not apply to nullity proceedings in the way it applies to divorce. As a result, a petition for nullity can be presented to the court within one year of the marriage.

As with a decree nisi in divorce proceedings, a decree of nullity gives rise to the court's powers to make financial provision. Prior to the pronouncement of a decree of nullity, once the petition has been presented the court can order interim periodical payments either for one of the parties or for a child. These are dealt with in more detail in the chapters dealing with divorce and ancillary relief.

Once a petition for a decree of nullity has been presented then either party may issue ancillary relief proceedings, in the same way as divorce proceedings. The court can exercise its powers in relation to nullity proceedings under MCA 1973, ss.23 and 24. The 's.25 factors' (contained in MCA 1973, s.25) will apply to any consideration of claims brought under nullity proceedings in the same way that they apply within divorce proceedings.

An obvious dichotomy arises from the financial powers which the court has following a decree of nullity if for example a decree of nullity is granted on the basis of a bigamous marriage. Under English law bigamy is a criminal offence under s.57 of the Offences Against the Person Act 1861 (as amended). Under MCA 1973, s.11, bigamy would render a marriage void yet the court's financial powers under MCA 1973, ss.22–24, would apply. As a matter of public policy, this raises the question of whether a bigamous spouse should be allowed to benefit and bring financial claims. This point was discussed in *Whiston* v. *Whiston* [1995] 2 FLR 268; in that case, the court found that such a spouse could not benefit from his or her bigamy, thus claims were not allowed. However, the matter was reconsidered in *Rampal* v. *Rampal* (No.2) [2001] 2 FLR 1179 where the court allowed claims to proceed. In *Rampal* v. *Rampal*, Thorpe LJ concluded that *Whiston* v. *Whiston* did not establish a rule preventing any bigamist from applying for ancillary relief. This was reflected in the more recent case of *Ben Hashem* v. *Al Shayif* [2009] 1 FLR 115, where Munby J emphasised that the court retains discretion to decide whether the existence of bigamy is relevant, seeing it as a circumstance of the case. In *Ben Hashem* v. *Al Shayif* the fact of bigamy was said to have 'marginal' impact and so did not preclude the parties from making financial claims.

2.5   OTHER EFFECTS OF MARRIAGE

2.5.1   Effect of marriage on wills

As a general rule, marriage (in England, Wales or Northern Ireland) will automatically revoke a will. The same is true of the creation of a civil partnership, which will also revoke any previous will.

Under the Wills Act 1837, s.18 (as substituted by the Administration of Justice Act 1982, s.18(1)), where a will is made on or after 1 January 1983 it will not be revoked by marriage provided:

(a)   the testator/testatrix was expecting to marry a particular person; and

(b)   the testator/testatrix did not intend for the will to be revoked by the subsequent marriage to that person.

In other words, provided that the will is written in contemplation of marriage to a named person it will not be revoked on marriage.

The formation of a civil partnership will also generally revoke a will unless it appears from the will that the testator/testatrix was expecting to form a civil partnership with a particular person and further that the testator/testatrix intended that the will should not be revoked by the formation of the civil partnership (see CPA 2004, Sched.4).

Note that a will made in Scotland is not automatically revoked by marriage.

It should be noted that a marriage which is voidable does, for the period in which it subsists and is valid, revoke all previous wills. A marriage which is void has no impact on earlier wills.

2.5.2   Effect of marriage on domicile

Prior to the Domicile and Matrimonial Proceedings Act 1973, s.1 (which came into force on 1 January 1974), on marriage a wife acquired her husband's domicile by virtue of dependence. For all marriages from 1 January 1974 onwards that law no longer applies and a woman in those circumstances retains her original domicile of origin/domicile of choice.

An assessment of a person's domicile is no longer dependent on marriage, where the marriage has taken place since 1 January 1974. Previously if a woman's marriage ended she retained her husband's domicile until she legally acquired a new domicile. (This may have tax implications.)

2.5.3   Effect on a person's legal status

As previously mentioned marriage alters a person's legal status in a way that cohabitation does not. It should be noted, as already commented on, that there is no such thing as 'common law marriage'. A common misconception is that, following the cohabitation, parties somehow acquire a new status and have a 'common law marriage'. That does not exist under English law. Cohabiting couples do not acquire the status, benefits, etc. flowing from marriage. To that extent couples who marry or enter a civil partnership are quite distinct from those who cohabit.

Duty to maintain

Historically there was a duty at common law for husbands to maintain their wives but, interestingly, no converse duty for a wife to maintain her husband. That position has largely been superseded by more recent statutory powers. The

Matrimonial Causes Act 1973 empowers the court to make interim financial provision and places spouses under a duty to provide reasonable financial provision, and an application can be made by either party to the marriage under the terms of that Act.

Duty to cohabit

There is no longer a statutory duty on married couples to cohabit as this is deemed to be against public policy.

Personal rights

Previously under common law, a wife lost her legal identity on marriage as she and her husband were treated as one legal person. This meant, by way of example, that she was unable to acquire property in her own name. That is no longer the case. Under the Married Women's Property Act 1882 and the Law of Property Act 1925 husbands and wives are deemed to be separate legal persons. As a result, ownership of property is determined by deed. If a husband and wife own property jointly the terms of that ownership are dictated by the deeds under which it is owned, i.e. whether it is stated to be owned as tenants in common or as joint tenants.

Debts

Husbands and wives do not assume responsibility for each other's debts (which is not always the case in other countries) and they are, as before, treated as individuals. It remains the case that they can both be subject, individually, to bankruptcy.

Name

There is no legal duty on either party to change their names, and it is entirely a matter for individuals whether or not to assume a different name on marriage. There are no provisions compelling them to do so.

Miscellaneous

To all intents and purposes married persons remain treated as individuals in terms of entering into contracts, exercising a power of appointment, etc.

Spouses are deemed able to transfer gifts to one another provided there is no undue influence or evidence of fraud. This is, however, subject to specific provisions in relation to inheritance tax and capital gains tax. Specific restrictions exist in relation to gifts in that context.

Unless there is evidence of a clear intention that a wedding gift was intended for one or other party or for both of them, it is assumed that gifts from the husband's family will be for the husband and gifts from the wife's family will be for the wife (*Samson* v. *Samson* [1960] 1 All ER 653).

2.6 RECOGNITION OF FOREIGN MARRIAGES

See also *International Aspects of Family Law*, 3rd edn (Resolution, 2009).

2.6.1 BACKGROUND

Why is it important for solicitors to know whether a foreign marriage is recognised in England and Wales?

1. To advise as to whether a client needs to have an English divorce and whether the client has any claims under divorce.
2. It can also affect:

   - legitimacy of children;
   - wills and inheritance;
   - nationality;
   - immigration; and
   - tax.

In short, clients will want to know whether they are 'married' in accordance with the local law.

In general, English law will strive to recognise foreign marriages as part of international comity and the English court's tolerance of other cultures. It will try and balance those marriages which, if recognised, would be 'offensive to the conscience of the English courts' with the need to take into account 'common sense, good manners and reasonable tolerance'. See *Cheni (otherwise Rodriguez)* v. *Cheni* [1962] 3 All ER 873; *M* v. *M* [2001] 2 FLR 6 and *City of Westminster* v. *C* [2008] 2 FLR 267.

There are two factors which need to be satisfied, independently, for a foreign marriage to be recognised. The marriage must be 'formally' valid and each of the parties to the marriage must have 'capacity'. If the question of whether a foreign marriage is valid is in issue, usually local advice from a foreign lawyer will be required.

For an explanation of the common law approach of the English court, see *Dicey, Morris and Collins on the Conflict of Laws*, 14th revised edn (Sweet & Maxwell, 2008).

In summary, form means the manner in which the marriage takes place and is governed by the law of the country where the marriage takes place. This is the *lex loci celebrationis*, with certain statutory exemptions. Therefore, unless the ceremony in the foreign country has been performed in accordance with the local law, the marriage will not be recognised in England, even if it was correct under English law.

Capacity relates to the legal ability of one person to marry another person. For example, under English law, a brother does not have the capacity to marry his sister and therefore a marriage on this basis would not be recognised (and, indeed, would be void under MCA 1973, s.11(a); see **2.2.1** above).

2.6.2 Formalities

Rule 66 of *Dicey, Morris & Collins on the Conflict of Laws*, 14th revised edn (Sweet & Maxwell, 2008) sets out the English common law position as to the formalities which are required before the English court will regard the foreign marriage as being formally valid. Rule 66 states:

> A marriage is formally valid when (and only when) any one of the following conditions as to the form of celebration is complied with:
>
> (i)   if the marriage is celebrated in accordance with the form required or recognised as sufficient by the law of the country where the marriage was celebrated (known as the *lex loci celebrationis* rule);
>
> (ii) if the marriage is celebrated in accordance with the requirements of the English common law in a country where the use of the local form is impossible;
>
> (iii) if the marriage is celebrated in accordance with the requirements of the English common law in a country in the belligerent occupation of military forces and one of the parties is a member of those forces or of other military forces associated with them (see *Taczanowska (otherwise Roth)* v. *Taczanowski* [1957] 2 All ER 563);
>
> (iv) if the marriage is celebrated in accordance with the provisions of s.22 Foreign Marriage Act 1892, as amended by s.2 Foreign Marriage Act 1947, between parties of whom at least one is a member of Her Majesty's Forces serving in any foreign territory or employed in such a territory in such other capacity as may be prescribed by order in council;
>
> (v)   if the marriage, between parties of whom at least one is a UK national, is celebrated outside the Commonwealth in accordance with the provisions of, and the form required by, the Foreign Marriages Act 1892–1947 (as amended).

The most important is the *lex loci celebrationis* rule.

2.6.3   Lex loci celebrationis (law of the place of celebration)

To reiterate, an English court will hold a foreign marriage to be valid if it complies with the local rules where the marriage is celebrated. If it does not comply with the rules of that jurisdiction, even if both parties complied with the rules from where they are both domiciled, the marriage will be invalid (see *Berthiaume* v. *Dastous* [1930] AC 79).

Practitioners should be aware that, in England, as explained at **2.3** above, a marriage can be obtained by either a religious or a civil ceremony. If checking the validity of a foreign marriage, it will be necessary to check whether the religious ceremony is valid in its local country in its own right or whether it requires a civil ceremony. If the country where the marriage was celebrated required a civil ceremony then just a religious marriage will not be recognised in England. See Deborah Levy and Tracy Kashi 'Getting married abroad' [2000] Fam Law 191 for further information in relation to the formalities of getting married abroad.

2.6.4 Capacity

Rule 67 of *Dicey, Morris & Collins on the Conflict of Laws* codifies the English common law position. This states that capacity to marry is governed by the law of each party's pre-marriage domicile.

This means that a marriage between two parties with different prenuptial domiciles celebrated in a foreign country will be void (and not recognised) where the law of the prenuptial domicile of one of them denies the individual the requisite capacity to marry (see *Sottomayor (otherwise De Barros)* v. *De Barros* (No.1) (1877–78) LR 3 PD 1).

However, the English courts, as part of an attempt to encourage the validity and recognition of marriages, have adopted a slightly different form of the 'dual domicile' theory. This is known as the 'intended matrimonial home' theory and states that, where the parties to a new marriage have the capacity under the law of the country with which the marriage has its most 'real and substantial connection' (i.e. where it is intended the parties will live) then the marriage will be regarded as valid even though it may be invalid under the dual domicile rule (see *Lawrence* v. *Lawrence* [1985] 2 WLR 86 (first instance) and [1985] 2 All ER 733 (Court of Appeal)). In the Court of Appeal, it was expressed that the court should try and uphold the marriage, by adopting either basis of recognition. See also *City of Westminster* v. *C* [2008] 2 FLR 267.

Note that there are two exceptions to the rule on capacity as follows:

1. Where the marriage is celebrated in England and one of the parties is domiciled in England (and has the necessary capacity under English law) the validity of the marriage will not be affected if the law of the domicile of the other party leads to an incapacity which the English court would not recognise.
2. The court will refuse to recognise the capacity or incapacity to marry imposed by the law of domicile if it is likely to be seen as unconscionable (see *Cheni (otherwise Rodriguez)* v. *Cheni* [1962] 3 All ER 873).

The following should also be considered.

1. Capacity to remarry after a foreign divorce.
2. Capacity to enter into a polygamous marriage (see **2.2.1** above).
3. The difference between capacity and formality – this can be difficult and will need help from local advisers.

4. The procedure for a declaration of status of marriage (see the Family Law Act 1986, s.55(1) and the Family Proceedings Rules 1991, SI 1991/1247 (FPR 1991), rule 3.12).
5. Consent: see Rule 68 of *Dicey, Morris & Collins on the Conflict of Laws*. No marriage will be valid if, by the law of either party's domicile, one party does not consent to marry the other. See MCA 1973, s.12(c) at **2.2.2** above, referring to the lack of consent by either party in consequence of duress, mistake, unsoundness of mind or otherwise which would render a marriage voidable. Regarding consent, see *Alfonso-Brown* v. *Milwood* [2006] 2 FLR 265.

If a marriage takes place abroad, and there is no dispute in relation to its validity, but the parties wish a divorce, practitioners must have regard to the requirements under FPR 1991 in relation to the documents required to be produced on a divorce (see FPR 1991, rule 10.14).

2.7 TERMINATION OF MARRIAGE

A marriage will end automatically on the death of either spouse.

A marriage can be brought to an end formally by way of a decree of nullity or divorce (decree absolute). Nullity is dealt with above and divorce is dealt with in **Chapter 3**. It is possible to apply for a decree of nullity at any stage, whereas divorce proceedings can only be commenced at least one year following the date of the marriage. The court will only grant a decree of divorce if it is satisfied that the marriage has irretrievably broken down. It should be noted however that in certain religions, to comply with the religious law, further steps are required such as, in the Muslim faith, the giving of a *talaq* and in Judaism, the giving of a *get*. Those matters fall outside the scope of this book.

The formal termination of marriage is divorce. The formal termination of a civil partnership is called dissolution.

CHAPTER 3

Divorce

David Woodward

3.1 SCOPE

This chapter provides an overview of the law and practice of divorce. Unless otherwise specified the Act referred to is the Matrimonial Causes Act 1973 (MCA 1973) and the Rules are the Family Proceedings Rules 1991 (FPR 1991). The person making the divorce petition is the 'petitioner' and the person receiving it is known as the 'respondent'.

3.2 JURISDICTION

A county court with divorce jurisdiction (which is most county courts) or the Principal Registry in England and Wales has jurisdiction if one or more of the following are established.

1. The petitioner and the respondent are both habitually resident in England and Wales.
2. The petitioner and respondent were last habitually resident in England and Wales and the petitioner or respondent still resides there.
3. The respondent is habitually resident in England and Wales.
4. The petitioner is habitually resident in England and Wales and has resided there for at least a year immediately prior to the presentation of the petition.
5. The petitioner is domiciled and habitually resident in England and Wales and has resided there for at least six months immediately prior to the presentation of the petition.
6. The petitioner and the respondent are both domiciled in England and Wales.

If none of the above applies there is the option of using either the petitioner's or the respondent's domicile if no contracting state has jurisdiction.

A contracting state is a European Union State which has signed the 1998 Brussels II convention replaced by a Council Regulation known as Brussels II bis. All members of the EU, except Denmark, are contracting states. Domicile and residence issues need to be treated with particular care because assertion of domicile and residence and nationality may carry other implications, e.g. tax. There are varying types of domicile and residence:

- domicile of origin;
- domicile of dependence;
- domicile of choice; and
- 'habitual residence', which is 'a concurrence of the physical element of residence and a mental state of having a "settled purpose" of remaining' (Clarkson and Hill, *The Conflict of Laws*, 3rd edn, OUP 2006).

It is possible to be habitually resident in two countries at the same time. Service out of the jurisdiction is dealt with at **3.6**.

3.3   ONE YEAR BAR

There is an absolute bar upon presenting a divorce petition to the court within one year of the date of the marriage (MCA 1973, s.3(1)). The bar does not apply to nullity or to judicial separation petitions and there is no prohibition upon referring to matters arising during the first year of the marriage.

3.4   GROUNDS FOR DIVORCE

3.4.1   Irretrievable breakdown

The sole ground is that the marriage has broken down irretrievably (MCA 1973, s.1(1)). This can be established in a number of different ways. The petitioner must satisfy the court of one or more of the following facts:

- the respondent has committed adultery and the petitioner finds it intolerable to live with the respondent (s.1(2)(a));
- the respondent has behaved in such a way that the petitioner cannot reasonably be expected to live with the respondent (s.1(2)(b));
- the respondent has deserted the petitioner for a continuous period of at least two years immediately preceding the presentation of the petition (s.1(2)(c));
- the parties to the marriage have lived apart for a continuous period of at least two years immediately preceding the presentation of the petition and the respondent consents to a decree being granted (s.1(2)(d)); and
- the parties to the marriage have lived apart for a continuous period of at least five years immediately preceding the presentation of the petition (s.1(2)(e)).

The standard of proof of irretrievable breakdown is on the balance of probabilities.

3.4.2 Reconciliation

The petitioner's solicitor must file a certificate with the divorce petition stating whether he has discussed with the petitioner the possibility of a reconciliation and provided names of counsellors (MCA 1973, s.6(1)). It is usually sufficient for the local address of Relate to be made available. At any stage the court may adjourn the process to explore the possibility of a reconciliation (MCA 1973, s.6(2)) although in practice, this will very rarely happen.

3.4.3 Adultery

The definition of adultery is as follows: consensual sexual intercourse during the subsistence of the marriage between a married person and a person of the opposite sex not being the spouse. The respondent has committed adultery 'and the petitioner finds it intolerable to live with the respondent' (s.1(2)(a)). The intolerability need have nothing to do with the adultery. The two parts of the test are disjunctive.

The petitioner can rely on the respondent's adultery even if after the petitioner is aware of the adultery they:

(a) live together for a continuous period of six months or less; or
(b) live together for two or more periods totalling six months or less (MCA 1973, s.2(1)).

Suspicion of adultery is not knowledge sufficient to start the 'six-month clock' running.

An expression of forgiveness does not disentitle the petitioner from relying on the adultery. The burden of proof is on the petitioner and is a civil standard of the balance of probabilities. Good evidence of adultery can include the respondent's signature on the acknowledgement of service, although inclination and opportunity or cohabitation provides a rebuttable presumption of adultery. The birth of a child may be evidence of adultery where evidence of adultery or paternity in other proceedings provides evidence for a petition.

Best practice is not to name the person with whom the respondent has committed adultery ('the co-respondent') and there is no obligation to do so. It is only usually considered appropriate to name the co-respondent if the petitioner seeks to recover the costs of the petition from that person.

3.4.4 Behaviour

Behaviour is a subjective assessment of the petitioner's complaints and criticisms of the respondent rather than the respondent's actions or inactions. As far as proof is concerned it is an objective assessment by the court looking at the petitioner's subjective complaints.

The test put forward in *Buffery* v. *Buffery* [1988] 2 FLR 365 is as follows.

1. Whether a right thinking person, looking at the particular husband and wife, would ask whether the one could reasonably be expected to live with the other taking into account all the circumstances of the case and the respective characters and personalities of the two parties concerned.
2. Sexual behaviour short of adultery (such as indecent familiarities) may be unreasonable behaviour.
3. An illness (physical or mental) is not behaviour in itself but the consequences and the impact upon the petitioner may be categorised as behaviour.
4. As in **3.4.3** above the petitioner and the respondent may live together for up to six months after the final incident relied upon (MCA 1973, s.2(3)). The six-month period needs to be considered when drafting the allegations.

When drafting the particulars of behaviour it is good practice only to include brief particulars sufficient to satisfy the court – see the Law Society's *Family Law Protocol*, 2nd edn (2006) para.2.5.1. It is also good practice to try to agree the contents of the particulars with the other party before issuing the petition. This reduces the risk of acrimony caused by misunderstandings – see the Resolution Code of Practice, para.16 (available online at **www.resolution.org.uk**).

3.4.5   Desertion

Desertion is a separation without cause for two years excluding the day of departure. The person is in desertion if they intend, without reasonable cause, to stop living with their spouse. Desertion is from a state of things rather than from an address and cannot be characterised as desertion if:

(a)   the separation is consensual; or
(b)   the separation is because third parties (e.g. employers or prison authorities) require spouses to live apart.

An honest and genuine offer to return can end the desertion.

As in **3.4.3** above the petitioner and respondent may live together for up to six months without breaching the two-year requirement. The period of living together does not count towards the two-year qualifying period (s.2(5)). There are very few desertion petitions because other grounds are normally available and are preferable.

3.4.6   Living apart and consent to divorce

The requirement is not living with each other in the same household for two years and consent by both parties to divorce. There is no need to explain why the parties have not lived with each other. It is possible to live apart under the same roof but may be difficult to prove. Indicators of living apart include:

- separate lives;
- no sexual relations;
- not socialising together;
- separate financial arrangements;
- no sharing of domestic chores;
- not eating together; and
- not being seen as a couple by third parties.

As in **3.4.3** above the two-year period is extended by up to six months if the couple resume living together. The period of living together does not count towards the two-year qualifying period (s.2(5)).

Consent is to the decree of divorce and not consent to the separation. The consent has to be subsisting at the date of the pronouncement of the decree and consent will normally be provided by the respondent's signature on the acknowledgement of service to the petition. In practice consideration of consent by the court will be the date the district judge considers granting his certificate for the decree nisi.

A respondent may delay the granting of the decree absolute by asking the court to consider the respondent's financial circumstances as they will be after the divorce (MCA 1973, s.10(2)). A decree absolute issued without compliance with the consideration of the respondent's financial circumstances is voidable rather than void. However, a decree absolute may be granted notwithstanding the respondent's request if the court considers it desirable (MCA 1973, s.10(4)).

3.4.7 Living apart for five years

The requirement is not living with each other in the same household for five years. As in **3.4.3** above the five years is extended by up to six months if the couple resume living together (MCA 1973, s.2(5)). There is no need to explain why the parties have not lived with each other.

As in two years' separation and consent the respondent may delay the grant of the decree absolute until his financial circumstances have been considered. Under MCA 1973, s.5(1) a respondent may oppose the grant of a decree on the ground that:

- the dissolution of the marriage will result in grave financial or other hardship; and
- it will be wrong in all the circumstances to dissolve the marriage. If the respondent proves his or her case the petition will be dismissed.

3.4.8 Stays

Obligatory and discretionary staying of the divorce will be ordered if there are concurrent proceedings in another jurisdiction. An application may be made to discharge a stay.

3.5 THE PETITION

3.5.1 Good practice

Reference should be made to Part 2 of the *Family Law Protocol* and to the Resolution Code of Practice for guidance on good practice.

Although rare, there are occasions when nullity or judicial separation petitions are an option. If so, solicitors should consider the advantages and disadvantages with the client. Prior to issuing a petition, solicitors should:

- unless there is a good reason not to, notify the respondent of the intention to issue;
- inform the respondent of the fact or facts and particulars to be relied upon; and
- provide the respondent with a copy of the statement of arrangements for approval.

3.5.2 Drafting the petition

In drafting the petition, solicitors should:

- discourage the petitioner from naming a co-respondent;
- notify the respondent that an admission of adultery on an acknowledgement of service is likely to be sufficient evidence;
- only include sufficient particulars of behaviour to secure the decree; and
- consider with the client the aggravating effect of claiming costs.

Filing of answer and cross-petitions should be discouraged and alternatives proposed, e.g. noting views in correspondence, requesting confirmation that particulars can be argued within ancillary applications, or marking the acknowledgement of service that allegations are not admitted. Clients should also be advised that they will be prejudiced if they remarry before making an application for ancillary relief.

The form of the petition is prescribed by FPR 1991, rule 2.3 which refers to Appendix 2 to FPR 1991. The court office provides a blank form of petition and notes of guidance. When completing the petition, note the following.

1. The details of the marriage should replicate exactly what is on the certificate including punctuation and spelling errors.
2. If a name is incorrectly noted on the certificate this should be explained in the 'introduction' so, for example, 'this petition is issued by Alison Jane Smith incorrectly referred to in the marriage certificate as Alison Smith ("the petitioner")'.
3. The marriage certificate or a certified copy has to be lodged with the court together, if necessary, with a certified translation.
4. If there are children of the family:

(a)   state their full names including surname;
(b)   state their dates of birth, or if over 18 years say so;
(c)   if a child is over 16 years but under 18 years state if the child is at school or college or is training for a trade, profession or vocation or working full time;
(d)   if there is a dispute as to whether a living child is a child of the family add a paragraph to that effect.

5.   Paragraph 10 should be deleted unless the ground is five years' separation.
6.   Paragraph 11 should be deleted if applying for judicial separation or nullity.
7.   Paragraph 12 requires the identification of the proof of the irretrievable breakdown by stating which paragraph(s) of s.1(2) are being put forward.
8.   Paragraph 13 requires the detail upon which the district judge will consider granting his certificate.
9.   The 'prayer' lists what orders the petitioner seeks (dissolution and costs) and what ancillary relief orders the petition may seek.

3.5.3   International elements

If the case has an international element:

1.   It is good practice to include all of the jurisdictional bases which may be relevant.
2.   If time is of the essence and the marriage certificate is not available leave of the court may be obtained to file the marriage certificate subsequently (FPR 1991, rule 2.6(2)).
3.   It is good practice to personally attend the court to ensure that the petition is issued without delay and to ask the court to note on the court file the exact time that the petition was issued.

Service is dealt with at **3.6**.

3.5.4   Statement of arrangements

A statement of arrangements is required if there is a child of the family who is under 16 years, or over 16 years but under 18 years if the child is at school or college or training for a trade, profession or vocation. The form is prescribed by FPR 1991, rule 2.2(2) and is known as a M4. The form has to be signed by the petitioner even if a solicitor is acting.

3.5.5   Amended, supplemental and further petitions (rule 2.11)

If the acts to be added occurred before the date of the petition/answer, amendment is appropriate; however, if the acts are after the date of the petition/answer, a supplemental petition/answer is appropriate. A further petition may be filed with leave where amended/supplemental pleadings are not appropriate, e.g. where after the date of the original petition two years of separation or desertion have elapsed or adultery has taken place.

No leave is required if the divorce petition is filed at the end of the period of 12 months from the date of the marriage alleging the same facts as in a judicial separation petition. Amended/supplemental petitions may be filed without leave before either an answer is filed or directions for trial given (FPR 1991, rule 2.14).

A prayer for judicial separation may be amended to dissolution and vice versa before decree absolute unless the judicial separation petition was filed within one year of the marriage.

A petition may be filed, without leave, by a respondent. This might be appropriate where the first petition is judicial separation and the respondent's petition is divorce. As an amendment to a petition dates back to the date of issue, a petition for judicial separation, which was issued before the parties had been married for 12 months, cannot be amended to a divorce petition after the 12-month period has lapsed.

3.5.6   Answers (rule 2.12)

An answer is the mechanism for either or both of:

- denying that the marriage has broken down irretrievably; and
- denying that the fact alleged is true.

Note the statutory hardship defence to five years' separation.

A simple denial that the marriage has broken down irretrievably is inadequate. Particulars of the facts supporting the defence are required, e.g. evidence of the couple consorting suggesting no irretrievable breakdown. Whilst a simple denial of adultery or behaviour might be adequate, the particulars for defending desertion, consent and five years' separation need to be set out.

3.5.7   Cross-petitions (rule 2.12(1)(b))

Cross-charges cannot be included in answers, but can be included in cross-petitions. Cross-petitions include:

- prayer for dissolution in response to a petition for dissolution;
- prayer for dissolution in response to a judicial separation petition;
- prayer for nullity in response to a judicial separation or divorce petition; and
- prayer for judicial separation in response to a prayer for judicial separation or nullity.

Answers may be filed in response to amended/supplemental and further petitions. If the petitioner does not proceed with the petition the respondent may proceed with the cross-petition.

3.5.8 Reply and particulars

A petitioner may file a reply within 14 days of receipt of the answer (FPR 1991, rule 2.13). As with an answer the reply may be a simple denial or may particularise the denial. If the particulars in petition/answer or reply are too vague a request and application for full particulars may be made.

3.5.9 Parties (rule 2.7)

The spouse who files the petition is the petitioner and the spouse who files the answer is the respondent. The adulterous third party if named in a petition is a co-respondent and if named in the answer is the party cited. If the third party adulterer dies prior to the presentation of the petition that person is not made a co-respondent. If a named co-respondent dies during the suit he will be dispensed with as a co-respondent and his name struck out of the title to the suit.

If the petition alleges adultery by way of rape the victim is not made a co-respondent. However, if there are allegations of improper association the court may direct that the third party is made a co-respondent. If a third party is served he may file an answer.

Note that foreign royalty and diplomats have special privileges as regards costs and services as a co-respondent.

3.5.10 Disability (rule 9.2)

A person under a disability, whether a minor or under the Mental Health Act 1983, may bring or defend divorce proceedings by a 'next friend'. If the petitioner believes the respondent is a patient he must seek the court's directions.

3.6 SERVICE (RULE 2.9)

The respondent is usually served by post by the court office. The respondent may be served personally but not personally by the petitioner and not on a Sunday without leave of the court. The petitioner cannot proceed until service is proved.

The respondent is served with the petition, a court form (D50A) entitled 'Notice of Proceedings and Acknowledgement of Service' and a copy of any statement of arrangements. The co-respondent is served with the petition and the 'Notice of Proceedings and Acknowledgement of Service'.

If service is either very difficult or even impossible, the petitioner can apply for one of the following orders:

- an order for substituted service (FPR 1991, rule 2.9(9)); or
- an order dispensing with service (FPR 1991, rule 10.3(3)); or

- an order deeming service if there is evidence that the respondent has received the papers (FPR 1991, rule 2.9(5) and (6)).

Specific rules apply to service on minors and on patients.

Service out of the jurisdiction is potentially complex and errors may have serious consequences including losing jurisdiction to another country. Solicitors should take the following steps.

1. Do not allow the court to serve.
2. Issue the petition and have the respondent's copy returned to you for service.
3. Complete Form N224 and send with duplicate copies of all documentation including necessary translations to the foreign process section (address: Room E10, Royal Courts of Justice, The Strand, DX 44450).
4. The fee varies depending on the country and telephone enquiries about this or any other aspect should be made to 0207 947 6691 (cheques should be made payable to 'The Foreign and Commonwealth Office').

3.7 APPLICATIONS FOR UNDEFENDED DECREE NISI (RULE 2.36)

If the decree nisi is undefended the petitioner files an affidavit of evidence on a standard form M7 together with a form requesting special procedure directions. (The standard directions are referred to as 'special procedure directions'.) The district judge will consider whether the petitioner has proved the contents of the petition, any claim for costs and where there are children whether the court should exercise its powers. If all is well notification of the date for pronouncement will be sent to all parties.

If not satisfied the judge may:

- give the petitioner the opportunity of filing further evidence;
- direct that costs may be dealt with upon receiving an application; or
- give directions as regards children.

Neither party is required to attend when the decree nisi is pronounced.

3.8 DEFENDED HEARINGS (RULE 2.32)

3.8.1 Notice

Notice of the desired place of trial, number and place of residence of witnesses is served on the other party by the party applying. Notice can be given by either petitioner or respondent. The recipient of the notice responds within eight days, with desired place of trial, number and residence of witnesses. Directions for trial are filed and the district judge will give directions for trial. The normal practice is to list for a pre-hearing review either before the district judge or the trial judge.

3.8.2 Withdrawal of consent (rule 2.10(2))

Where the fact is two years' separation and consent and consent is withdrawn the district judge will stay the proceedings. If this is the only fact relied upon either party may apply to have the petition dismissed.

3.8.3 Staying the prayer

In a defended suit if it is agreed to proceed on the cross-prayer the prayer of the petition should be stayed and leave sought to proceed on the prayer of the cross-petition. If the prayer of the petition were dismissed all of the proceedings would cease to subsist.

3.9 DEATH

Where a spouse dies before decree absolute the marriage is ended by that death and notice of abatement should be filed. The consequences of death upon ancillary proceedings are complex. Where a spouse dies, whether there can be further proceedings in the suit depends upon:

- the nature of the future proceedings; and
- the true construction of statutory provisions; and
- the applicability of the Law Reform (Miscellaneous Provisions) Act 1934, s.1(1).

Examples of further proceedings are as follows.

1. Applications to vary secured periodical payments or failure to provide reasonable provision orders if made within six months of the grant of probate or letters of administration. Applications may be by personal representatives or the payee.
2. Enforcing costs orders.
3. Enforcing secured provision orders.
4. Enforcing transfer of property orders if there has been part performance by the deceased.

The death of the payer terminates liability to pay periodical payments as well as a pending ancillary relief claim.

3.10 DISMISSAL AND TRANSFER

3.10.1 Dismissal

A petition which has not been served may be dismissed without notice. If the petition has been served either party may apply to have it dismissed: the petitioner because he chooses to do so and the respondent because the petitioner is not prosecuting the petition.

As there are no limitation periods in matrimonial proceedings the court is usually reluctant to dismiss for want of prosecution where the petitioner demonstrates a willingness to proceed.

3.10.2 Transfer of suits (rule 10.10)

A case may be transferred to another divorce county court which includes the Principal Registry. The application is on notice.

3.10.3 Queen's Proctor (section 8 and rule 2.46)

During the progress of the divorce either the court or any person may pass information to the Queen's Proctor who will, as directed by the Attorney General, instruct counsel to deal with the matter raised.

A decree absolute granted where the respondent has not been served is void if there is no order for deemed or substituted service. In that situation the Queen's Proctor may make application for relief.

3.11 DECREE ABSOLUTE (RULE 2.49)

The petitioner may apply any day after the expiration of six weeks from the day following the day of pronouncement of the decree nisi. A form M8 is accompanied by payment of a fee. It is possible for the petitioner to apply to abridge the six-week period (MCA 1973, s.1(5)) although such applications are rare.

If the petitioner delays beyond 12 months from the decree nisi an explanation in writing is required stating:

- reasons;
- whether there has been cohabitation since decree nisi; and
- whether the wife has given birth to a child since decree nisi (FPR 1991, rule 2.49(2)).

The respondent may make application three months from the first date the petitioner could have applied (i.e. four and a half months after the decree nisi). Notice is given to the petitioner and the district judge will hear the application (FPR 1991, rule 2.50(2)). When the court issues a decree absolute it is sent to both petitioner and respondent. The Principal Registry maintains a national register of decree absolutes which is open to the public.

3.12 JUDICIAL SEPARATION

A judicial separation petition may be issued at any time from the day of the marriage on the ground of any of the facts at MCA 1973, s.1(2). There is no requirement for irretrievable breakdown; either or both parties may apply for ancillary relief; interim orders may be made and upon pronouncement of the decree of judicial separation 'final' orders.

CHAPTER 4

Ancillary relief

Andrew Newbury

4.1 INTRODUCTION

The term 'ancillary relief' refers to the resolution of financial claims within divorce proceedings, i.e. financial relief ancillary to a divorce. Most commonly the phrase is used to refer to a specific application to the court for ancillary relief within a divorce.

For many family law practitioners, ancillary relief work will reflect the vast majority of their caseload. The main suit of a divorce is usually straightforward, is rarely contested and often parents are able to resolve disputes relating to children between them, without recourse to court proceedings. Even though it is not necessary to secure an order of the court to reflect arrangements for the children, it is always necessary to obtain an order in respect of financial terms of settlement. Without an order of the court any settlement reached between a husband and wife is not final and binding. More importantly, claims arising on a divorce remain live until they have been formally dismissed by way of an order of the court.

The three principal aspects of ancillary relief it is necessary to understand are as follows:

1. The specific powers of the court upon divorce, i.e. what specific orders can be made in favour of a party to the marriage.
2. The principles which are applied in quantifying or ascertaining the claims of a husband and wife on divorce.
3. The practice and procedure to be adopted in resolving those claims.

4.2 POWERS OF THE COURT

4.2.1 The orders which can be made by the court

The Matrimonial Causes Act 1973 (MCA 1973) remains the principal statute which sets out the orders that can be made by the court upon an application for ancillary relief. The main relevant sections of MCA 1973 are ss.23–25D. To those unfamiliar with the Act, the powers of the court appear surprisingly limited.

Unless the appropriate power is set out in MCA 1973, the court is unable to make such an order on divorce.

The powers of the court on divorce are as follows:

- spousal maintenance (otherwise known as periodical payments) (MCA 1973, s.23);
- payment of a lump sum or lump sums by one party to the other (MCA 1973, s.23);
- transfer of property by one party to the other (MCA 1973, s.24);
- creation of a settlement of property (MCA 1973, s.24);
- variation of an ante-nuptial or post-nuptial settlement (MCA 1973, s.24);
- sale of property (MCA 1973, s.24A);
- pension sharing orders (MCA 1973, s.24B);
- pension attachment orders (formerly known as earmarking orders) (MCA 1973, ss.25B and 25C);
- secured maintenance and secured lump sum provision (MCA 1973, s.23); and
- maintenance, lump sum, property settlement in favour of a child of the marriage (MCA 1973, ss.23 and 24).

4.2.2 Recitals – undertakings and agreements

Accordingly, a practitioner will seek to negotiate a settlement on divorce in the context of the court's powers. Often part of a settlement may fall outside the power of the court; for example, a wife may agree to resign as a director from the family business, or a husband may agree to continue to discharge the mortgage on the matrimonial home pending a certain date. Where such agreements are reached, they can only be recorded in a court order by way of a recital. Recitals can comprise a formal agreement between a husband and wife, an undertaking between the parties, or an undertaking to the court. Such provisions can however be difficult to enforce.

4.2.3 Spousal maintenance

The court can order one party of the marriage to pay to the other maintenance (otherwise known as periodical payments). Those payments are usually specified to be in a fixed sum of £X each month (as opposed to, say, a percentage of the payer's income) and are usually paid on a monthly basis. Orders are usually made for a husband to provide spousal maintenance to a former wife. Whilst the court can order a wife to pay periodical payments to a husband, in practice such orders tend to be rare. The court has the power to order payment of spousal maintenance during the joint lives of the parties or until the recipient's remarriage. By virtue of MCA 1973, s.28(1)(a), periodical payments cannot extend beyond the remarriage of the recipient or the death of either party.

Broadly speaking, spousal maintenance orders can be dealt with in one of four ways: a joint lives maintenance order; a term maintenance order; a clean break order; or a capitalised clean break.

Joint lives maintenance order

Such an order may be appropriate where it is a long marriage, where there is significant disparity between the income or earning capacity of the husband and wife and where there are young children of the marriage.

Term maintenance order

In many cases it may be inappropriate for a former wife to receive maintenance during joint lives although an immediate clean break may likewise be inappropriate. It is often the case that the recipient may require a period of adjustment before any claims to maintenance are dismissed. Spousal maintenance can therefore be ordered for a limited term or until a specific date in the future. Term maintenance orders fall into two sub-categories: those which are of an extendable term and those which are non-extendable and are therefore subject to a bar by virtue of MCA 1973, s.28(1A).

Clean break order

Many divorces may be unsuitable for a spousal maintenance order. For example, the husband and wife may earn broadly similar incomes and there may be no children of the marriage. In such cases, the parties' claims for periodical payments will be dismissed and a clean break will be achieved.

Capitalised clean break

Whilst there is no presumption in favour of there being a clean break, the court is under a duty to consider whether a clean break is appropriate and to bring about a clean break wherever possible by virtue of MCA 1973, s.25A. Where there is sufficient capital, one spouse may pay a lump sum or series of lump sums to the other in lieu of a future maintenance obligation. Where a lump sum is to be calculated in lieu of a joint lives maintenance obligation, such sum is usually calculated by reference to the *Duxbury* tables (*Duxbury* v. *Duxbury* [1987] 1 FLR 7).

4.2.4 Lump sums

The court can order one party of the marriage to pay to the other a lump sum or lump sums. Although a lump sum order can only be made on one occasion, the court can on that occasion order a series of lump sums to be paid.

Practitioners should also be aware of the difference between an order for a series of lump sums and an order for a lump sum payable by instalments. Whilst on the face of it they are the same, an order for a series of lump sums cannot be varied at a later date. By contrast, an order for payment of a lump sum by instalments can be varied. Note should, however, be had of the unreported decision of Coleridge J in *Lamont* v. *Lamont* (13 October 2006) in which he expressed the view that some orders which provided for a series of lump sum payments were in reality a lump sum payment in instalments. He suggested that the mere drafting of the order in that manner should not preclude the court's power under s.31.

Lump sum orders can be made for a number of reasons: they may include a payment in lieu of maintenance; a payment to buy out an interest in the matrimonial home or other assets of the marriage; and/or in lieu of pension provision.

4.2.5 Transfer of property

In the vast majority of divorces the power to order transfer of property will be exercised in relation to the former matrimonial home. For example, an order may include the transfer of property into the wife's sole name in exchange for the payment by the wife to the husband of a lump sum. Note should be taken of the specific power of the court under MCA 1973, s.24(1)(a): the court can only order the transfer of a property by one party to the other or to (or for the benefit of) the child of the family. Orders providing for the transfer of property for the benefit of a child are, however, rare.

Both real and personal property can be transferred under s.24. The power of the court is therefore most commonly exercised in respect of the following: the family home or any other real property; endowment policies; shares; bank accounts; cars; household objects and other personal possessions. The only qualification is that one of the parties must have an interest or entitlement in the property to be transferred.

Practical issues need to be addressed where a property is subject to a mortgage. Whilst the court can order one spouse to transfer a property to the other, a mortgagee is not a party to the proceedings and cannot be ordered to consent to the transfer. Where an application for ancillary relief includes an application for a transfer of property which is subject to a mortgage then Form A must be served upon the mortgage company in accordance with FPR 1991, rule 2.59. Where there are no ancillary relief proceedings or where Form A has not been served upon the mortgagee, a draft consent order which incorporates a transfer of property subject to a mortgage must be served upon the mortgagee at least 14 days before lodging it with the court (FPR 1991, rule 2.61). If no objection is received from the mortgagee within that 14-day period, the draft order may then be lodged with the court.

In practical terms, however, it is of course sensible to seek the mortgagee's consent to the transfer of property before any such agreement is finalised.

4.2.6 Sale of property

The court's power to order the sale of property is akin to its power to order the transfer of property. The court can order the sale of any real or personal property subject to the qualification that one of the parties must have a beneficial interest in the property itself or its proceeds of sale.

The court can order that a sale of property takes place immediately or on a deferred basis. When ordering a sale of property, the court will also usually order the following provisions: who should have conduct of the sale of the property; the estate agents and/or solicitors to be instructed on the sale; that the costs of sale and the outstanding mortgage be discharged from the proceeds of sale; how the eventual net proceeds of sale should then be divided between the parties. The net proceeds of sale can be divided in a number of ways: in some cases a simple percentage division may be appropriate; in other cases one party may receive a fixed sum and the other party the balance of the proceeds of sale, regardless of the sale price.

4.2.7 Pension sharing orders

Pension sharing orders are a relatively new concept and can be made where divorce proceedings were issued on or after 1 December 2000. In essence, the court can order that one or more pensions owned by one party to the marriage are divided between the parties. A 100 per cent pension sharing order would entail an entire pension policy being transferred from one party to the other.

The usual way in which pensions are valued upon divorce is by reference to their cash equivalent transfer value. The court can then order that the cash equivalent transfer value be divided on a specified percentage basis.

A pension sharing order can be effected by way of an internal or external transfer. Internal transfers are often the only option in respect of final salary schemes such as civil service pensions, teachers' pensions, etc. The net effect of an internal transfer is that the recipient of the pension share would become a member of that pension scheme with the fund transferred to them. By contrast, where there is an external transfer, the fund received by the recipient can be invested in a new pension fund of their choice.

It is worth noting that whilst a separating couple can agree to transfer or sell property at any time and a court order is not required, a pension share can only take effect subsequent to a court order made upon divorce.

4.2.8 Pension attachment orders

A power of the court to make pension attachment orders was introduced in 1996, although these orders were never particularly popular, especially since the introduction of pension sharing in December 2000. Such orders were initially known as earmarking orders, but are now known as attachment orders.

In essence, they are usually maintenance/periodical payments orders or lump sum orders, but instead of the payments being made via the former spouse, they are made direct by the pension provider. The legislation does however contain some useful powers: the pension holder can be compelled to nominate their former spouse to receive some or all of the death-in-service benefit and they can also be ordered to commute the pension lump sum upon retirement. It should, however, be noted that a pension attachment order and a pension sharing order cannot be made in respect of the same policy within the same divorce.

4.2.9 Variation of settlements

The court has the power to vary trusts or settlements on the basis that they are either ante-nuptial or post-nuptial settlements. Accordingly, only a settlement made in relation to the marriage that is the subject of divorce proceedings can be the subject of such an order. Such orders are relatively rare.

4.2.10 Settlement of property

Likewise, an order creating the settlement of property is uncommon, but where the circumstances warrant it, the court may make a *Martin* order or *Mesher* order (*Martin* v. *Martin* [1978] 3 All ER 764; *Mesher* v. *Mesher and Hall* (1973) [1980] 1 All ER 126). In essence, the court can order the transfer or the variation of title under which the matrimonial home (or other property) is held. The sale of that property may then be postponed until a specific later date such as the death of the transferee, remarriage or cohabitation of the transferee or the youngest child of the family reaching a specified age. Upon the happening of the appropriate event, the trust for sale comes into effect and the proceeds of sale are then divided in accordance with the specific order of the court.

4.2.11 Orders in respect of children of the family

In essence, since the introduction of the Child Support Agency (CSA) in 1993, the court's powers to order maintenance for children can only be exercised in limited circumstances. The court will only order capital provision for the benefit of the children should the circumstances warrant it, although such circumstances tend to be rare. See further **Chapter 7**.

4.3 PRINCIPLES APPLIED IN ANCILLARY RELIEF CLAIMS

4.3.1 Overview

The basic principles which are applied in considering and quantifying ancillary relief claims are set out in MCA 1973, s.25. The checklist set out in s.25

comprises the overriding statutory principles which must always be considered in any ancillary relief claim. Although the s.25 checklist has been in place for over 30 years, it has been interpreted and adapted by the courts in different ways since its inception. Ancillary relief case law has evolved as society has developed and attitudes have changed. First instance decisions and, more importantly, Court of Appeal decisions have led to the refinement and reinterpretation of s.25. On rare occasions, s.25 has come under scrutiny by the House of Lords. The leading cases on the interpretation and application of s.25 are the House of Lords decisions in *White* v. *White* [2000] 2 FLR 981 and *Miller* v. *Miller*; *McFarlane* v. *McFarlane* [2006] UKHL 24.

4.3.2   Matrimonial Causes Act 1973, section 25

When exercising its powers under MCA 1973, ss.23, 24, 24A, 25B and 25C, the court must have regard to the factors set out in s.25. The statutory provision can be broken down into three parts: s.25(1); the checklist under s.25(2); and the duty of the court to consider the clean break under s.25A.

4.3.3   Matrimonial Causes Act 1973, section 25(1)

The court must have regard to 'all the circumstances of the case'. In practice this means the court must look at all of the relevant issues in any particular case and therefore can take into account issues which are not specifically addressed in the s.25(2) checklist. Also under s.25(1) the court must give first consideration to the welfare of any child of the family who has not attained the age of 18. Although the welfare of the children is the court's first consideration, it is not necessarily of paramount consideration to the court in all cases (*SRJ* v. *DWJ (Financial Provision)* [1999] 2 FLR 176). In practice consideration of the children's welfare will usually mean having particular regard to their housing need and meeting their day-to-day income needs.

4.3.4   The section 25(2) checklist

The court must have regard to the factors set out in paras.(a)–(h) of s.25(2). The checklist is not set out in any order of priority (*Piglowska* v. *Piglowski* [1999] 3 All ER 632) and in certain cases particular factors may be of greater importance than others.

Financial resources

Section 25(2)(a) directs that the court must have regard to the income, earning capacity, property and other financial resources. That can include property and income which either party has or is likely to have in the foreseeable future and can include earning capacity. Before there can be any proper assessment of ancillary relief claims, both parties to a divorce must provide full and frank disclosure of their financial resources (*Jenkins* v. *Livesey (formerly Jenkins)* [1985] 1 All ER 106). The obligation to provide full disclosure is the bedrock of ancillary relief proceedings. In most divorces ascertaining and calculating the full extent of the property and income of the parties is a straightforward task. In more complex cases there may be detailed arguments over what exactly constitutes relevant assets or resources. Examples include whether assets owned prior to the marriage should be treated differently from those built up during the marriage, the true value of a spouse's earning capacity or even the financial resources of a cohabitee.

Financial needs, obligations and responsibilities of each of the parties to the marriage, or which they are likely to have in the foreseeable future (section 25(2)(b))

The needs should be viewed in the context of the available resources of the marriage. The needs of a wife in the context of a high net worth divorce would be very different from the needs of a wife in a limited means case. In the majority of divorces, needs will centre on the following two issues: housing need and income need. Reasonable housing needs will be ascertained by reference to the number of bedrooms required in relation to the number of children of the family and the cost of property in the local area. The estate agents' property particulars are often used as a guide for assessing housing need. Income needs are calculated by compiling lists of expenditure setting out income requirements on either a monthly or an annual basis. Such schedules must however be considered in the context of the available income of the parties to the marriage.

Standard of living enjoyed before the breakdown of the marriage (section 25(2)(c))

Whilst standard of living is a factor to be considered by the court, in the majority of cases the assessment of available resources and needs takes a more central role. In the majority of divorces, it is inevitably the case that standard of living will drop when two separate households have to be created out of one.

Age of each party to the marriage and the duration of the marriage (section 25(2)(d))

The age of the parties may have a direct impact upon other s.25 factors. By way of example, pension considerations will be significant for a couple in their 50s, but would be less important for a couple in their 30s. The potential income and earning capacity of a woman in her 30s or 40s may be of crucial importance to a divorce, whereas a wife in her late 50s or 60s would probably not be expected to exercise an earning capacity.

It might seem that the phrase 'duration of the marriage' is self-explanatory. That is not, however, the case. Although the courts are bound by the wording of statute, since the decision of *GW* v. *RW (Financial Provision: Departure from Equality)* [2003] 2 FLR 108 the courts have been taking into account any period of pre-marriage cohabitation which has moved seamlessly into marriage. That period can commence when cohabitation starts or at whatever point the courts feel that the parties truly became committed to one another. The change in the courts' approach is a reflection of society insofar as many people now choose to cohabit prior to marriage. As far as the end of the marriage is concerned, courts now tend to look at the date when the parties separated as opposed to the pronouncement of decree absolute.

Physical or mental disability of either of the parties to the marriage (section 25(2)(e))

This is of limited application, although where such issues do arise they tend to have a particular bearing upon a party's needs or their earning capacity.

Contributions (section 25(2)(f))

There has been particular focus in case law on the issue of contributions since the House of Lords decision in *White* v. *White* [2000] 2 FLR 981. The House of Lords made it clear that there should not be any discrimination between the roles of the breadwinner and the homemaker. Since the decision in *White* there has therefore been little scope for argument when evaluating the comparative worth of contributions during the course of the marriage itself. In the majority of cases, contributions arguments will not help to advance a case, although they can be relevant in certain circumstances. In particular, the court may wish to have regard to pre-marriage contributions where one party introduced a significant amount of capital at the outset. Such arguments tend to be of lesser relevance following on from a long marriage. Assets which have been inherited by either party to the marriage may be treated on a different footing from those acquired in a normal manner during the marriage itself: inherited assets could be viewed as a contribution. In wholly exceptional cases, there may be scope to argue the relevance of a truly special or stellar contribution during the course of the marriage. Such contributions would only be relevant when they have had a direct impact upon the welfare of the family, it would be inequitable to disregard them and they are 'obvious and gross'. This approach, which is akin to the approach on the relevance of conduct under s.25(2)(g), was adopted by the House of Lords in *Miller and McFarlane*.

Conduct of each of the parties (section 25(2)(g))

Bad behaviour or conduct is rarely taken into account by the courts. It will only be treated as a relevant factor if it would be inequitable to disregard it. Historically the test used to be that the conduct was 'obvious and gross'. In very few divorces is the conduct sufficiently serious to warrant being taken into account by the court. In practice, very few judges will be willing to allow conduct arguments. The limited application of conduct arguments was emphasised by the House of Lords in *Miller and McFarlane*.

Section 25(2)(h) – the loss of benefits which either party would have acquired were it not for the divorce

In practice, this generally refers to the loss of widow's pension benefits and any other rights of the pension schemes. It could, however, extend to any other benefit which may fall in at some point in the future, such as benefits under share options or inheritance prospects.

4.3.5   *White v. White*

The House of Lords decision in *White* v. *White* [2000] 2 FLR 981 is the leading case in ancillary relief work. Whilst the decision in *White* does not mean that all case law predating that judgment is no longer valid, a certain amount of caution should be adopted when relying upon such case law, particularly if the approach and principles of such decisions do not fit in with the clearly established principles of *White* v. *White*. The leading judgment in the case was given by Lord Nicholls of Birkenhead and can be broadly summarised as follows below.

The yardstick of equality

After the trial judge has considered and applied the factors in the s.25 checklist, that decision should be cross-checked by reference to the yardstick of equality. If there is to be an unequal division of the assets of the marriage, good reason must be shown. However, in the vast majority of cases where assets are limited, equality will not be the appropriate outcome. The court's consideration of children's housing needs will outweigh any issues of equality. By contrast, where the marriage is long, the assets outweigh the needs of the parties and there are no significant contributions arguments which would justify a departure from equality, then an equal division of the assets of the marriage would be the appropriate outcome.

Contributions

As stated above at **4.3.4** there should be no discrimination between the contributions made by the breadwinner and those made by the homemaker. In the absence of any striking arguments to the contrary, such contributions are viewed as equal.

Reasonable requirements

In pre-*White* big money cases, the needs of a claimant wife were often determined by reference to reasonable requirements, regardless of the value of the overall assets of the marriage. Lord Nicholls, however, took the view that such an approach was discriminatory and unfair.

Fairness

Fairness was the overriding hallmark of the *White* decision and it has since been echoed in subsequent decisions (for example, *Lambert* v. *Lambert* [2002] EWCA Civ 1685) that the overarching aim of the courts is to achieve fairness between the parties.

Inherited assets

In the vast majority of cases the fact that some of the assets were inherited by one party will carry little or no weight, particularly where the first consideration would be to meet the needs of the children. Where needs are less of a predominant factor, inherited assets may be treated differently from those acquired jointly by the parties during the course of the marriage and, where possible, should be retained by that party.

4.3.6 Post-*White* case law – *Miller and McFarlane*

The period following the House of Lords decision in *White* v. *White* has been one of change and uncertainty in ancillary relief work. Whilst the intention of Lord Nicholls' judgment was to assist litigants and clarify the law, there has since been a series of cases which have sought to further redefine the principles set out in the judgment. Despite such decisions, uncertainty remains.

The principal post-*White* authority is the House of Lords decision in *Miller* v. *Miller*; *McFarlane* v. *McFarlane* [2006] UKHL 24. Whilst the decision is not as clear in its application as *White* v. *White*, the principles to be drawn are as follows.

The requirements of fairness

Further guidance is given to the approach adopted in *White* v. *White*. Fairness requires consideration of the following: meeting needs; compensating a party who has suffered an economic disparity; sharing, although the yardstick of equality is an aid, not a rule. In the majority of cases, the search for fairness may largely begin and end in a consideration of needs.

Compensation

A periodical payments order can be made not only to meet the spouse's needs, but also to compensate them. The principle of compensation is aimed at redressing any significant prospective economic disparity which may arise from the way in which the parties conducted their marriage. Few reported cases have considered the application of the compensation principle since *Miller and McFarlane*, although note should be taken of the decisions in *Lauder* v. *Lauder* [2007] EWHC 1227 (Fam), *VB* v. *JP* [2008] EWHC 112 (Fam) and *McFarlane* v. *McFarlane* [2009] EWHC 891 (Fam), all of which were variation of maintenance cases.

Contributions and conduct

Arguments in respect of conduct or special/stellar contributions should only be pursued in cases where such contributions or conduct are 'obvious and gross'.

Short marriages

The principles of *White* v. *White* apply to short as well as long marriages. The right to share is applicable in all marriages. The approach adopted by the Court of Appeal in *Foster* v. *Foster* [2003] EWCA Civ 565 was upheld.

Matrimonial and non-matrimonial assets

The House of Lords in *Miller and McFarlane* was not agreed on what constitutes matrimonial and non-matrimonial assets. Lord Nicholls was of the view that the yardstick of equality should be applied to all matrimonial property, which comprises all assets built up during the marriage. The yardstick should apply whatever the character of the assets and whatever the length of the marriage. By contrast, Baroness Hale viewed matrimonial assets as comprising those which have been acquired by either spouse and used for the benefit of the family as a whole, as well as business/joint ventures in which both spouses work. She viewed non-matrimonial property in a broader manner than Lord Nicholls, with such a category incorporating business or investment assets generated solely or mainly by the efforts of one spouse during the marriage.

4.3.7 Post-*Miller and McFarlane* case law

Since the House of Lords decision in *Miller and McFarlane*, there has been some uncertainty regarding how its principles should be applied. The following are some examples:

(a) *Charman* v. *Charman (No.4)* [2007] EWCA Civ 503. Where the sharing principle met the parties' needs, then the sharing principle would take precedence. By contrast, if the sharing principle failed to meet needs, then needs would dictate a greater share of the assets. This approach was subsequently adopted in *L* v. *L* [2008] 1 FLR 142.

(b) *C* v. *C* [2007] EWHC 2033 (Fam). After a long marriage, a formulaic approach of having to identify matrimonial and non-matrimonial property should be resisted. The husband's substantial wealth created prior to the commencement of the relationship justified a departure from equality. The extent of that departure in any given case was not to be calculated according to a formula or clear mathematics.

(c) *B* v. *B (Ancillary Relief: Distribution of Assets)* [2008] EWCA Civ 543. It was stated that neither *White* nor *Miller and McFarlane* established any rule that equal division is a starting point in all cases. On the contrary, the starting point is the financial position of the parties and MCA 1973, s.25. In all cases the objective is fairness, which requires an individual assessment of each case. The court must follow *White* and look at the extent to which there has been a departure from equality, but that exercise is simply a cross-check. The primary objectives remain fairness and an absence of discrimination.

4.4 PRACTICE AND PROCEDURE

4.4.1 The overriding objective

When conducting an ancillary relief case, regard must always be had to the overriding objective set out at FPR 1991, rule 2.51B. The procedural rules which govern an application for ancillary relief are set out in FPR 1991 as amended. Rule 2.51B states that the Rules are a code with an overriding objective of enabling the court to deal with cases justly. That includes ensuring the parties are on an equal footing, saving expense, dealing with the case in ways which are proportionate, ensuring that it is dealt with expeditiously and fairly and allotting to it an appropriate share of the court's resources.

4.4.2 Voluntary disclosure and the pre-action protocol

In many cases it is possible to resolve matters between the parties without the need for the court timetable of an ancillary relief application. With the assistance of solicitors, the husband and wife may agree to produce their financial disclosure on a voluntary basis. The extent and format of that disclosure can be agreed between the solicitors, although reference should be made to the pre-action protocol set out at Part IV of the Law Society's *Family Law Protocol*.

The Protocol suggests that Form E should be used as a guide to the format of the disclosure and documents should only be disclosed to the extent that they are required by Form E. Excessive or disproportionate costs should not be incurred. Where further information is required that is not otherwise set out in the Form E, that can be raised by way of a concise questionnaire setting out further documents and information required from the other party.

4.4.3 Application for ancillary relief

An application to the court for ancillary relief may be required for a number of reasons. One party may refuse to provide disclosure on a voluntary basis, or it may be that the information provided is incomplete and further information is not forthcoming. On the other hand it may be the case that whilst comprehensive disclosure has been provided, an impasse has been reached regarding terms of settlement and matters may only be progressed with the benefit of a court timetable.

Some cases may be more suitable for court managed ancillary relief proceedings as opposed to voluntary disclosure. As the pre-action protocol states at para.2.2, 'in considering the option of pre-application disclosure and negotiation, solicitors should bear in mind the advantage of having a court timetable and court managed process'. In cases where there is a complex asset structure or where the parties are apart on fundamental points of principle, an application to the court may prove necessary.

The various steps of the ancillary relief procedure are set out at FPR 1991, rules 2.71 to 2.77, as amended. The following is an overview of the main steps of the process.

Issuing the application

The application can be made by either the petitioner or the respondent within the divorce proceedings. The application is lodged with the court in triplicate together with the requisite fee payable. The court will then issue the application and will set down the first stages of the court timetable up to and including the fixing of the first appointment.

Forms E

The date for exchange of Forms E will have been set down by the court upon the issuing of the ancillary relief application. Form E is a voluminous standard form document which must be sworn by each party and will include the financial information as required by the form. The form also requires each party to set out details of their income and capital needs as well as other relevant background information such as any allegations of contributions or conduct. Form

E also lists specific documents which must be exhibited to it including bank statements, payslips, P60 and pension valuations.

First appointment documents

Form C, issued by the court, will also set out a date for the exchange of documents prior to the first appointment. Those documents comprise questionnaire, statement of issues, chronology and Form G. Arguably the most important document is the questionnaire as this is each party's main opportunity to seek further information in respect of their spouse's finances. The questionnaire must be carefully drafted and must relate only to issues relevant to the case.

The first appointment

This is a procedural hearing, the purpose of which is to define issues and save costs. The principal issues to be considered by the district judge are as follows:

- the extent to which any questionnaires shall be answered;
- the instruction of expert witnesses – usually surveyors in respect of property or accountants in respect of businesses;
- whether any further evidence by way of affidavits is required either from the parties or from witnesses (whilst this is relatively uncommon, affidavits may be required on specific issues, such as contributions, conduct or by reference to the entire s.25 checklist); and
- any other timetabling issues that will need to be addressed, including the listing of the next court hearing.

Post-first appointment steps

Following the first appointment, the parties will compile their replies to the questionnaires. Any expert evidence that has been ordered will also be produced. It is usually the case that once such information has been marshalled, both parties will then be in a position to make and consider proposals for settlement. In certain cases, further applications may need to be made back to the court for more disclosure or expert evidence.

The financial dispute resolution hearing

The financial dispute resolution (FDR) hearing is effectively a meeting at court held for the purpose of conciliation and settlement. Seven days before the hearing, the solicitor for the applicant must lodge with the court any open or without prejudice proposals which have been submitted. Once at court, the parties and their representatives use their best endeavours to reach an agreement on the outstanding issues between them. Whilst the judge will not hear evidence and cannot impose any decision upon the parties, judges are encouraged to assist in the resolution of the matter by making appropriate comments and expressing their views. As the judge conducting the FDR hearing will have seen without prejudice correspondence, if an agreement is not reached at the FDR, then, save for very limited circumstances, that judge cannot have any further involvement with the case – see FPR 1991, rule 2.61E(2) and *Myerson* v. *Myerson* [2008] EWCA Civ 1376.

Final hearing

The FDR hearing is an effective filter. For those cases that have not been resolved by that stage, many ongoing disputes settle either at or soon after the FDR hearing, and relatively few matters therefore proceed to a fully contested final hearing. Such hearings can be expensive and draining for the parties involved. It is only at this stage in the process that the parties will usually be required to give evidence. Having heard such evidence and submissions made by the parties' representatives, the judge will then make a final decision, taking into account the s.25 checklist and appropriate case law.

4.4.4   Negotiations and settlement

The underlying purpose of ancillary relief procedure, whether in the context of voluntary disclosure or a court structured application is to achieve a settlement of claims arising upon divorce. Practitioners should always bear this aim in mind when conducting any part of ancillary relief work. Once a party is in a position to do so and once all of the necessary information is available, focus should be placed upon conducting negotiations. Such negotiations can be carried out in a number of ways including the following:

1. Historically the most common approach was by way of without prejudice *Calderbank* correspondence passing between the parties' solicitors. Following the introduction of new costs rules on 3 April 2006, without prejudice correspondence can no longer be relied upon when the court hears arguments on the issue of costs. Even though without prejudice correspondence will no longer have any impact on costs, it can remain an effective negotiating tool. Without prejudice correspondence can be used in conjunction with open correspondence.
2. In certain circumstances a round table meeting with both solicitors and the parties can be an effective tool to achieve a prompt settlement. Such meetings tend to be most effective where the issues between the parties have been narrowed and both parties have set out their proposals prior to such a meeting.
3. By use of mediation or collaborative law – see **Chapter 13**.

4.4.5 Consent orders

Once terms of settlement have been agreed between the parties, a consent order must be drawn up setting out those terms of settlement in the form of a court order. Such draft orders can be submitted to the court for approval on or after pronouncement of decree nisi of divorce.

Care must be taken in the drafting of consent orders. Particularly if issues arise at a later date, great focus may be placed upon the wording of the order itself. As emphasised at **4.2.1** above, as the court only has the power to make certain types of orders (for example periodical payments, lump sum payments, pension sharing orders, etc.), care must be taken to draw a distinction between parts of the agreement which can form a substantive order of the court and those elements which fall outside the scope of the court's powers. Terms of settlement which have been agreed between the parties, but which cannot be ordered by the court, need to be recorded as recitals, undertakings or agreements.

4.5 INTERIM ORDERS

4.5.1 Overview

The court's power to make substantive interim orders is limited. Whilst the ancillary relief procedure is geared towards dealing with procedural issues, the only substantive interim orders which can be made are in respect of periodical payments and injunctive relief. It should be particularly borne in mind that the court does not have the power to make interim capital orders, such as an order for an interim lump sum or for the sale of property (*Wicks* v. *Wicks* [1998] 1 All ER 977).

4.5.2 Maintenance pending suit/interim periodical payments

The court has the power to order maintenance pending suit by virtue of MCA 1973, s.22. That is to say the court has the power to order one party to pay to the other periodical payments for the other's maintenance, commencing not earlier than the date of the presentation of the petition and to continue not beyond the pronouncement of decree absolute. Where an application is made after decree absolute but before resolution of the substantive terms of settlement, an application could be made for interim periodical payments by virtue of MCA 1973, s.23. Whilst the terminology is different, the commonly held view is that the same principles apply.

Whilst the case law on maintenance pending suit applications is limited, the wording of s.22 gives the court a wide discretion so that it is able to make such orders as it 'thinks reasonable'. Whilst some judges will therefore focus upon simply meeting a spouse's basic needs pending conclusion of the case, others may take a more generous approach in the context of the overall available income. The inherent uncertainty and expense of such applications means that they are inevitably less common than they once were. Whilst the courts have been at pains to point out that the order made for maintenance pending suit should not be viewed as setting the yardstick for a longer term award of periodical payments (*M* v. *M (Maintenance Pending Suit)* [2002] 2 FLR 123), many practitioners are of the view that it is often the case that it is used as a useful yardstick.

Useful guidance on maintenance pending suit applications was given by Nicholas Mostyn QC in *TL* v. *ML* [2005] EWHC 2860 (Fam).

The procedure for applying for maintenance pending suit, interim periodical payments or a variation of such an order is set out in FPR 1991, rule 2.69F.

4.5.3 Injunctive relief

Under MCA 1973, s.37 the court can make an order preventing the disposition of property which is about to be effected with the intention of defeating a claim for financial relief. The court's power is also extended to setting aside any disposition that has already been completed if it would result in a different order for financial relief being made.

It is important to note that an application for relief under s.37 can only be made in the context of ancillary relief proceedings. It is also important to note the specific requirements set out in s.37: if a disposition is about to be made, it is necessary for the applicant to show that it is with the intention of defeating the claim for financial relief. Where a party is seeking to set aside a disposition, they must show that it would result in different financial relief being granted to the applicant. This can sometimes prove to be a high hurdle.

An alternative route to an application under s.37 is an application under the inherent jurisdiction of the court to preserve assets which are the subject matter of proceedings (*Shipman* v. *Shipman* [1991] 1 FLR 250) or by way of a freezing injunction (formerly known as a *Mareva*) by virtue of rule 2.5.1 of the Civil Procedure Rules (CPR) 1998.

4.6 VARIATION APPLICATIONS

4.6.1 Overview

The court's power to vary orders is governed by MCA 1973, s.31 which sets out the categories of ancillary relief orders that can and cannot be varied. The powers under s.31 also extend to the discharge and suspension of various orders. For a comprehensive list of those orders that are capable of variation, reference must be made to the provisions of MCA 1973, s.31, although the main categories are as follows:

1. A periodical payments order, including an interim order as well as a secured periodical payments order. The vast majority of variation applications under s.31 will concern reviews of periodical payments orders.
2. Order for lump sum by instalments. As noted at **4.2.4** above, by contrast an order for a series of lump sums cannot be varied.
3. Certain provisions relating to pension attachments orders.
4. An order for settlement of property or for variation of a settlement where the order has been made within judicial separation proceedings.
5. An order for sale of property.

4.6.2   Capitalisation applications

In 1998 MCA 1973, s.31 was amended to provide for the capitalisation of periodical payments orders. Upon hearing an application to vary, the court has the power to order one party to pay to the other capital provision in lieu of future maintenance and on the basis that a clean break is made either immediately or at some point in the future. Although in such circumstances it would be usual for the court to order the payment of a lump sum, the court also has the power to make an order for the transfer of property or a pension sharing order in lieu of ongoing maintenance. A pension policy shared on divorce cannot be shared again in the context of a capitalisation application under s.31.

4.6.3   Principles applied on variation applications

By virtue of MCA 1973, s.31(7), the court will consider any change in any of the matters to which the court was required to have regard when making the original order. In addition, the court must have regard to all the circumstances of the case, with first consideration being given to the welfare of any children of the family who are minors. In effect, this reflects the checklist under MCA 1973, s.25. Changes in circumstances could be the cohabitation of one of the parties, children leaving home or ceasing to be financially dependent or one of the parties changing their job or receiving significantly increased or reduced salary.

When considering a capitalisation application, courts have been keen to emphasise that such applications should not be viewed as a second bite of the cherry. In *Pearce* v. *Pearce* [2003] 2 FLR 1144 the Court of Appeal laid down the following test for capitalisation applications:

1. The court must consider what variation, if any, should be made to the original order for periodical payments.

2. The court must then consider the date from which the varied order is to commence.
3. The capitalisation of that maintenance is then carried out in accordance with the *Duxbury* tables. There is a narrow discretion to depart from the *Duxbury* tables to reflect special factors.

4.6.4 Procedure for variation applications

An application to vary under s.31 is a form of ancillary relief and therefore the same procedure as set out in **4.4** above must be adopted. It can be a cumbersome procedure for a variation application and the costs can therefore be disproportionate to the issues in dispute between the parties. In some cases it may be viewed as appropriate to move straight from the first appointment to a final hearing with a view to reducing potentially significant costs.

4.7 APPEALS

4.7.1 Appeals

Appeals are uncommon in ancillary relief proceedings. Most practitioners will probably experience few appeals, if any, during the course of their career. Robust advice needs to be given to clients who are considering appealing a decision of the court.

To succeed in an appeal, it is necessary to demonstrate that there has been a procedural irregularity, or that in carrying out the balancing exercise, the district judge has taken into account matters which are irrelevant or ignored matters which were relevant, or otherwise has arrived at a conclusion which was plainly wrong and which could only have been reached if the judge erred in the balancing exercise. A useful overview is contained in *Cordle* v. *Cordle* [2002] 1 FLR 207 and more recently in *S* v. *S* [2008] EWHC 519 (Fam).

For most practitioners, final ancillary relief hearings will take place before a district judge sitting in the county court. An appeal against a district judge's decision should be made to a judge of the county court following the procedure in FPR 1991, rule 8.1 and CPR 1998, Part 59.

An application for an appeal must be issued within 14 days of the date of the original order which is being appealed and must be served not less than 14 days before the date fixed for the hearing of the appeal. Leave of the original judge to make the appeal is not required.

Upon hearing the appeal, the judge of the county court does not hear evidence afresh, but simply considers the evidence on paper. Generally speaking, the appeal is limited to a review of the original order, unless the judge considers that it would be in the interests of justice to hold a rehearing.

By contrast, an appeal from a judge of the county court or the High Court is made to the Court of Appeal. The procedure for all appeals to the Court of Appeal is prescribed by CPR 1998, Part 52 as supplemented by Practice Direction – Appeals (PD52).

An application for permission to appeal to the Court of Appeal should be made to the original judge, if possible. Where refused, an application for permission should be made to the Court of Appeal.

4.7.2 *Barder* appeals

An appeal under the principles contained in *Barder* v. *Caluori* [1988] 1 AC 20 is an appeal out of time against an order where new events have occurred since the making of the order which invalidate the basis, or fundamental assumption, upon which the order was made. The new event must have occurred within a relatively short time after the order was made and the application must be brought reasonably promptly.

As Thorpe LJ stated in *Myerson* v. *Myerson (No.2)* [2009] EWCA Civ 282, 'very few successful applications have been reported'. As in *Barder* itself, successful applications have been brought where one party has died soon after the original order was made. By contrast, however, a significant change in the value of assets (such as property or shares in a limited company) does not give rise to an appeal under the *Barder* principles – *Cornick* v. *Cornick (No.1)* [1994] 2 FLR 530.

4.8 ENFORCEMENT

Enforcement of ancillary relief orders is a subject fraught with difficulty. In essence, ancillary relief orders are not always easily enforceable. When dealing with a difficult spouse, care should be taken in the drafting of the original ancillary relief order to limit recourse to enforcement procedure.

A detailed consideration of the different forms of procedure is beyond the scope of this chapter, save to say that there is not one single form of enforcement available to a party to the proceedings, but the form of enforcement used depends upon the breach of the original order. The most commonly used forms of enforcement include an attachment of earnings order, a charging order, a garnishee order or committal by way of judgment summons.

4.8.1 Attachment of earnings order

This is one of the most effective forms of enforcement and can be used where the debtor is in employment. The court has the power to order the debtor's employer to deduct fixed amounts from the debtor's earnings and to pay them to the court against the sums due under the order to be enforced. Such orders are usually used for maintenance orders.

4.8.2   Charging order

The court may impose a charge on the debtor's interest in land or securities. In practice, the effect of the remedy is to provide security for the debt as opposed to actually enforcing it. Having made a charging order, the court may eventually order the sale of the asset subject to such an order.

4.8.3   Garnishee order

An order may be made in respect of the creditor's bank or building society account.

4.8.4   Committal by way of judgment summons

The court may imprison for up to six weeks a person who has been ordered to pay maintenance or a lump sum and who has the means to pay it, but neglects or refuses to do so. In view of the criminal standard of proof required to obtain such an order, the judgment summons procedure has become less effective (*Corbett* v. *Corbett* [2003] 2 FLR 385).

CHAPTER 5

Inheritance Act claims

Emma Collins

5.1 INTRODUCTION

Whilst it is possible for individuals to make wills leaving their estates to whomever they choose, in certain circumstances the Inheritance (Provision for Family and Dependants) Act 1975 (IPFDA 1975) will enable a claim to be made against the deceased's estate where it is considered that inadequate provision has been made for certain categories of family or dependants. A claim can also be made where the deceased died intestate. This is an important additional tool for the family lawyer and should not be overlooked when advising clients in the context of marriage breakdown as well as in the event of the death of a spouse or former spouse.

Inheritance Act claims can be seen as a difficult area of the law for family lawyers. They sit slightly uncomfortably between family law and civil litigation, with practitioners having to apply family law type principles, with which they are familiar, within a CPR 1998 framework, about which they are usually less confident. In many ways, however, this area of the law is well suited to the family lawyer who is used to applying a discretionary set of criteria, particularly as the criteria and available remedies are similar to many ancillary relief concepts. A better understanding of IPFDA 1975 and the potential claims under it will inform the approach adopted in day-to-day ancillary relief proceedings and will ensure that practitioners are in a position to fully advise their clients as to the implications of the financial settlements to which they are agreeing.

Whilst the Resolution ethos and best practice should always be adopted where possible to try and promote an amicable settlement, it should be borne in mind that these cases will often be conducted for the personal representatives by non-family lawyers unfamiliar with the Code of Practice. Nonetheless, whilst it may be necessary to take a more litigious approach to protect the client, inflammatory correspondence should always be avoided. Inheritance Act cases can be amongst the hardest and most bitterly fought (by the parties) of any family lawyer's practice and it is the duty of the lawyer to minimise that acrimony where possible. The Association of Contentious Trust and Probate Specialists (ACTAPS) has produced Practice Guidance

Notes ('The ACTAPS Code') which are designed to promote the resolution of trust and probate disputes, including Inheritance Act claims, without expensive and difficult court proceedings. Whilst the Code has not been adopted as part of the CPR, consideration of it is recommended for anyone undertaking this work. The Code may be found on the Association's website: **www.actaps.com**.

5.2 PRELIMINARY CONSIDERATIONS

5.2.1 Is there a potential claim?

A detailed consideration of the law follows below; however, when a client first seeks advice, it will be necessary to make a preliminary assessment of whether there is a case worth pursuing on the client's behalf, particularly in view of the potential costs that could be incurred. There are several basic factors to consider.

1. What does the will say? Who is to benefit under it? If there is no will, who will benefit under an intestacy? A basic flow chart identifying which family members are entitled to the estate in the absence of a will is provided at the end of this chapter (at **5.7**). It should be borne in mind that even if the will or intestacy rules would result in the potential claimant receiving something, it may still be insufficient and thus give rise to a potential claim.
2. Is there any value in the estate? However good the potential claimant's claim is, there will be no point in pursuing it in the event that the estate has little or no value. In making this preliminary assessment, be wary of what falls inside and outside the estate: for example, pension benefits will not normally form part of the estate. This is not to say that pension benefits would be ignored in assessing an appropriate settlement; however, the court's powers of redistribution are limited to those assets which fall within the estate.
3. Does the claimant fall into one or more of the relevant categories? Simply being an aggrieved relative who anticipated receiving some or all of the deceased's estate is of itself insufficient to enable a claim to be brought. The potential claimant must be either the spouse/civil partner or former dependent spouse/civil partner of the deceased, the cohabitant of the deceased (of at least two years' standing), a child of the deceased (or treated as a child of the family), or a dependant of the deceased.
4. What are the potential claimant's own financial circumstances? These will be relevant when assessing both whether appropriate provision has been made for the potential claimant and the extent to which claimants are able to fund the legal costs of their claims. Do not, however, dismiss the possibility of a claim simply because clients have their own means. This in itself does not preclude them from having had an element of maintenance from the deceased. Consider the potential methods of funding which may

include public funding (in particular for child claimants), conditional fee agreements, or litigation loans.

5. Has there been a failure to make reasonable provision for the potential claimant? To answer this question properly, there will need to be full disclosure to include, for example, the estate accounts and HM Revenue and Customs form (IHT 200), as well as details of all of the assets of the deceased which might have fallen outside the estate, for example pension benefits. Before embarking on the process, it is essential to make a crude initial judgement as to what, if anything, the potential claimant will receive and whether in the circumstances that is reasonable.

6. Who else will benefit under the will or intestacy? What are their financial circumstances so far as the claimant is aware? The other potential parties in the case need to be identified at an early stage. For example, has anyone else with a potential claim been excluded from the estate distribution, such as a former wife with an ongoing maintenance claim? A broad assessment as to whether anyone might have a competing claim, for example minor children of the deceased, will affect the initial cost/benefit analysis to be undertaken with a potential claimant before deciding whether to take the matter further. If there are only very limited assets and several minor children to be provided for, whilst theoretically a cohabitant of the deceased may have a claim, it may not be worth the costs of pursuing.

5.3 PROCEDURAL CONSIDERATIONS

5.3.1 Was the deceased domiciled in England and Wales?

For there to be jurisdiction to bring a claim under IPFDA 1975, it is essential that the deceased was domiciled in England and Wales at the time of death.

5.3.2 Limitation period

A claim must be issued at court within six months of the date of grant of probate where there was a will, or letters of administration where the deceased died intestate. It is crucial that the potential claimant is made aware of this time limit at the outset since, save in exceptional circumstances, the claimant will not be able to bring a claim which falls outside the limitation period.

5.3.3 Permission to apply out of time

The court has discretion to allow an application brought outside the limitation period to proceed. The claimant must expressly request permission in the claim form including grounds, and should support the application with a statement explaining why the application was not made within the time limit.

In deciding whether to grant permission the court will balance the prejudice to the claimant and to the defendant. See *Bouette* v. *Rose* [1999] 2 FLR 466. Guidelines as to the factors to be considered in exercising the court's discretion are set out in *Re Salmon (Deceased); sub nom. Coard* v. *National Westminster Bank Ltd* [1981] Ch 167 and include:

- the length of delay;
- the reason for the delay and whether any fault lies with the claimant or the claimant's solicitor;
- whether the defendant was aware of the potential claim before proceedings commenced;
- whether negotiations had commenced when the time limit expired;
- whether the estate has already been distributed;
- whether the claim stands any realistic prospect of success;
- whether the claimant could pursue a claim against his or her solicitors if permission is not granted.

For examples of where leave was granted see *Re C (Deceased) (Leave to Apply for Provision)* [1995] 2 FLR 24 (an application on behalf of an illegitimate daughter two years out of time) and *Stock* v. *Brown* [1994] 1 FLR 840. In *Longley (Deceased), Longley and Longley* v. *Longley* [1981] CLY 2885 leave was refused where the estate had been distributed and the claimant had a good case against her solicitors.

5.3.4 Standing search

Whilst ideally contact should be made with those administering the estate (if known) and a copy of the will and grant of probate requested from them, if there is a lack of co-operation or if it is not known who will be dealing with the estate, it is advisable to lodge a standing search at the Probate Registry (see Form LFPR35, reproduced at **5.8**). This will ensure that a copy of the grant of probate/letters of administration and will, if any, will be forwarded to the claimant or his or her adviser once granted by the Probate Registry. In this way, the practitioner can ensure that the claimant has the maximum period available within which to bring a claim and is aware of the precise limitation date. The court will provide a copy of any grant that was issued not more than 12 months before receipt of the application or within six months thereafter. It is therefore important to apply to extend the search within the search period if no grant is received within that timescale.

5.3.5 Other options available?

It may be possible for a claimant who does not meet all of the criteria to bring an alternative course of action, for example, on the basis of proprietary estoppel or under the Trusts of Land and Appointment of Trustees Act 1996 (TLATA

1996). Consideration should be given as to whether such actions should be brought as an alternative to an Inheritance Act claim or in conjunction with such a claim. It is beyond the scope of this chapter to examine such a claim in detail and reference should be made to **Chapter 10**. However, a situation may arise, for example, where a cohabitant claimant cannot successfully establish a claim under IPFDA 1975 against property shared with the deceased, because of a failure to establish an element of dependency, but may be able to satisfy a court that by way of contributions to that property and agreement made with the deceased, the claimant had acquired, by way of implied trust, an interest in it. For a recent example of a claimant pursuing (unsuccessfully in respect of the beneficial interest claim) a dual claim see *Webster* v. *Webster* [2009] EWHC 31 (Ch). If it is appropriate to bring more than one claim under different Acts, the applications should be consolidated. By analogy see *W* v. *W (Joinder of Trusts of Land Act and Children Act Applications)* [2004] 2 FLR 321.

5.3.6   Pre-action protocol

As in all family and civil cases, disclosure should be dealt with on a voluntary and reciprocal basis. If possible, disclosure should take place prior to proceedings being issued and attempts to agree settlement terms without recourse to the courts should be made. In practice, however, the scope for this will be limited in IPFDA 1975 claims given the need to issue proceedings prior to the expiry of the limitation period. It is appropriate to do this to provide protection to the claimant even if it is anticipated it may be possible to agree settlement terms. Do not forget, however, that a short stay of proceedings, once issued, can be requested, to enable negotiations to continue. If a settlement is possible the court will usually allow a stay of up to six months.

5.3.7   Client interview checklist

A suggested checklist which is intended to serve as an aide-mémoire of the information needed from a potential claimant can be found at **5.9**. It is unlikely that all of this information will be available at the first interview or even known to the claimant; however, the more information that is obtained at the outset, the better the judgement that can be made as to the prospects of success.

5.4   THE LAW

5.4.1   Categories of claimant

Section 1(1) of IPFDA 1975 provides that the following may apply for relief:

- a surviving spouse/civil partner (s.1(1)(a));
- a former spouse/civil partner who has not remarried or entered into a civil partnership (s.1(1)(b));

- a surviving cohabitant who lived with the deceased throughout the whole of the period of at least two years immediately before the death (s.1(1)(ba));
- a child of the deceased (s.1(1)(c));
- a person who was treated as a child of the family (s.1(1)(d)); and
- any person not included in the above categories who was being maintained in whole or in part by the deceased immediately before their death (s.1(1)(e)).

It is therefore possible for a potential claimant to qualify under more than one category. For example, a surviving cohabitant may also be a person who was being maintained in whole or in part by the deceased. Since the introduction by s.2 of the Law Reform (Succession) Act 1995 of the category of surviving cohabitant, in respect of a death after 1 January 1996, cohabitants can make a claim on the basis of their status as a cohabitant rather than having to rely solely on s.1(1)(e) as a dependant.

The status of the claimant will directly affect the relief that the claimant may receive. A surviving spouse or civil partner will be able to make a claim based purely on whether or not reasonable financial provision has been made for him or her, without reference to whether that provision is required for the claimant's maintenance. All other categories of claimant are required to establish both strands of the test, i.e. that reasonable provision for their maintenance has not been made.

Surviving spouse/civil partner

This is a self-explanatory category of claimant. Claimants falling under this section do not have to establish anything beyond their legal status to be entitled to bring a claim. The fact that they might be informally separated at the time of death will not affect their eligibility to bring a claim. In certain circumstances where there has been a decree absolute/decree of judicial separation/dissolution order, the court has the power to treat a claimant as a surviving spouse/civil partner in spite of the decree (IPFDA 1975, ss.14 and 14A). This applies where the defendant has died within 12 months of the decree/dissolution and there has been no application for relief and/or final order in the divorce/dissolution proceedings. This will have a significant bearing on the potential entitlement of the claimant, as a spouse or civil partner is in a far stronger position as to entitlement than a former spouse or civil partner.

Former spouse or civil partner

This category of claimant is automatically eligible to make a claim by reason of their status although whether they will receive anything is dependent on the considerations dealt with below.

Surviving cohabitant

The claimant must meet a three-part test to be defined as a surviving cohabitant for the purpose of a claim under IPFDA 1975.

1. Cohabitation for two years immediately preceding the death of the deceased. The cohabitant must satisfy the court that they cohabited for the whole of the two years immediately preceding the death of the deceased. The court will adopt a realistic approach to this requirement in defining what is meant by 'immediately preceding'. See *Re Watson (Deceased)* [1999] 1 FLR 878, where the deceased had been in hospital for some weeks immediately before dying. Also see *Gully* v. *Dix* [2004] 1 FLR 918, where the claimant was living separately from the deceased when he died, although the relationship was continuing. In both cases, the court accepted that there was the requisite cohabitation for the claimant to be eligible under IPFDA 1975.
2. Shared household. It is implicit in the requirement for cohabitation that there will be a shared household. The courts adopt a flexible attitude to what amounts to a household (see above).
3. Living together as husband and wife or civil partners. The court will make this judgment based on the reality of the situation and whether 'in the opinion of a reasonable person with normal perceptions' it could be said that two people were living together as husband and wife or civil partners (see *Re Watson (Deceased)* [1999] 1 FLR 878). See *Baker* v. *Baker* [2008] 2 FLR 767 for a recent application of *Re Watson (Deceased)*. For more recent judicial consideration of this point see *Lindop* v. *Agus* [2009] EWHC 1795 (Ch).

Same-sex cohabitants will be able to make a claim as cohabitants under this section following the introduction of the Civil Partnership Act 2004 (CPA 2004).

Child of the deceased

This category extends to any illegitimate children of the deceased and also any child conceived but not born (*en ventre sa mère*) at the date of death (s.25(1)). Adult children are included. An adopted child is a legitimate child (Adoption Act 1976, s.39).

Child of the family

Although there is no definition in the statute it is submitted that by analogy matrimonial cases on this point may assist. The court will consider the evidence as to the nature of the relationship between the deceased and the claimant seeking to make a claim under this category. See *Re Callaghan (Deceased)* [1985] Fam 1 and *Re Leach, Leach* v. *Lindeman* [1984] FLR 590. This is another scenario where a claim may be made under two different categories, for example, as a child of the family and dependant. An adult child is included.

Other dependants

This category of claimant can only bring an action if the claimant satisfies the following three elements.

1. Maintained by deceased. This can be in whole or in part and is not restricted to a narrow definition of maintenance such as periodical payments. The court will look at the reality of the situation in the light of all of the facts. See *Bishop* v. *Plumley* [1991] 1 FLR 121, *Rees* v. *Newbery and the Institute of Cancer Research* [1998] 1 FLR 1041 and *Graham* v. *Murphy and Another* [1997] 1 FLR 860. For a recent consideration of maintenance of a non family member (where the claims were unsuccessful) see *Baynes* v. *Hedger* [2008] 2 FLR 1805.
2. Immediately before death. It is submitted the courts will take a common-sense approach in assessing the situation which prevailed leading up to death, rather than the precise arrangement at the moment of death. See *Re Beaumont (Deceased)* [1980] 1 All ER 266, *Jelley* v. *Iliffe and Others* [1981] 2 All ER 29 and *Witkowska* v. *Kaminski* [2006] All ER (D) 357.
3. Substantial contribution without consideration. Section 1(3) defines maintenance as 'a substantial contribution in money or money's worth' by the deceased to the reasonable needs of the applicant otherwise than for full valuable consideration. This precludes those who might be said to be paid housekeepers from bringing a claim. See *Re Wilkinson (Deceased) Neale* v. *Newell* [1978] 1 All ER 221 for what may or may not amount to full valuable consideration. Valuable consideration expressly excludes marriage or promises of marriage (s.25(1)).

5.4.2 Basis of the claim

In order to qualify for potential relief, all claimants must satisfy IPFDA 1975, s.1(1) which provides that a person may apply on the ground that 'the disposition of the deceased's estate effected by his will or the law relating to intestacy, or the combination of his will and that law, is not such as to make reasonable financial provision for the applicant'.

What is reasonable financial provision?

In the case of a husband or wife, reasonable financial provision is defined as such provision as it would be reasonable in all the circumstances of the case for a husband or wife to receive, whether or not that provision is required for his or her maintenance (IPFDA 1975, s.1(2)(a)). Since the introduction of

CPA 2004, the same would be true in the case of an application by a civil partner of the deceased (IPFDA 1975, s.1(2)(aa)).

As has been noted, claimants other than a spouse or civil partner must additionally meet the requirements of IPFDA 1975, s.1(2)(b) which stipulates that reasonable financial provision is 'such financial provision as it would be reasonable in all the circumstances of the case for the applicant to receive for his maintenance'. What amounts to reasonable financial provision is an objective test and will largely turn on the facts of the case (see *Re Coventry (Deceased)* [1979] 3 All ER 815). The question to be considered is whether the effect on the claimant of the provision made by the defendant is such as to provide reasonably for that claimant in the light of the responsibility assumed by the defendant for the claimant. The needs of a claimant alone are not enough. In deciding whether the provision is reasonable or unreasonable the court must consider IPFDA 1975, s.3.

5.4.3   Factors for the court to consider

A non-exhaustive checklist is provided in the statute. The court must have regard to the checklist in deciding first, whether reasonable provision has or has not been made for the claimant and secondly, if the provision which has been made is not adequate, whether and how the court should exercise its powers.

The general factors which the court must consider in respect of all claimants, whether they be a former spouse or civil partner or one of the other categories of claimant, is found at IPFDA 1975, s.3(1)(a)–(g) inclusive. Those factors may be summarised as follows.

1. The financial resources and needs which the claimant/any other claimant or any beneficiary has or is likely to have in the foreseeable future (s.3(1)(a)–(c)).
2. Any obligations and responsibilities which the deceased had either towards the claimant or towards any beneficiary of the estate (s.3(1)(d)).
3. The size and nature of the net estate of the deceased (s.3(1)(e)).
4. Any physical or mental disability of either the claimant or any beneficiary of the estate (s.3(1)(f)).
5. Any other matter including the conduct of the claimant or any other person which in the circumstances of the case the court may consider relevant (s.3(1)(g)).

Financial resources/needs

The court will consider the needs and resources of all the relevant parties together with those of the beneficiaries as part of this exercise to establish whether reasonable provision has been made for the claimant. The exercise here will not be dissimilar to that in a matrimonial case. Details of needs and resources should be set out in the statements of the parties. 'Financial needs' is a relative term which must be looked at in the context of the standard of living enjoyed during the deceased's lifetime. See *Harrington* v. *Gill* (1983) 4 FLR 265. The court can take account of earning capacity where appropriate (IPFDA 1975, s.3(6)). It follows there must be full disclosure of all material financial circumstances of all the parties, although there is a greater emphasis on the claimant since claimants need to establish their cases. The court will also take account of an individual's financial obligations and responsibilities (IPFDA 1975, s.3(6)).

Obligations/responsibilities

The deceased's obligations will not be defined too narrowly (see *Espinosa* v. *Bourke* [1999] 1 FLR 747). Obligations will include a moral obligation (see *Re Goodchild (Deceased) and Another* [1997] 2 FLR 644, CA).

Net estate

Where the estate is limited, the court will be reluctant to intervene (*Gora* v. *Treasury Solicitor* [2003] Fam Law 93). The costs of proceedings (which are often borne by the estate) are likely to significantly deplete what is available, particularly as Inheritance Act cases often involve multiple parties and competing claims.

Physical/mental disability

See *Re Debenham* [1986] 1 FLR 404 where an award was made to an adult daughter with health problems where the court considered that the deceased had a moral obligation towards her.

Any other matter including conduct

Under this section the court will consider evidence of the deceased's wishes and the deceased's reasons for the provision made (see *Re Coventry (Deceased) Coventry* v. *Coventry* [1979] FLR 142). Conduct is likely to be looked at in a similar manner to conduct in matrimonial cases (see *Re Snoek (Deceased)* (1982) 13 Fam Law 18). Following the House of Lords decision in the matrimonial case of *Miller* v. *Miller* [2006] 1 FLR 1186, it is submitted the court will be reluctant to take conduct into account save where it is 'conduct which it would be inequitable to disregard'.

5.4.4 Additional category specific factors

In addition to the above, for each category of claimant there are specific further considerations to which the court must have regard.

Spouses and civil partners/former spouses and former civil partners

For claimants under any of these categories, the court must also consider:

(a) the age of the claimant and the duration of the marriage or civil partnership; and

(b) the contribution made by the claimant to the welfare of the family of the deceased including any contribution made by looking after the home or caring for the family.

In addition, in the case of a spouse or civil partner where the marriage or civil partnership was subsisting at the date of death (save where there is a judicial separation), the court must also consider what the applicant might reasonably have expected to receive had the marriage or civil partnership been terminated by a divorce or dissolution order, rather than on death (IPFDA 1975, s.3(2)). For a recent consideration of the application of this section, see *P* v. *G (Family Provision: Relevance of Divorce Provision)* [2006] 1 FLR 431.

It is important to remember that consideration of what provision might have been made in a divorce/dissolution is not an overriding consideration and is only one factor for the court to weigh in the balance. For consideration of a short marriage case see *Fielden* v. *Cunliffe* [2005] 3 FCR 593, although see *Adams* v. *Adams* [2001] WLR 493 for a contrasting view. For a recent application of *Fielden* v. *Cunliffe* see *Baker* v. *Baker* [2008] 2 FLR 1956.

Cohabitant applicants

In the case of cohabitants, in addition to the general checklist, the court must consider:

(a) the age of the claimant and length of the cohabitation (i.e. the period during which the claimant lived as husband/wife or civil partner of the deceased in the same household); and

(b) the contribution made by the claimant to the welfare of the family of the deceased including any contribution made by looking after the home or caring for the family (IPFDA 1975, s.3(2A)).

These are the same matters the court must consider for former spouses or civil partners and may form the basis for an argument that cohabitants represent a hybrid category of claimant, having a claim for something more than just what is reasonable for their maintenance, albeit not as extensive a claim as a spouse or civil partner. These matters were considered in *Re Watson (Deceased)* [1999] 1 FLR 878, where the claimant's contribution to the welfare of the family was viewed as substantial. For a recent consideration of reasonable financial provision for a dependent cohabitant see *Negus* v. *Bahouse* [2008] 1 FLR 381.

Child of the deceased or claimant who was treated by the deceased as a child of the family

Applications by either a child of the deceased or someone who was treated by the deceased as a child of the family are subject to a supplemental requirement that the court should 'have regard to the manner in which the applicant was being or in which he might expect to be educated or trained' (IPFDA 1975, s.3(3)). For a natural child of the deceased the additional consideration will only be relevant if that child remains in full-time education. The issue for the court will be whether there was an actual or at least reasonable expectation of education funding, rather than whether the estate can afford it (see *Re C (Deceased) (Leave to Apply for Provision)* [1995] 2 FLR 24).

For a 'child of the family' claimant the court must also consider three further elements.

1. Whether the deceased had assumed any responsibility for the applicant's maintenance, the extent and basis of that responsibility and the length of time that the responsibility was discharged (s.3(3)(a)).
2. Whether in assuming and discharging the responsibility the deceased did so knowing that the claimant was not the deceased's own child (s.3(3)(b)).
3. The liability of any other person to maintain the claimant (s.3(3)(c)).

The additional considerations for a child of the family claimant are simply that, not preliminary hurdles.

Minor children are in a far stronger position than adult children, as generally they have no resources of their own, although they may face a competing claim, for example, from a spouse.

Adult children are in a far weaker position and their resources will be closely scrutinised. It has been said that they will need to establish special circumstances, which may be in the form of a moral obligation (see *Re Jennings (Deceased)* [1994] 3 All ER 27; see also *Re Abram (Deceased)* [1996] 2 FLR 379, *Re Goodchild (Deceased) and Another* [1997] 2 FLR 644 and *Re Hancock (Deceased)* [1998] 2 FLR 346). For recent consideration of an adult child's claim (which failed) see *Garland* v. *Morris* [2007] 2 FLR 528.

Person being maintained by the deceased

Where a claimant makes a claim on the basis that he or she was being maintained wholly or partly by the deceased immediately before death, the court must have regard, in addition to the general checklist, to the extent and basis upon which the deceased assumed responsibility for the maintenance of the claimant and the length of time for which the deceased discharged that responsibility (IPFDA 1975, s.3(4)). See *Rhodes* v. *Dean* [1996] 7 CL 593 where the application failed.

Summary

In summary, the court will first decide whether the claimant fulfils the criteria to come within one of the categories of claimant. In some cases this will be beyond dispute, for example, where the parties were married and living together at the time of death. In other cases, it will not be entirely straightforward, for example, where claimants might seek to suggest that they fall within the category of cohabitant; however, if they fail on this, they may still be able to bring their claims under the category of dependant of the estate.

Having made that decision, the court will go on to decide whether or not reasonable financial provision (for maintenance, depending on the category of claimant) has been made. To reach this decision, the court will first apply the general checklist as outlined and in addition, the relevant individual checklist which applies to the specific category of claimant. If, having considered all the relevant matters, the court concludes that reasonable provision (for maintenance, if applicable) was not made, the final stage will involve the court considering whether and in what manner it should exercise its powers. In other words, what, if any, orders it should make.

It is not therefore a foregone conclusion that just because it is established that reasonable provision has not been made by the estate, this means the court will automatically make orders in favour of the claimant. When deciding whether and which orders to make, the court will again refer to the general checklist and to the specific checklists which are relevant to the particular category of claimant.

In doing all of this, the court must take into account the facts known to the court at the date of the hearing (IPFDA 1975, s.3(5)). See *Re Hancock (Deceased)* [1998] 2 FLR 346 where a sixfold increase in the value of land by the time of the hearing was taken into account.

5.4.5 Property available for financial provision

Before the court can make an assessment as to what orders it might make in favour of a claimant who has successfully established that inadequate provision was made, it must assess what monies/assets are available. Section 25(1) defines the net estate of the deceased to be:

(a) all property of which the deceased had power to dispose by his or her will (otherwise than by virtue of a special power of appointment) less the amount of the deceased's funeral, testamentary and administrative expenses, debts and liabilities, including capital transfer tax (inheritance tax since Inheritance Tax Act 1984) paid out of the deceased's estate on his or her death;

(b) any property in respect of which the deceased held a general power of appointment (not being a power exercisable by will) which has not been exercised;

(c) monies treated as part of the estate by virtue of s.8;

(d) property treated as part of the estate by virtue of an order under s.9; and

(e) monies ordered to be provided by ss.10 or 11.

Sections 8 and 9 provide for certain monies to be treated as part of the estate by the court. The most common example that a practitioner is likely to come across is a jointly held property. The right of survivorship means normally the deceased's share would automatically pass to the surviving joint tenant and fall outside the estate. However, s.9 allows the court to treat the deceased's severable share as part of the net estate for the purpose of assessing what payment should be made. In *Jessop* v. *Jessop* [1992] 1 FLR 591 this resulted in the deceased's cohabitant, who retained a jointly owned house, having to make a lump sum payment to the deceased's widow. There is no cap on value created by the words 'at the value thereof immediately before his death' in s.9(1) (*Dingmar* v. *Dingmar* [2006] EWCA Civ 942). When seeking disclosure from the beneficiaries and estate care should therefore be taken to ensure information is obtained as to all material money and property, including that which on the face of it would not normally form part of the estate. Examples might include joint property, pensions, and life policies in trust.

Avoidance

The court has powers similar to those available in matrimonial cases to effectively set aside transactions which seek to defeat applications under IPFDA 1975 by ordering the recipient of monies from such a transaction to make available a sum of monies. For the court to be able to make such an order, the following criteria must be fulfilled:

(a) the transaction must have taken place less than six years before death;

(b) there must have been an intention by the deceased to defeat a claim under IPFDA 1975;

(c) there must not have been full valuable consideration;

(d) the court must be satisfied that making an order would facilitate making provision under IPFDA 1975.

See IPFDA 1975, ss.10, 11 and 12 and *Re Kennedy (Deceased)* [1980] CLY 2820 as to the intention of the deceased.

5.4.6 Orders available to the court

If satisfied that reasonable financial provision has not been made, the court has the power to make a variety of orders against the estate. These are not dissimilar to the orders available to a matrimonial court and include periodical payments, lump sum order, transfer of property, a settlement of property and an order varying an ante-nuptial or post-nuptial settlement (including the civil partnership equivalent) to which the deceased was one of the parties (IPFDA 1975, s.2(1)).

Periodical payments

These will normally be made from the date of the deceased's death unless there has been an interim order. They will terminate on the death of the claimant or on remarriage or formation of a civil partnership in the case of a spouse or civil partner (or former spouse or former civil partner) (IPFDA 1975, s.19).

In the case of a minor child, payments would normally cease upon the child reaching majority or completing full-time education. Periodical payments can be varied or discharged or replaced by a lump sum order on a variation application (IPFDA 1975, s.6).

Lump sum

This is the most common form of order and may be used to provide for rehousing the claimant or to capitalise maintenance. In the latter case, it is likely that a *Duxbury* calculation (*Duxbury* v. *Duxbury* [1987] 1 FLR 7) or similar will be used to quantify the amount. Historically, it was considered appropriate, where the estate was large enough, for a lump sum order to be made as a cushion to protect against contingencies (*Re Besterman* [1984] FLR 503). In a matrimonial context, it is not considered that this concept remains good law; however, it may still be appropriate in an Inheritance Act claim, particularly where the estate is large.

A lump sum order can be made by instalments in which case the court has power to vary it (IPFDA 1975, s.7(2)).

Settlement of property

It may be appropriate in the particular circumstances of a case to make a life-time settlement of property upon a claimant, for example, to provide for the claimant's housing needs, which then reverts to the estate on his or her death, rather than an outright transfer.

Interim orders

Section 5 allows the court to make interim provision for a claimant from the estate where it is satisfied that:

(a) there is an immediate need; and
(b) there are available monies in the estate to meet that need.

The court can impose conditions and restrictions on any payments it orders, which will be such sums as the court thinks reasonable. Payments will not be ordered beyond the date of the final order or final adjudication.

In deciding whether to make an interim order, the court must consider as far as possible, given the urgency, the s.3 factors which are set out above.

THE ORDER

A copy of the order must be sent to the Principal Registry of the Family Division and a memorandum of the order endorsed to the probate or letters of administration (IPFDA 1975, s.19(3)).

THE FORFEITURE RULE

This rule disentitles a person from acquiring benefit from the estate of a person whom he or she has unlawfully killed (Forfeiture Act 1982). However, see *Land* v. *Land* [2006] All ER(D) 71 for circumstances in which such a claimant did receive relief.

5.5   PROCEDURE/APPLICATION

5.5.1   Application

The procedure is governed by CPR 1998, Part 57. High Court (Chancery or Family Division) and county courts have jurisdiction. The application should be made by Part 8 claim form with the heading 'In the Estate of Deceased' and 'In the Matter of the Inheritance (Provision for Family and Dependants) Act 1975'. It should be supported by a witness statement or affidavit exhibiting an official copy of the grant of representation, will, death certificate and in the case of an application by a child, the birth certificate. The defendants will be the personal representatives, beneficiaries and any other persons affected.

The witness statement should include:

- the name, date of death and country of domicile of the deceased;
- the category of applicant to which the claimant belongs;
- the date of grant and names and addresses of the personal representatives;
- whether/what provision is made (will or intestacy);
- other persons interested in the estate and their interest;
- the claimant's financial resources now and in the future; and
- the provision sought.

The defendants must file and serve the acknowledgement of service together with a statement or affidavit in answer within 14 days.

Directions can be requested when issuing the claim form or the court will give directions after the filing of the acknowledgement of service (or time limit to do so).

5.5.2 Disclosure checklist

A checklist of the standard documents it is suggested will need to be obtained is provided at **5.10**.

5.5.3 Costs

What might be considered a general starting point of costs following the event is not necessarily routinely followed in these claims. Frequently the costs of both sides are borne by the estate, even in the case of an unsuccessful claimant (see *Re Fullard (Deceased)* [1981] 2 All ER 796). For a more recent authority where a successful claimant did not recover all of his costs see *Graham* v. *Murphy and Another* [1997] 1 FLR 860.

5.6 IMPLICATIONS OF THE ACT WHEN ADVISING MATRIMONIAL CLIENTS

5.6.1 Dismissal clauses in consent orders

Where a clean break as to both income and capital is intended in a divorce or civil partnership financial settlement it is imperative that an order is made preventing either party from making any application under IPFDA 1975 (s.15) to ensure that the clean break is also effective on death. Without this there may be the potential at least for a former spouse or civil partner to bring a claim against the estate of the deceased.

Equally important is to ensure s.15 provision is not inadvertently made which applies to both parties when one of them has an ongoing maintenance order in his or her favour.

Clearly any such orders only affect adult spouses/civil partners and have no effect on a child's ability to bring a claim.

5.6.2 Wills

Clients are routinely advised on separation to consider making a will, severing the joint tenancy of jointly owned property, and lodging an expression of wish with the trustees of their pension fund. All of this is intended to protect the assets of the client from their spouse in the event of death, particularly prior to final settlement or order. In view of the provisions of the Inheritance Act such steps must be considered carefully so as not to inadvertently leave the estate open to a potential claim from a separated but not divorced spouse or civil partner after death of the client but before financial settlement.

5.7 INTESTACY RULES FLOW CHART

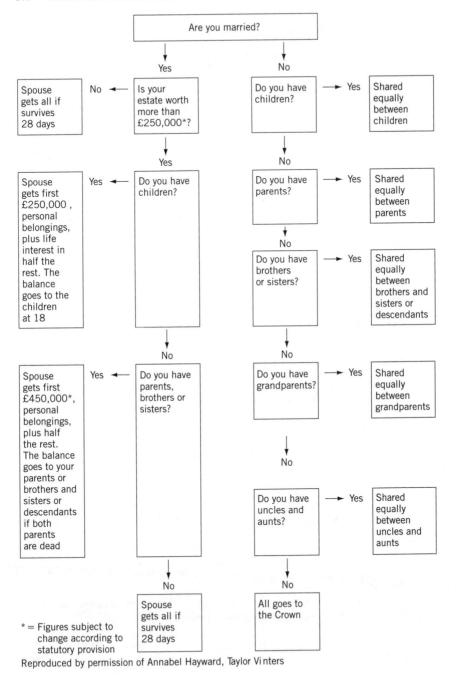

* = Figures subject to
    change according to
    statutory provision

Reproduced by permission of Annabel Hayward, Taylor Vinters

Figure 5.1 Intestacy rules

5.8   STANDING SEARCH FORM – FORM LFPR35

Application for Standing Search

IN THE HIGH COURT OF JUSTICE

FAMILY DIVISION
[PRINCIPAL] [**DISTRICT PROBATE] REGISTRY**[1]

IN THE ESTATE OF

DECEASED

I/We[2]

apply for the entry of a standing search so that there shall be sent to me/us an office copy of every grant of representation in England and Wales in the estate of:-

Full name of the deceased:[3]

Full address:

Alternative or alias names:

Exact date of death:[3]   day of

which either has issued not more than 12 months before the entry of this application or issues within 6 months thereafter.

Signed

(Solicitor for the applicant(s))

Name in block letters

of

reference (if any)

Notes

1.   Delete as appropriate.
2.   Name(s) of applicant(s).
3.   The name and date of death of the deceased as recorded in the Register should be inserted.
     Failure to give correct details may render the search ineffective.

Revised 3/99   © Laserform International Limited 1994   **LFPR35**

5.9 CLIENT INTERVIEW CHECKLIST

1. Full name, address, contact details, date of birth of client.
2. Full name, address (at time of death) (if different), date of birth, date of death and place of death of deceased.
3. Full name, address, date of birth (if known) of any beneficiaries.
4. Full name, address, date of birth of any other potential parties (if known), e.g. children, spouse, former spouse, etc.
5. Details of the executors/trustees and who is representing them.
6. Full details of any assets of the deceased including:

   - property
   - bank accounts
   - policies
   - pensions
   - trust interests
   - investments/shares

   and income during lifetime.

7. Full details of income and assets of the claimant and the claimant's needs (income and capital).
8. Details (if known) or a general assessment of the income/assets of other potential parties/beneficiaries.
9. Information as to the contents of the will (if known).
10. Any information as to the deceased's intentions/wishes.

5.10 SUGGESTED DISCLOSURE CHECKLIST

Estate

1. Estate accounts/interim accounts.
2. IHT 200 form.
3. Documentation in relation to any other assets of the deceased falling outside the estate (e.g. life policies in trust, pensions, property owned as joint tenants).

Defendants/beneficiaries

1. Documentary evidence of income and assets.
2. Details of expenditure.

Claimant

1. Evidence of income.
2. Evidence of assets.

CHAPTER 6

Costs in family proceedings

Nigel Shepherd and Sue Brookes

6.1 INTRODUCTION

An understanding of the law, practice and procedure in relation to costs in family proceedings is essential for the family law practitioner. The impact of costs has to be considered at every stage of a case, from initial contact with the client through to final hearing.

The subject of costs is complex and extensive. It would not be possible within the scope of this chapter to provide an exhaustive analysis of every aspect of the issue. Rather, the objective is to highlight and summarise key areas with the emphasis being on the application of the main principles to the family solicitor's day-to-day practice. Accordingly, some areas are covered only briefly and many have had to be omitted completely.

With the exception of some limited references to legal aid, this chapter deals only with costs in privately funded family work.

The issues to be covered are:

- definition of family proceedings;
- professional obligations, client care and best practice;
- types of costs orders, terminology and assessment;
- costs orders in different types of proceedings;
- Forms H and H1;
- interest on costs orders; and
- enforcement of costs orders.

6.2 DEFINITION OF FAMILY PROCEEDINGS

The distinction between family and other proceedings so far as costs are concerned is important, at least in theory. The general principles in relation to costs are set out in CPR 1998, Part 44. Rule 44.3(1) provides that the court has discretion as to whether costs are payable, the amount of those costs and when they are to be paid. Rule 44.3(2)(a) goes on to say, however, that the 'general rule is that the unsuccessful party will be ordered to pay the costs of the successful party'.

The Family Proceedings Rules 1991 (FPR 1991), rule 10.27 (as inserted by the Family Proceedings (Amendment) Rules 2003, SI 2003/184) provides that the majority of Parts 43 and 44 apply to family proceedings (except rules 44.9–44.12). However, the general rule that costs follow the event (rule 44.3(2)) is also specifically disapplied by FPR 1991, rule 10.27(1)(b). Also rules 44.3(1) and 44.3(3)–(5) do not apply to 'new' ancillary relief proceedings (this is dealt with in more detail in **6.5.4** below).

It is to be noted that not all disputes between those in a family relationship fall within the definition of family proceedings. An example is proceedings under TLATA 1996 for the sale of a jointly owned home. However, the wide discretion given to the courts under CPR 1998 means that in practice the distinction between family and other proceedings, when it comes to costs orders, is not as significant as may at first appear.

6.3 PROFESSIONAL OBLIGATIONS, CLIENT CARE AND BEST PRACTICE

6.3.1 The retainer

The business relationship between a solicitor and client is a contractual one, known as a retainer. The issue of costs is a key aspect of that retainer. Clients need to know where they stand, and providing the best information about how costs affect the client is essential, not only in terms of client service but also for the profitability of the solicitor's business.

6.3.2 Costs information

Costs information is governed by rule 2.03 of the Solicitors' Code of Conduct 2007 and the non-mandatory guidance which accompanies it. Clients must be given in writing the best possible information to understand the cost of legal services, both at the outset of a matter and as it progresses. However, what is meant by 'best possible' is far from straightforward in practice.

The retainer letter needs to give all the relevant information about the charging rates of the fee earner(s) who might be working on the file at any time during the course of the case. It needs to set out billing frequency and practitioners need to address with the client how they are going to pay. Clients also need to be told about their potential liability for the other party's costs.

It is the information about likely overall costs that causes the real difficulties. In some areas of work a fixed fee can be agreed, for example, in relation to the costs of an undefended main suit for divorce, which is dealt with below, but the open-ended nature of almost all other family law work makes a fixed fee inappropriate in the vast majority of cases. It has been common practice in the past simply to say that it is not possible to give even broad estimates, because there are so many uncertainties and variables, but that is not now sufficient to discharge the professional obligations of the solicitor.

As highlighted in the cases of *Mastercigars Direct Ltd* v. *Withers LLP* [2007] EWHC 2733 and *Reynolds* v. *Stone Rowe Brewer (a firm)* [2008] EWHC 497 (QB), it is essential to be as accurate as possible with estimates. The court in *Mastercigars* held that although solicitors are not limited to recovering the sum in the estimate, the court will use the estimate as a yard-stick when considering the reasonableness of the costs. It can therefore act as a cap upon the costs the client is expected to pay. In *Reynolds*, the client was given an initial estimate of £18,000, which was revised several times over a two-year period and the total costs amounted to £60,000. The client applied for detailed assessment and the judge found that £31,000 was a reasonable amount for the fees. He found that if the client had been given an accurate estimate from the outset she would not have acted as she did and the revised estimates had been too haphazard. The solicitors had therefore breached the Solicitors' Code of Conduct.

Perhaps the best approach in family law cases is to give, at the outset, a range of possible costs outcomes based on experience or a detailed analysis of different types of case. Each time a bill is delivered, or if there is a significant development in the case, for example an application that was not originally anticipated or the instruction of an expert, the estimate can be either confirmed or amended. Care should be taken about the use of the word 'estimate', as experience suggests that clients will often construe this as a fixed quotation. If a reasonable estimate is given at the outset and it is revised subsequently because of a change in circumstances, the solicitor will not be bound by it. However, the solicitor must have explained the assumptions on which the estimate is based and the revised estimate should not be given at the last minute if it is clear earlier on that the original estimate will be exceeded. Solicitors should also make it clear to the client that they can never quantify accurately the total cost of the work unless they are agreeing a fixed fee.

Clients must be given the opportunity to set an upper limit on costs, which must not be exceeded without the client's consent. This should be included in the retainer letter.

Clients must also be notified about the costs of third parties. This is partic-ularly important with counsel, as by custom barristers look to the solicitor for payment of their fees and not to the lay client, and the client's agreement should therefore be obtained before the cost is incurred.

A detailed bill/breakdown must be provided if requested, so proper time recording and file notes are essential. If a client challenges the solicitor's costs, remember that an application can be made to the court for an assessment. This will often be the response of the client when it becomes necessary for the solicitor to sue for outstanding costs.

Dissatisfaction with costs is one of the most common causes of dispute between clients and solicitors. As with the *Reynolds* case, a breach of the professional obligations can lead to all or part of the costs being disallowed or to a compensation payment, which was increased from £5,000 to £15,000 with effect from January 2006. Even less serious disagreements will take considerable time to resolve and are likely to lead to bills having to be reduced.

In summary, giving accurate information about costs at the outset, and as the case progresses, and managing clients' expectations, undoubtedly makes good business sense.

It is important to note what is covered by the term 'disbursements'. Items where there is a profit element for the solicitor must not be described as disbursements on bills, in estimates or in any other communications with the client. Getting this wrong can lead to criticism from the regulator and the repayment of what might be substantial sums. Examples of items with a profit element can include bank charges (e.g. telegraphic transfer fees including international payments and banker's draft fees), photocopying charges and fax charges.

6.3.3   Approaches to funding costs

Most practices will require clients to pay for the work being undertaken as it progresses. This means that in every case the way in which the work is to be funded will need to be addressed at the outset and kept under review. Where the client does not have readily accessible income or capital, the principal methods of funding can be summarised as follows.

Public funding

It is the professional duty of all solicitors to assess whether any potential new client might be eligible for public funding (legal aid). If the firm does not undertake legal aid work, but the client has other means of funding available and wishes to proceed with the instruction to the firm, the advantages and disadvantages of legal aid should still be explained. The advantages include the lower hourly chargeable rate (which of course may be recovered if the statutory charge applies) and the disadvantages include the potential for delay and the need in many situations to get authority in advance for steps to be taken. The retainer letter should refer to the advice given. It is good practice for firms that do not do legal aid to have a list of those that do to which the client can be referred.

Assistance from family and friends

Many clients may be able to call upon help from family or friends. The contract in respect of costs, however, remains between the client and the solicitor and both client and solicitor need to be aware of the particular tensions that can arise with this source of funding.

Practitioners need to explain to the client that the debt owed to a family member or friend for costs, even if evidenced by a written requirement to repay, may be considered as a 'soft debt', which may be treated in a different light from a 'hard' commercial debt when the court comes to consider the client's liabilities. However, the advantages of what is likely to be an interest-free loan will usually outweigh the disadvantages of the court questioning whether it will in fact have to be repaid.

Commercial borrowing

Some firms now accept credit cards.

A client may also be able to borrow from the bank to fund legal fees whether by using an existing or renegotiated overdraft or taking out a separate loan. Many banks and other financial institutions also offer tailor-made loans to fund the costs of family proceedings. A number of these will rely upon a certificate or similar confirmation from the solicitor to say that in due course the client will receive a settlement that will enable the client to repay the loan. Most of these institutions will be looking not only to the interest payable on the loan, but for an investment opportunity at the end of the case. Some will require security, but many do not.

Solicitors need to be careful about how they refer clients to commercial lenders. Various regulations, including the Financial Services and Markets Act 2000 and the Consumer Credit Act 1974, govern what solicitors are authorised to do. Charles Marquand of 4 Stone Buildings has prepared a helpful summary of the legal position, which is contained in Issue 136 of *The Review* (November 2008).

Maintenance pending suit/interim maintenance

For some time the courts have accepted that a maintenance pending suit/interim maintenance order can include an element of provision for legal fees. This is to guard against inequality of arms between the parties. The leading decision is that of the Court of Appeal in the case of *Currey* v. *Currey* [2007] 1 FLR 946. Whilst confirming the power for the courts to include legal fees in such orders, the case makes it clear that this will not be allowed as a matter of course. Essentially, the applicant will need to show that it is not possible to get appropriate legal advice by any means other than a costs allowance or as part of an interim maintenance order and the court will also look at other considerations including the parties' stance in the proceedings. The applicant will need to explore first the availability of commercial funding, a *Sears Tooth* agreement (see below), and public funding. However, sadly, it is now rare that highly specialist solicitors and counsel experienced in the most complex cases undertake publicly funded work, so the availability of legal aid as a potential source of funding may not be fatal to the application to include legal fees in the interim maintenance.

Sears Tooth *agreement*

It is possible to enter into a deed of assignment with the client by which the costs will be paid at the end of the case from capital to be recovered in the ancillary relief proceedings. This is called a *Sears Tooth* agreement after the case of *Sears Tooth (A Firm)* v. *Payne Hicks Beach (A Firm) and Others* [1997] 2 FLR 116. The court held that this is not a conditional fee agreement, which is unlawful in family proceedings. Strict procedures must, however, be complied with. The client must take independent legal advice (or must at least have been strongly urged to do so) and the court and the other party must be notified of the deed's existence.

6.3.4 Solicitor's lien

A solicitor is entitled to retain the client's file until the solicitor's costs have been paid. This is called a lien. Generally, a court will not force solicitors to hand their papers over until they have been paid, but there is a distinction to be drawn between the situation where the retainer is ended by the client and when it is ended by the solicitor. In the latter case, although the lien still applies, the court will not allow it to be exercised if doing so would unreasonably interfere with court proceedings (*Ismail* v. *Richards Butler (A Firm)* [1996] 2 All ER 506). However, the court can impose conditions on the client such as requiring a payment into court or security for costs.

6.4 TYPES OF COSTS ORDERS, TERMINOLOGY AND ASSESSMENT

6.4.1 Standard and indemnity bases

When one side is ordered to pay the other side's costs, this will be on either the standard or the indemnity basis. If the order is silent as to the basis, it will be standard.

When assessing costs on the standard basis (which is the normal basis) CPR 1998, rule 44.4(2) states that the court will only allow costs which are proportionate to the matters in issue, with any doubts as to whether costs are reasonable being resolved in favour of the paying rather than the receiving party.

Rule 44.4(3) provides that on the indemnity basis any doubts are resolved in favour of the receiving party. Indemnity costs are accordingly a more generous assessment basis.

Where costs are assessed on the standard basis, the court will normally apply the hourly charging rates for different levels of fee earner that will be set out each year for their particular court area. The four levels of experience are:

- solicitors with over eight years' post-qualification experience (i.e. irrespective of whether or not a partner);

- solicitors and legal executives (which means a Fellow of the Institute of Legal Executives) with over four years' post-qualification experience;
- other solicitors and legal executives and fee earners of equivalent experience; and
- trainees, paralegals and other fee earners.

If the actual charging rate agreed between the solicitor and the receiving client is higher, the client will have to bear the shortfall. Also, if the receiving client has required a particularly high level of attention from the solicitor, on the standard basis the paying party is unlikely to be ordered to pay for all of that. On the indemnity basis, however, the actual charging rates and the time spent will usually be recovered, although it is important to note that an order for indemnity costs does not equate to carte blanche. Costs that are clearly unreasonably incurred or unreasonable in amount will still be disallowed on the indemnity basis.

Wall J emphasised in *Re B (Indemnity Costs)* [2008] 1 FLR 205 that an order for indemnity costs is a 'wholly exceptional order to make in family proceedings and needs to be very carefully thought through and justified'. They will usually be appropriate only in extreme cases where the paying party has been deliberately dishonest, misled the court or abused court procedures, or has acted in some other way that is clearly unreasonable. The majority of costs orders will therefore be made on a standard basis.

6.4.2 Terminology of costs orders

There are different types of costs orders that can be made by the court. The first three and the last of these relate to interlocutory (interim) hearings. It is important to understand these as they impact upon the eventual final costs order.

Costs in the case/application

This order means that the costs of the interlocutory application will be awarded to the party that succeeds in obtaining an order for costs at the end of the case. This is the usual order at interlocutory hearings. If there is no order for costs at the final hearing, each party remains responsible for its own costs of the interlocutory application.

Costs reserved

This order means that the decision as to whether there should be a costs order is postponed to be dealt with at a later date. It is essential that reserved costs orders are not overlooked later as if they are not revisited the costs will be lost. A reserved costs order will be appropriate where more information is required to assess responsibility for those costs, e.g. on a without notice injunction application, where it would be wrong to impose an order on a party who is not present to argue the merits of the case. Instead, the question of costs would be dealt with at the later on notice hearing.

Applicant's/respondent's costs in the case/application

The successful party in the interlocutory application will recover the costs of that application only if he or she gets costs at the end of the case. If the successful party does not get costs at the end of the case, there is still no obligation to pay the other party's costs of the interlocutory application, even if the other party gets an overall costs order. This is a fairly uncommon order in family cases.

No order for costs

Neither party recovers the costs of the application/hearing. This can be very important in relation to interlocutory applications. If there is no order for costs, the costs of the application cannot be recovered at the end of the day. As noted above, if this order is made at the end of the case, any orders for 'costs in the case/application' at an interlocutory stage will fall by the wayside. If the court order is silent on the question of costs (although this should only happen in error) this is the same as no order for costs. As noted below at **6.5.4** this is the usual order in ancillary relief proceedings for divorces started after 3 April 2006.

Costs in any event

The party receiving this order will get the costs of the interlocutory application, irrespective of the final outcome of the case or any final costs orders made. Accordingly, a 'costs in any event' order at an interlocutory hearing will be unaffected by a 'no order for costs' order made at the end of the case, unless the final order specifically provides that any earlier unpaid costs are not to be enforced.

6.4.3 Assessment of costs, costs options and time for payment

The party awarded costs will need to have them assessed by the court, if they cannot be agreed with the other side. The assessment will be either summary or detailed.

Summary assessment

By virtue of para.13.2 of the Practice Direction About Costs to CPR 1998, Parts 43–48, the general rule is that there should be a summary assessment of costs at the conclusion of any hearing (whether interlocutory or final) which has lasted not more than one day, unless there is good reason not to do so, e.g. where the paying party shows substantial grounds for disputing the sum claimed that cannot be dealt with summarily, or where there is insufficient time to carry out a summary assessment. The summary assessment procedure applies where appropriate to the full range of family proceedings but does not apply where either party is in receipt of public funding.

The party who intends to claim costs in a situation where summary assessment has to be considered must prepare a written statement of those costs. This must set out the hours claimed, the hourly rate of the various fee earners, the grade of fee earner, disbursements and the costs claimed for solicitor and/or counsel attending the hearing in question. The statement must follow Form N260 as closely as possible. It must be filed at court and served on the other side as soon as possible and in any event not less than 24 hours before the date fixed for the hearing (para.13.5).

Failure to comply with these rules may result in costs being disallowed in part or completely, which could turn a successful hearing into a pyrrhic victory. The practice of district judges varies widely in this respect. For example, some apply the 24-hour deadline rigidly, whereas others will still allow costs if it is considered that the paying party has not been prejudiced by the late service of the schedule. In some courts, if the paying party objects to having insufficient time, the judge will suggest an adjournment, which in practice will make arguing further about the time limit uneconomical.

The only safe approach is to prepare the schedules correctly and file/serve them in time. In terms of the procedure adopted by the court on summary assessment, the schedule prepared by the receiving party will be that party's 'evidence' so usually the paying party will be invited to go first with his submissions. Assuming that there is no argument as to the suitability of summary assessment as such, the paying party's representatives are likely to focus not only on the issues of the charging rates and time spent but also on the grade of fee earner undertaking certain tasks (could the work have been done at a more junior level) and the receiving party's conduct of the litigation, for example failure to negotiate. It is still possible to argue about litigation conduct even though that will probably have been aired very fully in the substantive representations at the stage when the court was being asked to rule on whether there should be a costs order at all.

The receiving party will have the right to respond. The paying party will have the right to reply to that response and the judge will then make the decision. It will be necessary to have a calculator ready to work out the impact of the judge's decision on the schedule of costs so that everyone can agree on the final figures.

As ever, the court has a wide discretion. The principles relating to standard and indemnity costs (see **6.4.1** above) apply to the summary assessment procedure. The advocate for the paying party will need to be able to explain and justify each item of work that is being challenged. This can present difficulties if the hearing is being dealt with by counsel and, in these circumstances, the fee earner who has had day-to-day conduct of the case will either need to be at the hearing or will need to ensure that counsel is fully briefed on the costs arguments. Issues that may arise include why a particular statement may have taken a long time to prepare and why it may have been necessary for a senior fee earner to have dealt with an interlocutory hearing rather than a more junior one. Consideration may also be given to whether it was necessary to use counsel.

The schedule that may have been prepared by the paying party can provide a useful response to their arguments, but will not be determinative as there may be good reasons justifying differences between the work undertaken by each side.

Finally, it goes without saying that it is essential for solicitors to know the standard hourly rates allowed for the different levels of fee earner in the court group in which they are appearing.

Detailed assessment

Where, in a privately paying case, a summary assessment is not appropriate, and the parties have not been able to agree the costs, they will need to be subject to a detailed assessment. The law and procedure for this is set out in CPR 1998 and the Practice Direction About Costs.

Rule 47.7 provides that the receiving party must commence detailed assessment proceedings within three months of the date of the relevant judgment. This is done by a notice of commencement in the prescribed form being served on the paying party along with the bill of costs. Under rule 47.8, if this time limit is not complied with, the costs may be disallowed in part or completely.

Rule 47.9 provides that the paying party has 21 days from the service of the notice of commencement and bill to raise points of dispute. Failure to comply with the time limit will almost certainly mean that the paying party will lose the right to make representations, enabling the receiving party to apply for a default costs certificate. The points of dispute have to be detailed but concise, so that the receiving party knows the case that is being argued against him or her. It is not sufficient for the paying party simply to make general comments to the effect that too long has been taken over a piece of work. The points must be more specific than that. The receiving party will almost always want to exercise the right provided in rule 47.13 to reply. The receiving party then requests the hearing. The court has to be provided with details of what is in dispute and what is agreed, thereby narrowing the issues to be argued about.

The above is only a brief summary of the detailed assessment procedure. Most firms will either have a costs expert in-house or will outsource the preparation (and often the advocacy) to an external costs draftsman, as the process is complex and time consuming. However, a fee earner with day-to-day responsibility for the file will still have a central role to play.

Other orders that the court can make

In addition to setting out the general principles CPR 1998, rule 44.3 gives the court a range of other options when dealing with costs. They are often overlooked, but can prove very useful.

Rule 44.3(6) provides that the court may make an order that a party must pay a proportion of the other party's costs, a stated amount of costs, costs from or until a certain date only, costs incurred before proceedings have begun, costs relating to particular steps in or a distinct part of the proceedings and interest from or until a certain date.

Rule 44.3(8) allows the court to order a payment on account of costs. Paragraph 12.3 of the Practice Direction About Costs specifically provides that whenever the court awards costs to be assessed by way of detailed assessment it should consider ordering a payment on account. This can be particularly useful. If the client is successful at final hearing and a costs order is made in the client's favour, getting an order from the judge for a significant payment on account will usually act as a powerful encouragement to the opponent to agree the balance of the costs, rather than risk the expense involved in a detailed assessment.

Rule 44.3(9) allows the court to set off the receiving party's costs against any costs owed by that party (for example from an earlier order) to the paying party.

Time for payment

Rule 44.8 states that a party must comply with an order for costs within 14 days of the date of judgment (if the amount of those costs are stated in the judgment) or of the date of the costs certificate (if the amount is determined at a later date). However, it is always open to the court to specify a later date.

There is an interesting point here in relation to the costs of the main divorce suit. A costs order in relation to the decree proceedings will be made at the same time as the pronouncement of the decree nisi. If, which will often be the case, those costs have been agreed in advance, rather than remaining to be agreed or assessed at a later date, rule 44.8 provides that they will be payable in 14 days. This will obviously be before the decree absolute. However, there is an argument that the respondent should not have to pay the divorce costs (which will include the decree absolute fee) before the proceedings covered by the costs have been completed. What would happen if the decree were never made absolute? Although the strict position seems to be that provided by rule 44.8, in practice payment will often be delayed until decree absolute, not least because if the respondent refuses to pay earlier, the costs of enforcing the position are likely to be disproportionate.

6.5 COSTS ORDERS IN DIFFERENT TYPES OF PROCEEDINGS

This section of the chapter considers types of proceedings where costs orders may commonly be made. These are:

- undefended decree proceedings for divorce (or judicial separation);
- injunction proceedings under Part IV of the Family Law Act 1996;
- Children Act cases;
- ancillary relief cases; and
- other cases (claims under TLATA 1996, *Barder* events and applications for set asides).

6.5.1 Undefended decree proceedings

The costs of the main suit relate only to the decree procedure itself, not to any separate applications in respect of finances, children or otherwise. Where those proceedings are undefended and are dealt with under the 'special procedure', they are reasonably self-contained and for this reason this is one area of family work in which a fixed quote can and often will be given.

The petitioner seeking costs must do so by claiming them in the prayer in the petition. They can be claimed from the respondent and, if applicable, any co-respondent. The respondent and co-respondent can of course object to paying all or part of the costs by stating to this effect in the acknowledgement of service to the petition. In an undefended divorce, petitioners in the affidavit in support of the petition can either give up the claim for costs in the face of objections, accept or propose a compromise position, or confirm that they wish to proceed with the prayer as originally stated.

The district judge will consider the issue when dealing with directions for trial under the special procedure. FPR 1991, rule 2.36(3) provides that the judge can either determine that the petitioner is entitled to the costs claimed or, alternatively, require the objecting party to attend the pronouncement of the decree nisi to argue the matter. Obviously, the petitioner will be able to attend as well. As noted at **6.4.3** above, any order for costs will be made at the nisi pronouncement.

The practitioner needs to consider with the client at the outset whether to claim costs and in accordance with the Resolution Code of Practice and the Law Society's *Family Law Protocol* efforts should be made to agree the position wherever possible. It will usually be appropriate to claim all of the costs only where the petition is based on one of the fault-based grounds of adultery, unreasonable behaviour or (although rare) desertion. A two-year separation case is by its very nature by consent, so if any costs are claimed it is common practice for them to be shared. It is not usually appropriate to seek costs in a five-year petition.

The objection to costs must be one of principle not of affordability. Practice varies very considerably between district judges when it comes to deciding at the special procedure stage how to deal with a disputed costs claim. Many will simply grant costs for any adultery or unreasonable behaviour petition. However, others will list a hearing when faced with the common response from a respondent that, although he does not intend to defend the divorce, he could have done and indeed could himself easily have issued his own fault-based petition, or that the admitted adultery was a symptom rather than the cause of the breakdown of the marriage. Although there is no procedure set out in FPR 1991 to this effect, some district judges will make an order of their own motion requiring written submissions on the costs dispute ahead of the decree nisi pronouncement.

In view of the fact that in most cases the costs of the main suit are modest in the context of the overall costs, it is nearly always uneconomical to take any dispute about them as far as a contested hearing at the decree nisi pronouncement. The risks are simply too high. Also, bear in mind that the decree nisi hearing is in open court so solicitors would need to attend in gowns, etc!

6.5.2 Injunction proceedings

In contrast to other family proceedings, it is usually easier to persuade a judge to make a costs order where an injunction under Part IV of the Family Law Act 1996 is found to be justified, but of course the court still has to exercise its discretion and take account of all relevant factors. As noted already, a reserved costs order is likely at an initial without notice hearing, on the basis that it would be inappropriate to decide costs without hearing the respondent's case. It may be of course that the without notice injunction is discharged after the court has heard evidence and that the applicant may be ordered to pay the costs.

6.5.3 Children Act proceedings

There is no distinction in CPR 1998 between Children Act proceedings and other family proceedings when it comes to the question of costs. Accordingly, the court has the power to order them. In practice, however, it will only be where one party's conduct has been particularly unreasonable or obstructive that a costs order will be contemplated.

In proceedings involving children, the welfare of the children is the paramount concern. Whilst the court may have to hear contested evidence and make findings of fact and a decision, proceedings are viewed essentially as a means of finding out what is best for the child. The court will always urge on the parties the benefits of an agreed outcome and emphasise the value to the child if they are able to work together as parents in the future, notwithstanding the breakdown in their relationship. This is a key component also of the Resolution Code of Practice. For this reason, the general view is that the parties should not be discouraged by the threat of costs from being able to present their arguments fully.

The recent case of *Re N (A Child); A* v. *G and N* [2009] EWHC 2096 (Fam) highlights how difficult it can be to obtain a costs order in Children Act cases. Munby J held that the fact that a parent had litigated in an unreasonable fashion did not of itself necessitate the making of a costs order. Although the father's behaviour had come close to justifying it, the judge refused to make a costs order because of the likely effect it would have on relations between the parents and thus on the child. However, Munby J made it clear that if the father continued to pursue the litigation by making further unsuccessful applications, a costs order may have to be made.

However, there is a limit to the allowance which a judge will make for a parent who deliberately and persistently fails to comply with, for example, a contact order in circumstances where the court has investigated the concerns fully and has determined that contact is clearly in the interests of the child. Costs orders are therefore made in certain cases (see by way of example the judgment in *Re T (A Child) (Order for Costs)* [2005] 1 FCR 625).

In summary, the latitude afforded to parties in the conduct of children proceedings is considerably greater than in even post-April 2006 ancillary relief proceedings, where, as explained below, the general rule is no order for costs. This presents the family lawyer with a challenge in managing the expectations and frustrations of the client who is likely to have to meet the costs of dealing with a former partner who adopts a stance that, on any objective analysis, may be considered to be unreasonable.

6.5.4 Ancillary relief proceedings

Ancillary relief work will often be at the heart of the family lawyer's day-to-day practice. A full understanding of the costs rules in relation to ancillary relief proceedings is therefore essential.

Following the changes introduced into FPR 1991 by the Family Proceedings (Amendment) Rules 2006, SI 2006/352, there are two separate costs regimes in financial cases: the 'old' *Calderbank* rules and the 'new' rules.

Although it may seem obvious, in order to work out whether the old or new costs rules apply in a particular case, regard must first be had to the definition of 'ancillary relief'. FPR 1991, rule 1.2 confirms that it means the following:

- an avoidance of disposition order under the Matrimonial Causes Act 1973 (MCA 1973), s.37(2)(b) or (c) or para.74(3) or (4) of Sched.5 to CPA 2004;
- a financial provision order (under MCA 1973, s.21(1) except an order under s.27(6) of the Act);
- an order for maintenance pending suit;
- a property adjustment order;
- a variation order;
- a pension sharing order.

By definition, all other family law cases (including all other financial matters) are not 'ancillary relief' applications and the 'new' rules do not apply. This is explained in more detail below.

Although the majority of ancillary relief proceedings will now be governed by the new rules, the *Calderbank* rules still apply to all cases in which the application was issued before 3 April 2006. For this purpose an application is by prayer in a petition or answer or, where there is no such prayer, an application made in Form A or Form B.

Pre-3 April 2006 proceedings – Calderbank *rules*

In respect of ancillary relief applications issued (as defined above) before 3 April 2006, the key provisions were to be found in FPR 1991, rules 2.69, 2.69B and 2.69D (rule 2.69C having already been revoked). When an application is made after 3 April but is heard at the same time as one made before, the relevant date is the original application.

Rule 2.69 provided that:

(1) Either party to the application may at any time make a written offer to the other party which is expressed to be 'without prejudice except as to costs' and which relates to any issue in the proceedings relating to the application.

(2) Where an offer is made under paragraph (1), the fact that such an offer has been made shall not be communicated to the court, except in accordance with rule 2.61E(3), until the question of costs falls to be decided.

Rule 2.61E(3) is the provision that requires all offers and responses to them to be disclosed in connection with the FDR.

An offer made 'without prejudice except as to costs' is called a *Calderbank* offer, after the Court of Appeal case of *Calderbank* v. *Calderbank* [1975] 3 All ER 333. Rule 2.69B provided that where the judgment or order in favour of the applicant or respondent is more advantageous than a *Calderbank* offer made by the other party, the court *must* (our emphasis) order the other party to pay any costs incurred after the date beginning 28 days after the offer was made, unless *the court considers it unjust to do so* (again, our emphasis).

Rule 2.69D sets out the factors that apply when determining whether or not it would be just or unjust to make a costs order. These include the terms of any offers, when in the proceedings they were made, the information available to the parties at the time, the conduct of the parties in respect of the giving or refusing of information needed to evaluate the offer, and the respective means of the parties.

The objective of course has always been, and remains, to encourage parties to negotiate a settlement. Making sensible offers, and responding sensibly to them, is critical to this. Rule 2.69 was intended to give teeth to the search for a settlement by keeping the threat of costs hovering like the Sword of Damocles above the heads of the parties. Once appropriate disclosure has been given, and sufficient time allowed to assess a proposal, the party refusing to negotiate reasonably should be at risk on costs. In view of the likely high level of those costs by the end of a contested hearing, that risk is clearly significant in most cases.

However, notwithstanding the use of the word 'must' in rule 2.69D, the court retained its overriding discretion. Often the parties have both made a series of offers as the case progresses towards trial. Both may genuinely be trying to compromise and the court's eventual decision will often fall between the respective offers. For example, one party may have judged the capital award accurately, but have been wide of the mark on maintenance. Although there was a perception before April 2006 that in the Principal Registry in London the judges may have been more willing to make costs orders, the feeling of practitioners outside London was generally that 'no order' was a much more likely outcome, unless the way in which a party had negotiated (or failed to negotiate) had been clearly blameworthy.

There was increasing criticism of the old regime, primarily from judges, who pressed for change through comments both within reported judgments and in commentary outside the courtroom. One of the main difficulties identified in practice was that the judge might have reached a carefully considered decision after hearing the evidence and balancing all the MCA 1973, s.25 criteria, and taking into account the openly stated position in respect of both parties' costs from their Form H, only to have that discretionary exercise undermined by the production, like rabbits out of a hat, of *Calderbank* offers. Furthermore, if a settlement only just meets a party's needs, a judge will not want to order that party to pay costs to the other and, in doing so, be left without their needs being met, no matter how close the other party's *Calderbank* proposals may have been. The momentum for change therefore gathered pace and, after lengthy consultation, resulted in the Family Proceedings (Amendment) Rules 2006.

Post-03 April 2006 proceedings – new rules

The Family Proceedings (Amendment) Rules 2006 deleted rules 2.69, 2.69B and 2.69D from, and inserted a new rule 2.71 'Costs Orders' into, FPR 1991. As stated above, CPR 1998, rule 44.3(1)–(5) are specifically disapplied to 'new' cases. Note, however, that CPR 1998, rule 44.3(6)–(9) is retained, so that the court can still make payments on account, set off costs, etc. – see **6.4.3** above.

Rule.2.71(4) provides:

(a) The general rule in ancillary relief proceedings is that the court will not make an order requiring one party to pay the costs of another party; but
(b) the court may make such an order at any stage of the proceedings where it considers it appropriate to do so because of the conduct of a party in relation to the proceedings (whether before or during them).

Having set out the general rule of no order for costs, rule 2.71(5) goes on to list the factors which the court must take into account in deciding what order (if any) to make under rule 2.71(4)(b). These are:

(a) any failure by a party to comply with these Rules, any order of the court or any practice direction which the court considers relevant;
(b) any open offer to settle made by a party;
(c) whether it was reasonable for a party to raise, pursue or contest a particular allegation or issue;
(d) the manner in which a party has pursued or responded to the application or a particular allegation or issue;
(e) any other aspect of a party's conduct in relation to the proceedings which the court considers relevant; and
(f) the financial effect on the parties of any costs order.

It is to be noted that (c) and (d) mirror exactly CPR 1998, rule 44.3(5)(b) and (c). Also, importantly, rule 2.71(5)(f) retains the provision in the old rule 2.69D(e) that regard must be had to the means of the parties.

Rule 2.71(5)(b) directs the court to have regard to *open* (our emphasis) offers and rule 27.1(6) specifically confirms that, apart from in relation to FDR proceedings, only open offers will be admissible. There is nothing to stop parties making without prejudice letters, but they offer no protection on costs and there are no sanctions in making or rejecting them as they cannot be drawn to the court's attention.

There is a consequential amendment to rule 2.61D(e) which deals with the possibility of making a costs order at the first appointment and directs the court to have regard in particular to the extent to which each party has complied with the requirement to send documents with Form E.

Open offers now take centre stage in ancillary relief cases. Rule 2.69E still applies so that not less than 14 days before the date fixed for the final hearing, the applicant must file an open offer, and not more than seven days later the respondent must do likewise. However, whereas before open offers would nearly always be below/above the more 'realistic' *Calderbank* offer, open offers have to be closer to what the parties think the judge may order, in case unreasonable offers are viewed by the court as justification for a costs order.

Without prejudice offers can still be made. They remain relevant in the run-up to the FDR (FPR 1991, rule 2.61E) and, even though they are not capable of being referred to in support of an application for a costs order, they may continue to be used to encourage settlement.

The new rules were supported by a President's Practice Direction issued on 20 February 2006. Apart from confirming that costs orders will be made only where justified by the litigation conduct of one of the parties, and that only open offers will be relevant, the Practice Direction goes on to deal with two practical points.

First, it makes it clear that a maintenance pending suit order that includes an element of legal fees provision is not a 'costs order' and that such provision can continue to be made where appropriate (see **6.3.3** above).

Secondly, a party intending to seek a costs order should usually make this claim in open correspondence or skeleton arguments prior to the hearing. The purpose of this is to set out the arguments to enable the court wherever possible to rule on the issue of costs at the end of the hearing, rather than having to adjourn to a later date.

The 'new' rules – three years on

When the new rules were introduced, practitioners thought that more applications for costs would be made in interlocutory proceedings in relation to specific aspects of a case, to compensate for the fact that an overall costs order was less likely. In our experience this has not happened and interim costs orders are still rarely made in practice. However, the practice may vary up and down the country.

Although the new regime applies only to ancillary relief proceedings there is a perception that it influences judges when they consider costs in other family proceedings, for example, under the Children Act 1989, Sched.1 and when they hear ancillary relief cases which fall within the old *Calderbank* rules.

The future of costs in ancillary relief cases

Resolution and the Family Law Bar Association share the view that the new rules have not had the desired effect and *Calderbank* proposals should be re-introduced. In practice, the new rules are being applied as a presumption of no order as to costs unless there has been 'litigation misconduct', notwithstanding the fact that this is not the test set out in FPR 1991, rule 2.71. It is therefore extremely difficult to persuade judges to make costs orders, which can be detrimental to many parties and is potentially very unfair in some cases. For example, the no order principle makes interim maintenance applications all the more risky.

Furthermore, without the ability to make *Calderbank* proposals, there is less of an incentive on parties to negotiate and more cases end up at a final hearing as a result.

The Family Procedure Rules Committee Costs Group has been established to review the position in the light of practitioners' concerns. However, the impression is that the judges are reluctant to see the return of the *Calderbank* offer, for the same reasons that they called for the law to be changed in the first place. We can therefore only watch this space to see how this debate is resolved.

6.5.5 Other cases – non-ancillary relief

FPR 1991, rule 2.71 confirms that the new rules apply only to ancillary relief applications issued on or after 3 April 2006. As such, they do not apply to any family proceedings which are excluded from the definition of 'ancillary relief' under FPR 1991, rule 1.2, regardless of when the application is made. We have summarised the position with costs in undefended divorces, Family Law

Act 1996 claims and Children Act claims above. The other family proceedings which are omitted from the definition of ancillary relief and which therefore remain within the old *Calderbank* rules are:

- Children Act, Sched.1 claims;
- Inheritance (Provision for Family and Dependants) Act claims;
- proceedings under Part III of the Matrimonial and Family Proceedings Act 1984 (financial provision following a foreign divorce);
- applications for set asides on the grounds of mistake, misrepresentation or duress;
- appeals; and
- applications for leave to appeal out of time (including *Barder* events).

In our view (which is supported by other commentators), if applications for orders to be set aside and appeals are successful, the costs rules applying to the substantive rehearings are determined by the date of the original application for ancillary relief, i.e. whether this was pre- or post-3 April 2006. However, we are not aware of any reported decisions dealing with this point.

As stated at **6.2** above, claims made under TLATA 1996 are outside the definition of 'family proceedings' completely, so neither the *Calderbank* rules nor the new rules apply. These cases are covered by the CPR and costs follow the event pursuant to CPR 1998, rule 44.3(2) (see *Hannan* v. *Maxton* [2009] EWCA Civ 773).

6.6   FORM H AND FORM H1

As a result of the Family Proceedings (Amendment) Rules 2006, Form H was expanded to provide better information at interlocutory hearings and Form H1 now has to be filed and served not less than 14 days before the final hearing. The purpose of Form H1 is to enable the court to see clearly each party's costs liability when deciding what ancillary relief order to make. It is not intended to replace the statement of costs on Form N260 (or equivalent) that is required to be filed and served if a summary assessment is being sought.

A point in practice is that Forms H and H1 deal only with the costs of the ancillary relief proceedings. Practitioners are specifically asked to exclude any other costs which may have been incurred. The parties may of course have other unpaid costs in relation to, for example, Children Act proceedings. Although these should not be included as a liability on Form H1, they should be drawn to the court's attention as any unpaid costs are a debt which the court needs to take into account.

6.7   INTEREST ON COSTS ORDERS

Unless ordered otherwise, interest accrues automatically on all costs orders made in the High Court (Judgments Act 1838, s.17) and on any orders made in the county courts of £5,000 or more (County Courts (Interest on Judgment Debts) Order 1991, SI 1991/1184).

The rate of interest is the judgment debt rate (currently 8 per cent). The general rule is that where interest is payable it begins to run from the date of the order, unless the court orders otherwise. This applies even to orders which are to be the subject of detailed assessment. However, if the detailed assessment is not applied for as prescribed by the rules, the interest can be disallowed (in part or completely). Practitioners are referred to the provisions in CPR 1998, Parts 44 and 47.

Pursuant to CPR 1998, rule 44.3(6)(g), the court can order that a party must pay interest on costs from or until a certain date, including a date before the order was made.

6.8   ENFORCEMENT OF COSTS ORDERS

In order to be able to enforce an order for costs, the amount due, including any interest that has accrued, must be quantified and the time for payment must have passed. Subject to these two conditions, a costs order may be enforced in the same way as any lump sum, i.e. by way of judgment summons, attachment of earnings, charging order, order for sale, bankruptcy, receivership, sequestration or writ of fieri facias/warrant of execution. A detailed analysis of the methods of enforcement is outside the scope of this chapter.

CHAPTER 7

Financial provision for children

James Pirrie and Stephen Lawson

Where financial provision for children is sought other than in the context of divorce proceedings there are two ways it can be achieved:

- by applications to the CSA; or
- by application under Schedule 1 to the Children Act 1989.

In relation to each, first, the law is different from that we are used to in our divorce work, being either highly technical and regulation based (child support) or lacking clarity, through absence of sufficiently diverse cases (Schedule 1 work). Secondly, each system may involve ethical challenges. We will need to keep a grip on our Resolution code and on a structured and grounded approach. So for example, when acting for respondents to the child support process, we will be cautious about advising on steps which amount to avoidance of child support liabilities, encouraging clients to keep a firm focus on the needs of their child. When acting for applicants for Schedule 1 provision, we will need to avoid confusing the claims of the child with the needs of the residential parent.

7.1 CHILD SUPPORT CASES

7.1.1 Introduction

The main source for our child support system is the Child Support Act 1991 which has been very significantly amended by further Acts in 1995, 2000 and 2008. The original Act established the CSA as a limb of the relevant government department (originally the Department of Social Security, then the Department for Work and Pensions). The latest Act created the Child Maintenance Enforcement Commission (CMEC or 'the Commission'), an independent body corporate that has taken over many of the tasks and resources of the original Agency.

The key to child support work is the formula that the 1991 Act established and by which maintenance awards are fixed – agreements to opt out of the structure are not enforceable. The original formula was very complex.

Though replaced with effect from 3 March 2003, there are (as at 2009) still over half a million 'old rules' cases in existence. Specialist advice may well be required to deal with them.

Each legislative refinement created clusters of changes, introduced at different stages aimed at addressing flaws in the original system. The current formula is described below. This is due to be replaced in 2011 by a similar structure save that:

- it will focus on gross income not net (the percentages are correspondingly lower);
- the preceding year's income will be looked at and only in the event of a significant change would adjustment be considered.

One of the most significant changes introduced by the 2008 Act was in relation to benefit claimants who had throughout the operation of the system until that point been threatened with benefit reductions if they would not name the fathers of their children. From October 2008 the 'requirement to co-operate' which had taken up so much policy and adviser time was abolished and benefit claimants keep the first £20 per week of maintenance monies paid.

7.1.2　Some truths about the Commission

There can be a lot of frustration dealing with the Commission. Sometimes this is because of difficult circumstances, sometimes it is because of poor service, but very often it is because of a lack of understanding about what the Commission can do and the rules by which it operates. Causing further problems is the history of poor service that dogged the old CSA, whilst it was underfunded and struggled with the complexities of the 'old rules' formula and whilst, according to Parliament's social security select committee, it was poorly led.

7.1.3　Ethics

Practitioners will want to help clients maintain a clear focus on the needs of children that this system endeavours to address. A client who is unhappy with the level of child support due must be discouraged from using this to justify withholding contact. The client owing money must be helped to see the bigger picture rather than pursuing further overnight stays so as to reduce the level of payments or adopting other manipulative strategies.

7.1.4　Abbreviations used in relation to child support

There are a number of abbreviations used in this chapter, which are listed here for ease of reference.

The 'parent with care' (PWC) is the parent with whom a child lives. In shared arrangements it is the one who has slightly more overnight stays in the 12 months leading up to the application.

The 'non-resident parent' (NRP), formerly the pejorative 'absent parent', is the other parent.

The obligation to pay under the old rules is referred to as the 'assessment' and the 'calculation' is the obligation to pay under the new.

7.1.5 Points to note regarding child support

Remember that clients will need to send to the Commission (either directly or through their solicitor) an authority for the Commission to speak to the solicitor before any of its officers will speak to the solicitor at all. The solicitor will then receive all documentation generated in the case.

See **www.childmaintenance.org** for information about the Commission's activities, but for useable information about child support generally, go to its website at **www.csa.gov.uk** which is a well-designed and accessible resource. The application and enquiry (response to an application) forms can be downloaded there. The national helpline number is 08457 133133.

7.2 JURISDICTION OF THE COMMISSION

The Commission has jurisdiction where:

- the parent is connected to the child because the child is the parent's natural or adopted child or the rules under the Human Fertilisation and Embryology Act 1990 apply (e.g. following IVF treatment);
- the child is under 16 or in full-time secondary education;
- the child is living in the UK and the NRP is resident in the UK, or if overseas then at least the NRP is on government service or employed by a UK-based company; and
- there are two separate households: only where the NRP has separated from the family can an application be made against the NRP.

There are a number of limited exceptions which all relate to where the parents have made their own separate arrangements. Where the Commission does not have jurisdiction then the case will fall within the limited range of cases where an application for child maintenance is made to the court and the court has power to *impose* a maintenance award. Case law (*GW* v. *RW* [2003] 2 FLR 108) gives strong suggestion that the child support formula should be used as a guide by the court in considering the appropriate level of award to make.

7.3   THE FORMULA

1.   First work out who is the PWC. There are detailed rules for dealing with the situation if care is broadly equal.
2.   Take the NRP's income after tax and national insurance.
3.   Deduct pension contributions (the maximum income after pension contributions that can be considered is £104,000 per annum).
4.   Deduct a slice from this income to represent the financial responsibility for any children in the NRP's new household. (This slice is worked out as 15 per cent for one child, 20 per cent for two children and 25 per cent for three or more children.)
5.   Apply the same rate (15 per cent or 20 per cent or 25 per cent) to what is left to give the basic liability for child support.
6.   Adjust this in line with overnight stays. (If the children stay with the NRP for more than one night on average a week then reduce by one-seventh; if for two nights, then two-sevenths, three nights is three-sevenths and if there are 175 nights or more then there is a reduction of 50 per cent plus £7 per week.)
7.   Consider whether any of the categories of 'variation' apply.

Note that there are special rules for those on low incomes or in particular circumstances:

- A flat rate of £5 applies to those earning £100 per week or less.
- The reduced rate applies to those earning £100 to £200 per week, which is broadly the flat rate plus between 17.5 per cent and 45 per cent of the remainder of the NRP's income up to £200.
- The nil rate applies to students, children, prisoners and those with an income of £5 per week or less.

7.4   THE PROCESS

7.4.1   Commencement

The process generally commences through the PWC making contact with the Commission by telephone or in writing. Often then contact is made with the other parent by phone. Usually the 'maintenance enquiry' form (also on the website) is completed. The Commission then carries out its calculations on the basis of the information that it is given and issues notification to each party about the basic information as to income and the calculation – the sum that must be paid.

In many cases, the Commission will then start to collect the sum it records as being due from the non-resident parent, receiving the money in and paying it across to the parent with care. The Commission may broker an

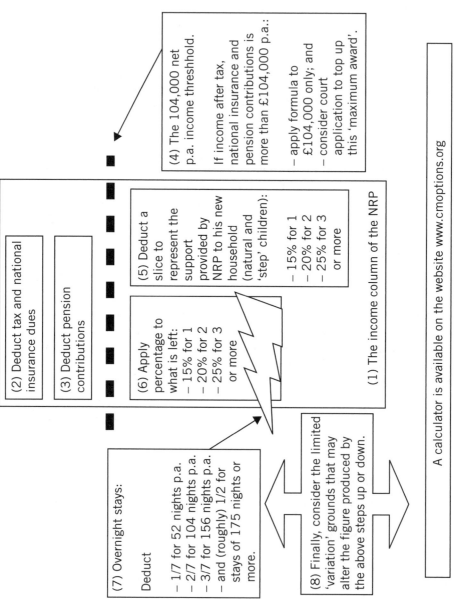

(4) The 104,000 net p.a. income threshold.

If income after tax, national insurance and pension contributions is more than £104,000 p.a.:

– apply formula to £104,000 only; and
– consider court application to top up this 'maximum award'.

(2) Deduct tax and national insurance dues

(3) Deduct pension contributions

(5) Deduct a slice to represent the support provided by NRP to his new household (natural and 'step' children):

– 15% for 1
– 20% for 2
– 25% for 3 or more

(6) Apply percentage to what is left:

– 15% for 1
– 20% for 2
– 25% for 3 or more

(1) The income column of the NRP

(7) Overnight stays:

Deduct

– 1/7 for 52 nights p.a.
– 2/7 for 104 nights p.a.
– 3/7 for 156 nights p.a.
– and (roughly) 1/2 for stays of 175 nights or more.

(8) Finally, consider the limited 'variation' grounds that may alter the figure produced by the above steps up or down.

A calculator is available on the website www.cmoptions.org

Figure 7.1 The child support formula under the Acts of 1991–2000

arrangement for the NRP to pay the money directly to the PWC and the Commission only becomes involved again if either side asks for the figures to be reviewed or if the PWC complains that the payments are not being made.

The process has three particular additional areas to this basic structure:

1. Parentage – where the NRP denies he is the father of the child.
2. Non-co-operation – where the NRP refuses to provide any information or refuses to abide by the calculation issued by the Commission.
3. Challenges – what to do if the result is wrong?

7.4.2 Denying parentage

The Commission is entitled to presume that a person is the father of the child in the following circumstances:

- where he is named on the birth certificate;
- where he was married to the mother at the time of conception or birth; or
- where he refuses to take a DNA test.

It is then for the father to make application to the court to make a declaration as to parentage.

7.4.3 Non-co-operation by the non-resident parent

Sanctions available to the Commission include the following.

1. An NRP who refuses to provide information, or who provides misleading information, commits an offence, punishable as a crime with a fine of up to £1,000.
2. The Commission has rights to demand information from a variety of bodies, including employers and has access to the government national insurance records, etc. to obtain information about the up-to-date situation. Accountants of the self-employed have duties to co-operate. More extreme cases may involve the appointment of inspectors who have rights of entry to non-domestic premises, including those of professional advisers. Solicitors may seek to deny access to records on the basis of legal privilege in this situation and the Solicitors Regulation Authority should be contacted for guidance.
3. Where there is an assessment in place, which is not being paid, the Commission has the power itself to impose a deduction from earnings order (DEO). This is an internal decision. There are no fixed rules as to when it is imposed: the Commission will use this route where the NRP will not respond.
4. The Commission acquired powers in 2009 to impose 'a regular deductions order' or 'a lump sum deductions order': directions to a bank or building society to send monies through to the Commission either as a lump sum to pay off arrears or on a repeating basis to meet ongoing liabilities.

5. If the DEO is not regarded as effective, the Commission may seek a liability order. The magistrates' court has very little discretion to refuse such an order, thus providing the Commission with a passport enabling it to obtain further orders from the court, for example, freezing monies in bank accounts or charging property with the debt that has accrued. The Commission may also make a reference to credit agencies, which will impede the NRP from borrowing. In the Autumn of 2009, the Commission began piloting new 'administrative enforcement' powers, passed in the 2008 Act, permitting it to pursue such enforcement measures independent of court sanction.

6. In the ultimate analysis, the Commission can ask for an order to remove the driving licence of a non-payer or impose a term of imprisonment.

7.4.4 Challenging the result

There are only five avenues by which the outcome can be challenged.

(1) Appeal

An appeal can be brought where the Commission has misinterpreted the facts or misapplied the law. Where an error of law has occurred, the stages of appeal are as follows.

1. The Commission *reviews* its case (usually a new case worker is appointed).
2. *An appeal* is made (usually within 28 days): the tribunal service then reviews the decisions of the Commission.
3. The Upper Tribunal considers whether the tribunal service made legal errors in the way that it dealt with the case.
4. The Court of Appeal considers whether the Upper Tribunal made legal errors in the way that the Commissioner dealt with the tribunal's decision.

The application for CSA and tribunal review must generally be made within one month of the decision. There is an absolute bar to proceeding with an appeal 13 months after the decision.

(2) Supersession

This avenue is used where an event has taken place that will change the level of payments by a figure in excess of a tolerance level (5 per cent is a good rule of thumb, but there are detailed rules). The Commission then embarks on a new set of calculations in a way that is similar to making a new application for child support.

(3) Variation

The third option outcome is a variation. A variation is the limited play within the formula that reflects a broader range of circumstances that could not be accommodated within the basic formula but which were, nonetheless, seen as sufficiently significant to demand recognition. An application should be made within a month of the decision if possible, otherwise any altered figure will only be effective from the date the variation was applied for.

(4) Complaint

The fourth option to challenge a final resolution is pursuing a complaint. If the service has been so bad, and in particular where loss has resulted, then an application for compensation can be made. This might be because the initial process was slow and a maintenance enquiry form was not issued to the NRP. Where this is not done, the liability does not start to clock up and so loss may have resulted. Similarly, where enforcement steps were taken only after long delay, resulting in major inconvenience or loss, compensation can be considered. The awards are often at derisory levels for inconvenience.

(5) Judicial review

The Commission must apply its own rules and where it fails to do so, the court may intervene following an application for judicial review. Judicial review proceedings will need specialist consideration, which is beyond the scope of this book.

7.5 FINANCIAL PROVISION FROM THE COURTS (OTHER THAN IN MATRIMONIAL PROCEEDINGS): CHILDREN ACT 1989, SCHEDULE 1

7.5.1 What is a Schedule 1 case?

The primary use of Schedule 1 is by parents who:

- cannot make use of the comprehensive scheme of MCA 1973 to resolve their financial questions (generally because they have never been married); and/or
- have claims beyond the scope of the system of the Child Support Act 1991, for example, where:
  - the provider is outside the jurisdiction of the Commission (e.g. because he or she lives abroad);
  - the income of the NRP exceeds the child support formula's upper limit;
  - the application concerns educational costs or disability costs; or

- the applicant seeks capital provision to provide a home for the child or other capital needs.

The Schedule would also be used by the child seeking provision from separated parents who have not been married to each other to pay university fees. The court's permission is needed (FPR 1991, rule 2.54(1)(f)).

7.5.2   Legal guidance

There is insufficient clarity from the statutory code for a practitioner to advise as to how these claims will be addressed by the courts in all cases. Most of the principles must be worked out from the cases. As most of the cases have involved fathers of high net worth, practitioners may find difficulty in identifying the principles that should apply to the situations usually encountered. Furthermore, even in the cases that we have, there are logical inconsistencies, which mean that it can be hard to sift out principles to be applied in particular circumstances.

Unlike divorce cases, for example, practitioners may have little experience of how a local court will react as the cases are far less numerous. Therefore, counsel may be required at an early stage. Those wanting further information may want to make use of Resolution's book, *Claims under Schedule 1 to the Children Act 1989* (2009).

7.5.3   Funding

Funding can also be difficult as (again, unlike divorce) the applicant may not be permitted to use the resources that are secured in the claim for costs (often awards are earmarked for specific issues and the substantial lump sum – for housing – if secured is likely to be held by trustees on a loan basis till the child comes of age). Even those who qualify financially for public funding may find their applications refused by the Legal Services Commission (LSC) on a merits basis. At last there have been indications that the courts will consider making lump sum awards at the outset of a case to enable the costs of the case to be funded. The availability of such provision is likely to be a strong inducement to parties entering into negotiations at an early stage. But counsel's advice and guidance are likely to be needed with such applications.

7.6   THE BOUNDARIES OF THE APPLICATION

7.6.1   What is or is not permitted

Where the Commission has jurisdiction, the court will not make provision for maintenance, other than:

- to top up a maximum award or to meet the costs of disability;
- for school fees; or

- by agreement. Where matters proceed by agreement particular care is needed as the parties have the absolute right 12 months after the order is made to apply to the Commission anyway and the eventual child support award will replace any terms of the court order.

Further, *Phillips* v. *Peace* [1996] 2 FLR 230 makes it clear that it is not for the court to make up for the deficiencies of the child support system, e.g. by awarding a lump sum to bolster the formula-based award to a level that the court might regard as appropriate.

7.7 THE MENU OF CLAIMS

Periodical payments orders:

(a)   cannot start earlier than the date of the application (although special rules apply to applications where there has been a previous CSA calculation, which may permit longer backdating);

(b)   may not last beyond the date when the child attains the age of 17 (unless the court thinks it right to specify a later date);

(c)   must end at the date when the child attains the age of 18, unless:

  –   the child is attending an educational establishment or undergoing training; or
  –   there are special circumstances to justify a later date;

(d)   must end with the death of the payer (unless it is a secured order);

(e)   are ended if applicant parent and respondent parent live together for six months or more.

7.7.1   Housing

It is an established principle that where money is provided for housing, there is a need to avoid 'creating an excessive disparity between' the parents' homes (*Re S (Child: Financial Provision)* [2005] 2 FLR 94).

Only one order for housing may be made. The court should not subsequently use the device of a lump sum order or a transfer of property order to make further provision (*Phillips* v. *Peace (No.2)* [2005] 2 FLR 1212). The practitioner who fails to confirm an arrangement by a court order, thus leaving open the possibility of a second bite at the cherry, without clear instructions will put him/herself at risk of a claim.

7.7.2   Terms on which housing is provided

Respondents have some rights to veto an unsuitable investment (*Re P (Child: Financial Provision)* [2003] 2 FLR 865).

Estate

There are a number of ways in which property can be held or owned following an order being made. The court will stipulate the method of ownership at the time of making the order. Some options are:

1. The property is held by trustees, who would be nominees of mother and father.
2. The property is held in the joint names of the parties.
3. The property is held by the mother outright, with her then providing the father with a mortgage to secure his claims and protect his position.

Term

A variety of trigger events have been taken for the end date, when the respondent can recover his investment. The earliest has been the child's finishing secondary education. The latest has been six months after the last of the children has completed tertiary education.

Tax advice

The effect of capital gains tax and stamp duty land tax should be taken into account when advising upon the best method of owning property for the benefit of a child.

Variation

Provision should be made for variation where circumstances change (*Phillips v. Peace (No.2)* [2005] 2 FLR 1212). Though the applicant is not permitted to have a further housing award, account may need to be taken of the mother finding a new partner, her earning or receiving capital windfalls. Bear in mind that the trustees of a bankrupted respondent might have powers to call in this asset even before the trigger events of the order.

Improvements

It may be necessary to deal with improvements at the property. The mother might ask for these to be funded by the father as a lump sum payment (e.g. where the child's needs have changed). Alternatively, it may be appropriate to build in a system to enable her to recover the increased value reflected in the property's selling price as a result of the improvements that she carries out.

The father is entitled to proof that all of the money has been spent on the home, if that was the purpose of the lump sum order (*Re P (Child: Financial Provision)* [2003] 2 FLR 865).

7.7.3   Lump sums

Lump sums are not designed to revert to the payer. It is of their essence that they are paid once and for all and are used to reimburse past expenditure or are spent on current or future needs (*Phillips* v. *Peace (No.2)* [2005] 2 FLR 1212) and where the value of what is purchased will depreciate rendering recovery by the respondent inappropriate.

So lump sums may be ordered to meet the cost of furnishing and equipping the property and the cost of the family car and other incidentals, such as computers or musical instruments. These are capital (as opposed to recurring) spends because the purchased asset is likely to depreciate significantly so that there would be nothing for the respondent to recover at the end of the day.

7.7.4   Carer's allowance and global maintenance

Terminology in the cases has changed over the years, making it hard to see a consistent message from the cases. Sometimes 'carer's allowance' is used to refer to the element of the applicant's budget that is to meet her own needs. Sometimes it refers to the global award. Essentially, where the respondent's income is off the top of the child support scale (currently £104,000 net p/a) then the court must decide what maintenance should be paid globally to enable the applicant to maintain an appropriate household for the child. The approach which is adopted by the court is set out in *Re P*:

* start with the housing that bears an appropriate relationship to the housing and lifestyle of the father;
* establish what income is needed to maintain that household;
* adopt a broad and commonsense approach; and
* try to prevent the parties from bickering over budgets.

The current value of the awards in the recent cases has been for annual payments to be in the region of £36,000 upwards to around £80,000. However, these sums would only be payable where the father is able to afford this and the higher awards have been in cases involving immensely wealthy fathers.

7.7.5   Claims for monies to fund future legal costs

Specialist guidance from counsel is likely to be required as regards the developing law on applications for legal costs.

7.8   THE APPROACH

The court must take various factors into account in making an order or orders.

The court is directed to take into consideration all the circumstances of the case including, in relation to each of the applicant and the parents/respondents:

- income, earning capacity, property, financial resources they have or are likely to have in the foreseeable future;
- financial needs, obligations and responsibilities they have or are likely to have in the foreseeable future;
- financial needs of the child;
- income, earning capacity, property and other financial resources of the child;
- physical or mental disability of the child;
- the manner in which the child was being or was expected to be educated or trained.

Where a person is not the mother or father, additionally, the court must consider:

- whether the person had assumed financial responsibility for the mainte-nance of the child and if so:
  - the extent;
  - the basis;
  - the period; and
  - whether he knew the child was not his (and then the court must record that the child was not his on the order);
- the liability of any other person to maintain the child.

This is a list with which practitioners will be familiar from applications made under the Matrimonial Causes Act 1973, because it largely mirrors the factors that are relevant. Case law suggests that apparent differences are not significant:

1. There is no specific provision that the welfare of the child be the first and paramount consideration in this list. However, its omission does not materially affect the approach likely to be taken, as explained by Hale J in *J* v. *C (Child: Financial Provision)* [1999] 1 FLR 152.
2. There is no reference to standard of living. However, in *F* v. *G (Child: Financial Provision)* [2005] 1 FLR 261 at [33]–[34], Singer J expressed the view that in an appropriate case, that might be the dominant feature.

7.8.1 Parents' financial responsibility

Parents have a responsibility to support their children throughout the period of the children's dependency (*J* v. *C (Child: Financial Provision)* [1999] 1 FLR 152).

7.8.2 Focus on the child's needs

The welfare of the child is a constant influence on the discretionary outcome. In the 2006 Court of Appeal case of *Re S*, Thorpe LJ ruled that a child's security was a major factor in determining what was in the child's best interests (*Re S (A Child)* [2006] EWCA Civ 479).

7.8.3 Proportionality between father's and mother's standard of living

The child is entitled to be brought up in circumstances that bear some sort of relationship to the father's current resources and the father's present standard of living (Hale J in *J* v. *C (Child: Financial Provision)* [1999] 1 FLR 152). (However, keep in mind that where the court has no freedom to impose a periodical payments award, because of the restrictions imposed by child support legislation, this may be a hard thing to achieve.)

7.8.4 Duration

Children are entitled to provision during their dependency and for their education, but they are not entitled to a settlement beyond that, unless there are exceptional circumstances such as a disability (Hale J in *J* v. *C (Child: Financial Provision)* [1999] 1 FLR 152). The case lists a variety of trigger events that determine the end of dependency.

7.8.5 Cohabitation

The effect of a parent with the care of a child cohabiting with a new partner will depend upon all the circumstances of the cohabitation (*F* v. *G (Child: Financial Provision)* [2005] 1 FLR 261).

7.8.6 Mother earning

A parent who has the care of a child is expected to contribute to the child's financial support where that parent is earning (*F* v. *G (Child: Financial Provision)* [2004] EWHC 1848, [2005] 1 FLR 261).

CHAPTER 8

Children proceedings

Punam Denley and Noel Arnold

PRIVATE PROCEEDINGS

8.1 INTRODUCTION

Most children proceedings are governed by the Children Act 1989 (CA 1989). In addition, wardship and the inherent jurisdiction of the court still apply to a small minority of cases, and this is dealt with below.

8.2 THE PRINCIPLES

Essentially there are three principles to which the court must have regard:

- the welfare principle;
- the 'no delay' principle; and
- the 'no order' principle.

8.2.1 The welfare principle

Section 1(1)

Also known as the 'paramountcy principle', s.1(1) is the guiding light behind CA 1989 and the court is compelled to apply it in every case concerning children, even if that case is not brought under the auspices of the Act.

> When a court determines any question with respect to –
>
> (a) the upbringing of a child; or
> (b) the administration of a child's property or the application of any income arising from it,
>
> the child's welfare shall be the court's paramount consideration.

It obliges the court to put a child's welfare first when there is a conflict between the interests of that child and a parent. It is mandatory for the court to consider the welfare principle and checklist when making any order under CA 1989, s.8 (see below).

The welfare checklist

The court must consider:

(a) the ascertainable wishes and feelings of the child concerned (considered in the light of the child's age and understanding);
(b) the child's physical, emotional and educational needs;
(c) the likely effect on the child of any change in circumstances;
(d) the child's age, sex, background and any characteristics which the court considers relevant;
(e) any harm which the child has suffered or is at risk of suffering;
(f) how capable each of the parents (and any other person in relation to whom the court considers the question to be relevant) is of meeting the child's needs; and
(g) the range of powers available to the court in the proceedings.

The court can of course take into account all relevant facts and attach varying degrees of weight and importance to those factors according to the circumstances of each case. No single issue will necessarily be considered as more important than another.

8.2.2 The 'no delay' principle

Under s.1(2):

> In any proceedings in which any question with respect to the upbringing of a child arises, the court shall have regard to the general principle that any delay in determining the question is likely to prejudice the welfare of the child.

The court has a positive duty to consider delay at every stage of the proceedings, on the basis that delay is likely to be detrimental to the child's welfare.

8.2.3 The 'no order' principle

Under s.1(5):

> When a court is considering whether to make one or more orders under this Act with respect to a child, it shall not make the order or any of the orders unless it considers that doing so would be better for the child than making no order at all.

This is known also as the 'non-intervention' principle: basically, the court should not make an order unless making one would be of positive benefit to a child. Parental agreement on issues is commonly asserted to be the reason why no order should be made, but the court must consider carefully whether no order would lead to further disputes between the parents.

8.3   JURISDICTION

The courts have jurisdiction to make orders under CA 1989 although if there is any foreign element to a child's position, the court's jurisdiction to make an order must be carefully checked.

8.4   THE ORDERS

8.4.1   Parental responsibility (section 4)

What is parental responsibility?

Parental responsibility is defined in CA 1989, s.3(1) as:

> . . . all the rights, duties, powers, responsibilities and authority which by law a parent of a child has in relation to the child and his property.

This is somewhat vague as definitions go and has given rise to much litigation. The list that follows is not exhaustive.

Parental responsibility does cover:

(a)   chastisement;

(b)   consent to medical treatment for the child;

(c)   decisions about education and adoption;

(d)   consent to marriage;

(e)   the appointment of a guardian for the child;

(f)   matters concerning the child's assets;

(g)   what amounts to rights of 'custody' for the purposes of the Hague Convention on International Child Abduction;

(h)   the right to apply for a passport and refuse a passport application; and

(i)   the removal of the child outside the jurisdiction for the purposes of a holiday of more than one month's duration or permanently.

In addition, there is a commonly held perception that parental responsibility gives rise to a right to information about the child. This is not supported by statute, but the Department for Education and Skills guidelines impose a requirement on teachers in schools to communicate with both parents. See Guidance, Schools, Parents and Parental Responsibility (Ref: DfEE 0092/2000), issued to headteachers in June 2000.

The Act intends that parents exercise parental responsibility independently of one another, but that parents should work together wherever that is possible. However if one person/parent seeks to remove a relevant child from the jurisdiction of England and Wales, they must obtain the consent to do so from every person with parental responsibility. The exception is where the person intending to remove has a residence order (see below), whereupon they are entitled to take the child out for 28 days without anyone's agreement.

How is parental responsibility obtained?

The area of parental responsibility has been expanded as a result of the Adoption and Children Act 2002. Parental responsibility is obtained in one of the following ways:

1. By marriage. When the mother is married to the father either at the time of the child's birth or subsequently the father attains parental responsibility. This category is by far the strongest type of parental responsibility, and can only be brought to an end by a court order, except by adoption.
2. By the natural father entering into a parental responsibility agreement with the mother. This needs to be witnessed by a Justice of the Peace or nominated court official and lodged at the Principal Registry of the Family Division (see below).
3. By the natural father obtaining a parental responsibility order from the court (see below). The court takes into account the following factors in determining whether an order for parental responsibility is appropriate:

    (a) the degree of commitment that the father has exhibited toward the child hitherto;
    (b) the degree of attachment between father and child; and
    (c) the father's motives behind making the application.

    This test was set out in the case of *Re H (Minors) (Adoption: Putative Father's Rights) (No.3)* [1991] 2 All ER 185 and is known as the tripartite test.

4. By becoming a testamentary guardian for the child, on the death of the natural mother. The appointment (by will) does not take effect unless and until there is no natural parent with parental responsibility.
5. By any person obtaining a residence order from the court. However, the parental responsibility aspect of this will also lapse if the residence order is discharged. Therefore it is important that where a natural father is granted a residence order, he should also consider obtaining a parental responsibility order alongside a residence order. An unmarried father's parental responsibility must be brought to an end by a specific order to that effect (CA 1989, Sched.1, para.16(2)).
6. A local authority can obtain parental responsibility upon the granting of a care order in its favour. This is covered more fully later in this chapter (see **8.16**).
7. If the child was born on or after 1 December 2003, an unmarried father who is registered on the birth certificate at the time of initial registration shall automatically attain parental responsibility (Adoption and Children Act 2002, s.111).

8. By re-registration of the birth certificate, to include the natural father if there is no father already mentioned and if the re-registration takes effect with the mother's consent.
9. A parent can acquire parental responsibility by marrying the parent with parental responsibility, provided that the marriage takes place after 30 December 2005. This applies equally to a non-parent who has entered into a civil partnership with a parent with parental responsibility. He or she can enter into an agreement with the biological parent or obtain it by way of court order. The former will require the agreement of all parties with parental responsibility (Adoption and Children Act 2002, s.112).

The parental responsibility agreement

A parental responsibility agreement must be in writing and must be in accordance with the Parental Responsibility Agreement Regulations 1991, SI 1991/1478, reg.2, as amended.

This provides that:

(a) the agreement must contain the full names of the child's parents and of the relevant child;
(b) the agreement must contain the signature of both parents and be witnessed;
(c) there must be one agreement for each child;
(d) both parents must have their signature witnessed at court by a Justice of the Peace or court official and provide evidence of their identity (including a photograph and signature); the child's full birth certificate must be provided.

The agreement will not come into force until it has been received and recorded at the Principal Registry of the Family Division.

How is parental responsibility lost?

Parental responsibility may be lost in two circumstances:

(a) where the child attains the age of 18; or
(b) where a court order is made terminating parental responsibility for reasons connected with the child's welfare, adoption or where parental responsibility had been obtained by way of a residence order and the residence order is discharged.

This application may be made as of right by a person who already has parental responsibility but also by the child himself or herself. The court will need to consider the child's maturity when looking at such a case (see *Re C (Care: Consultation with Parents; Not in Child's Best Interests)* [2005] EWHC 3390 (Fam)).

Testamentary guardianship (section 5)

A guardian of a child is someone who is appointed by will to take over responsibility for a child in the event of the death of the child's parent or other carer. The guardian will have the same right to decide on all matters as a parent with parental responsibility. This is unrelated to the appointment of 'special guardians' in public law care proceedings.

Guardians are governed by CA 1989, s.5, which provides that the following may make the appointment:

(a)   a parent with parental responsibility for the child (s.5(3)); or
(b)   an existing guardian of the child (s.5(4)); or
(c)   a court, by order in family proceedings (s.5(1) and (2)).

The appointment in (a) and (b) becomes effective when the person who makes the appointment dies, unless there is a surviving parent with parental responsibility, or the appointor did not have a residence order in his or her favour. In these circumstances, the appointment will only take effect on the death of the surviving parent.

The court can also appoint a guardian if there is no one to exercise parental responsibility, or where the deceased parent had a residence order in force at the date of death (s.5(1)).

8.4.2   Section 8 orders

These are outlined in Part II of CA 1989, ss.8–16:

> In any family proceedings in which a question arises with respect to the welfare of any child, the court may make a section 8 order with respect to the child . . .
>
> (CA 1989, s.10(1))

The four main private law orders which the court can make in relation to the child are:

- residence;
- contact;
- prohibited steps; and
- specific issue.

Who can apply for a section 8 order?

Section 8 creates a two-tier system for applicants: those who may apply to court as of right, and those who must seek the court's permission. The only persons who can apply as of right are those with parental responsibility.

Other applicants must first make an application to the court for permission. Notice of the application must be served on anyone with parental responsibility. The court may also make any s.8 orders of its own motion where it is dealing with proceedings under the Act, whether or not such an order has been applied for. In those circumstances the judge must give the parties an opportunity to make representations.

There are additional classes of persons who may apply for contact and residence orders, who are defined in s.10(5). They are:

(a) a party to a marriage in relation to which the child was/is a child of the family;

(b) any civil partner in a civil partnership in relation to which the child was/is a child of the family;

(c) any person with whom the child has lived for at least three years;

(d) if there is a residence order or care and control order in force, any person who has the consent of the holder(s) of that order;

(e) if there is a care order in force, any person who has the consent of the local authority; or

(f) a local authority foster parent can apply, where the child has resided with the foster parent for at least one year immediately preceding the application and where he or she has the consent of the local authority.

Who is the child?

The child must be under 18 years of age (s.105(1)), although the order cannot endure beyond the child's sixteenth birthday, unless the court is satisfied that the circumstances are exceptional (s.9(6), (7)). If over the age of 16 the child must be the subject of the application.

Directions and conditions

A section 8 order may –

(a) contain directions about how it is to be carried into effect;

(b) impose conditions which must be complied with by any person –

(i) in whose favour the order is made;

(ii) who is a parent of the child concerned;

(iii) who is not a parent of his but who has parental responsibility for him; or

(iv) with whom the child is living,

and to whom the conditions are expressed to apply;

(c) be made to have effect for a specified period, or contain provisions which are to have effect for a specified period;

(d) make such incidental, supplemental or consequential provision as the court thinks fit.

(CA 1989, s.11(7))

Conditions are not usually imposed upon the holder of a residence order, particularly in relation to geography.

Interim orders

These are usually applicable to residence and contact orders. The Act makes no reference to interim orders, although it is clear that the court has power to make a s.8 order at any time during the proceedings, even though it is not in a position to dispose finally of those proceedings (CA 1989, s.11(3)). Orders made in these circumstances are commonly referred to as interim orders. It is also clear that the court can impose whatever conditions are appropriate and specify the duration of the order (CA 1989, s.11(7)(a)–(d)).

Variation/discharge of orders

People who can apply for full orders are also able to apply for variation or discharge. The test that the court will apply is that the child's welfare is the paramount consideration, and the court has all the powers applicable to a s.8 application.

Expert evidence

The judge has a wide discretion as to what evidence is admissible or required for the disposal of children matters. Upon determination of major contact and residence matters, it is usual for a member of the Children and Family Court Advisory Support Service (CAFCASS) to become involved. By virtue of CA 1989, s.7, the court has the power to make an order that a report be prepared. Such reports are referred to as 'welfare reports'.

By virtue of CA 1989, s.37, the court can also direct that social services prepare a report, or it may perhaps direct an educational psychologist to do so if this is warranted in a specific issue application concerning schooling.

8.4.3 Residence orders

Introduction

> 'a residence order' means an order settling the arrangements to be made as to the person with whom a child is to live; . . .
>
> (CA 1989, s.8).

A 'residence order' is the name of the order which defines with whom the child shall live. The order usually lasts until the child's sixteenth birthday, but can be extended to the date when the child attains the age of 18 where it is in the child's best interests to do so, for example in the case of a disability. It allows the holder of a residence order to remove the relevant child from England and Wales without the consent of all others with parental responsibility for a period not in excess of one month. It does not allow permanent removal from the jurisdiction. See **8.6.3.**

The court has jurisdiction to grant an order even where the parents are living under the same roof provided they are in separate households (CA 1989, s.11(4), and *Re H (A Child)* [2002] EWCA Civ 2005).

Where an order has been made in favour of one parent where both have parental responsibility, and the parties subsequently begin to cohabit, it will lapse where they cohabit for more than six months (s.11(5)).

A child can seek the court's permission to issue a residence application himself or herself. The court must be satisfied that the child has sufficient understanding, and the test is the best interests of the child (*Re C (Residence: Child's Application for Leave)* [1995] 1 FLR 927).

It is most unusual for a court to impose geographical restrictions on a residence order, unless there are exceptional circumstances (*B v. B (Residence: Condition Limiting Geographic Area)* [2004] 2 FLR 979).

Where the court has to make decisions in relation to the upbringing of a child there is no presumption in favour of the wishes of the natural parent (*Re G* [2006] UKHL 43).

Joint and shared residence

A residence order can be made jointly with another party who does not have to be a parent. There is a distinction, however, between joint residence and shared residence.

Joint residence orders are rarer and generally cover the situation where one of the applicants does not automatically have parental responsibility.

Shared residence orders are appropriate where both applicants have parental responsibility and are becoming more usual and deal with splitting a child's time between two parties who no longer live in the same home. Where a shared residence order is sought a judge will need to give good reasons for refusal of such an order (*Re P (Children) (Shared Residence Order)* [2006] 1 FCR 309). Where a shared residence order is made, it does not mean that the child's time has to be divided equally between the parents (*D v. D (Shared Residence Order)* [2001] 1 FLR 495).

Termination of residence order

A residence order will terminate:

(a) on the child's sixteenth birthday, if it has not been ordered to extend beyond that date (s.9(6));

(b) by a further order of the court varying or discharging the order (s.8(2));

(c) upon the making of a care order;

(d) where the child's parents live with the child for a period in excess of six months, when the order is automatically discharged (s.11(5)).

8.4.4   Contact orders

Introduction

> 'a contact order' means an order requiring the person with whom a child lives, or is to live, to allow the child to visit or stay with the person named in the order, or for that person and the child otherwise to have contact with each other; . . .
>
> (CA 1989, s.8)

The Act defines contact in terms of being the right of a child to continue to have a relationship with the person with whom the child does not live following a relationship breakdown (see *Re R (A Minor) (Contact)* [1993] 2 FLR 762).

Orders should not last beyond the child's sixteenth birthday, but can be extended to the date when the child attains the age of 18 in exceptional circumstances (s.9(6)). An order can be made in favour of any person; the recipient need not be a parent. Parental responsibility is not gained from the granting of a contact order.

There is an effective presumption in favour of contact (although this does not feature in the welfare checklist) (*Re P (Contact: Supervision)* [1996] 2 FLR 314), and the party opposing it must produce good reasons as to why an order should not be made.

There is no presumption as to the amount of contact that should be ordered; only that it should be reasonable (*Re P*, above).

Interim contact

The comments made above in relation to interim orders apply equally to interim contact. It is considered undesirable to make an interim staying contact order in the face of the resident parent's objections where there has not been an investigation of the motives behind them.

Types of contact

INDIRECT

This may be ordered where a judge considers it unwise for a child to come into direct contact with a person, such as where the adult may have been the perpetrator of injury to that child, or a close relative of that child or even someone not connected with the family (see *Re P (Contact: Discretion)* [1998] 2 FLR 696 and *Re S (Violent Parent: Indirect Contact)* [2000] 1 FLR 481).

Indirect contact can consist of writing letters or emails, or sending cards and presents. The court may order the child's mother to send school reports and photographs on a regular basis.

SUPERVISED

Such an order would permit contact to take place only under the supervision of another adult. Such an order may be utilised where there may be some form of risk to the child or the resident parent.

STAYING

This involves the child having overnight and holiday contact with the non-resident party.

NO CONTACT

There will be occasions when it is not in the best interests of the child for contact to take place. The court will have to weigh the welfare test against the risk presented to the child should contact take place. In such circumstances the court can make a no contact order.

The effect of domestic violence on contact

Violence in itself will not necessarily lead to a denial of contact, but there is judicial appreciation of the impact that it has on the children and the resident parent (see *Re L (A Child), Re V (A Child), Re M (A Child), Re H (A Child) (Contact: DV)* [2000] 2 FLR 334).

When an application is made for a s.8 order on Form C100 (see **8.7.2**, table), if the applicant believes that the child(ren) subject to the application have suffered or are at risk of suffering any harm from any form of domestic abuse, violence within the household, child abduction or other conduct or behaviour by any person who has had contact with the child, then Form C1A (supplemental information form) must also be completed.

The President of the Family Division issued a recent *Practice Direction on Residence and Contact Orders: Domestic Violence and Harm*, to be found at [2008] 2 FLR 103.

This sets out fully the procedure to be adopted by the judge where there is an allegation or supposition of domestic violence upon the child or upon one of the parties by another party. The court must identify at the earliest opportunity the factual and welfare issues involved, and consider the nature of the allegations. The court cannot approve a consent order on residence and contact unless it is satisfied that there is no risk of harm to the child in so doing. The judge must decide whether or not to conduct a 'fact-finding hearing' in relation to any disputed allegation of domestic violence. Once that point has been adjudicated upon, the court can then go on to consider whether it is in the best interests of the child for a contact order to be made.

The Court of Appeal recently stressed the importance of carrying out the fact-finding exercise in full, in the case of *Z (Children)* [2009] EWCA Civ 430.

8.4.5 Prohibited steps

'a prohibited steps order' means an order that no step which could be taken by a parent in meeting his parental responsibility for a child, and which is of a kind specified in the order, shall be taken by any person without the consent of the court; . . .

(CA 1989, s.8)

This is a limited type of order which can only be made against a parent. It is generally utilised to prevent the removal of a child from the jurisdiction, or changing the child's schooling or name. It cannot be used to regulate contact or residence (s.9(5)), nor can it provide injunctive relief (see *Re D (Prohibited Steps Order)* [1996] 2 FLR 273).

As with other s.8 orders, a prohibited steps order will end on the child's sixteenth birthday, unless there are exceptional circumstances.

8.4.6 Specific issue

'a specific issue order' means an order giving directions for the purpose of determining a specific question which has arisen, or which may arise, in connection with any aspect of parental responsibility for a child; . . .

(CA 1989, s.8)

This is a limited type of order which can only be made against a parent. It is generally utilised to direct issues such as a child's religious upbringing, or medical treatment. The court can also adjudicate upon matters of schooling within this provision (*Re P (Parental Dispute: Judicial Determination)* [2003] 1 FLR 286).

As with other s.8 orders, a specific issue order will end on the child's sixteenth birthday, unless there are exceptional circumstances.

8.5 CHANGE OF NAME

There is a general restriction on changing a child's name after registration unless the permission of all the other holders of parental responsibility is obtained. Where a parent with a residence order wishes to apply, then this is governed by CA 1989, s.13. Where the parents are unmarried, but both retain parental responsibility, then consent or leave of the court must be sought under s.8 by way of specific issue. Where the mother has expressed such an intention but no application has yet been made, the father's recourse is to apply for a prohibited steps order.

Where the mother alone has parental responsibility for her child, then she alone can determine that child's name (Births and Registration Act 1953, s.2).

For the issues that the court will take into account in determining a change of name application see *Re W, Re A, Re B (Change of Name)* [1999] 2 FLR 930.

8.6 THE COURT'S ADDITIONAL POWERS

8.6.1 Court's own motion

The court may also make any s.8 orders of its own motion where it is dealing with other proceedings under CA 1989, whether or not such an order has been applied for.

8.6.2 Restrictions on further applications: section 91(14)

The court can restrict future applications by a party, if the judge feels that such applications may be harmful to the welfare of the child concerned. The party so restricted must first make an application to the court for permission. This provision is used sparingly and exceptionally (*Re P (Section 91(14) Guidelines) (Residence and Religious Heritage)* [1999] 2 FLR 573).

8.6.3 Leave to remove

If a residence order is in force with respect to a child, leave to remove the child from the United Kingdom is governed by CA 1989, s.13. Where a parent does not have a residence order in his or her favour, he or she must seek the permission of all the other holders of parental responsibility to remove the child from England and Wales (s.13(1)). If the parent does not do so, then he or she will be committing the crime of child abduction under the Child Abduction Act 1984.

If the parent does have a residence order, then he or she can take the child out of the jurisdiction for a period of one month only (s.13(1)(b)). For the factors which will govern consideration of applications permanently to remove see *Payne* v. *Payne* [2001] 1 FLR 1052.

In *Payne* the Court of Appeal confirmed that it is guided by the paramountcy test. The Court of Appeal said that there is no presumption in favour of an applicant parent. There also had to be 'genuine motivation for the move', that is the applicant was not seeking to leave the jurisdiction merely to frustrate contact, and conversely, the resisting parent must also have genuine motivation for refusal; not just because he or she sought to frustrate the applicant's plans. Other important elements included:

(a) the effect of refusal of leave upon the applicant parent;
(b) the effect on the child's new family; and
(c) the effect upon the child of denial or limitation of contact with the other parent (and in some cases that parent's family).

8.7 PROCEDURE FOR APPLICATION UNDER THE CHILDREN ACT 1989

8.7.1 The courts

Any application under CA 1989 can be made to the Family Proceedings Court, the county court or the High Court. All these courts may hear children cases to differing degrees.

Under the Children (Allocation of Proceedings) Order 1991, SI 1991/1677 there are three types of county court with differing functions:

- Divorce Centres: can hear uncontested s.8 matters, and applications under Parts I and II of CA 1989.
- Family Hearing Centres: can hear all contested private law applications concerning children, and applications under Parts I and II of CA 1989.
- Care Centres: can hear all contested private and public law applications concerning children, and applications under Parts I and II of CA 1989.

Certain district and circuit judges are 'ticketed'; i.e. they alone are qualified to hear contested proceedings. They are based at the Family Hearing and Care Centres.

8.7.2 Procedural tables

Application	Who can apply	Form	Fee	Supplements
Parental responsibility order	A parent/step-parent/ civil partner	C1	£180	C1A if violence is an issue
Residence, or contact orders	Parent/guardian; has parental responsibility; has leave of court to apply; a party to a marriage in relation to which the child was/ is a child of the family; any civil partner in a civil partnership in relation to which the child was/is a child of the family; any person with whom the child has lived for at least three years; or if there is a residence order/care and control order in force, the consent of the holder(s) of that order; if there is a care order in force, the consent of the local authority; a local authority foster parent where the child has resided with the foster parent for at least one year immediately preceding the application and where he or she has the consent of the local authority	C100 or C2 if existing proceedings	£180	C1A if violence is an issue
Prohibited steps or specific issue order	Parent/guardian; has parental responsibility; has leave of court to apply	C100 or C2 if existing proceedings	£180	C1A if violence is an issue
Leave to remove	Parent/guardian; has parental responsibility; has leave of court to apply	C1	£180	C1A if violence is an issue

In relation to all these applications, the respondents will be:

- parents/guardians;
- all persons with parental responsibility;
- a person with whom the child is living;
- local authority where the child is being accommodated.

The service period is 21 days, unless application has been made to abridge time for service.

Documents to be served include:

- original issued C100/C2 (at least three copies must be submitted to court for issue; one copy for court file, one copy for the applicant and one copy for each respondent);
- C6 Acknowledgement;
- C7 Notice of proceedings;
- C1A Supplement, if applicable;
- C43 Order, if made without notice.

It is normal practice now to list all s.8 and s.13 applications for conciliation, as per *District Judge's Direction (Children: Conciliation)* [2004] 1 FLR 974. This means a CAFCASS officer will be on hand to assist the parties in reaching an agreement. If the application is issued in the Principal Registry of the Family Division in London, there is a requirement that all children aged nine years and above who are the subject of the application must attend court. If there are younger siblings who are also involved in the application, they can also come to court to be seen by the CAFCASS officer. The children's attendance is generally not required in other courts.

8.8   RECOVERY OF COSTS

The usual order in children proceedings is that each party bears their own costs. However, where one party's conduct is clearly unreasonable and goes beyond what would be expected of a concerned parent attempting to protect what the parent sees as the child's best interests, the court can make a costs order (see *R v. R (Costs: Child Case)* [1997] 2 FLR 95).

8.9   APPEALS

An appeal from the decision of the Family Proceedings Court is made to the High Court. An appeal from the county court district judge is made to a circuit judge and from a circuit judge or High Court will be to the Court of Appeal as per CA 1989, s.94(1). The appeal must be in writing and clearly set out the grounds. It must be served and filed within 14 days (from a decision of the Family Proceedings Court) and 21 days (from a decision of the county court) of the original hearing against which the appeal is being sought.

An application for permission to appeal may be made orally to the judge at the time of the hearing. If no such application was made or if permission is refused, then an application must be made to the Court of Appeal (see CPR 1998, Part 52).

The following documents must be lodged as soon as possible after the filing of the appeal (FPR 1991, rule 4.22(4)):

- a certified copy of the order and the application;
- a copy of any notes of the evidence given; and
- a copy of any reasons given.

Appeals upward from the High Court are only permissible where there is an important point of principle or practice or where there is some other reason to hear it (CPR 1998, rule 52.13).

8.10 ENFORCEMENT OF SECTION 8 ORDERS

Enforcement has always been a difficult issue for the family courts. There was a time when the courts felt powerless to do anything in the face of a mother who refused to allow the father any contact. The only remedy for not following a contact order was imprisonment or a fine for contempt of court. Understandably the courts were reluctant to put a mother in jail, but there were a few notable cases where this was done (after many fruitless court hearings where the mother ignored all orders to allow contact), and ultimately transferred residence of the children to the father. But this was still a rare occurrence, so recently, in December 2008, new enforcement powers were brought in to run alongside the old ones.

The court now has the power to make the following orders:

8.10.1 Contact activity directions (CADs) and contact activity conditions (CACs)

There are three types of CACs requiring one parent or both to attend:

1. Information/assessment meetings about mediation.
2. Parenting information programmes.
3. Domestic violence prevention programmes.

The judge will ask CAFCASS whether he should make orders for CAD or CAC. The judge will look at the availability locally of such contact activities and their accessibility. He will take into account the religious beliefs and work/education commitments of the parents or those involved in the children court case. Also the judge has to look at the likely effect of undertaking the activity.

The court may monitor the activities through reports from CAFCASS.

8.10.2　Warning notices

All court orders after December 2008 now carry a *warning notice* which states the consequences of not complying with an order.

For contact orders made prior to 8 December 2008, applications can be made to have a warning notice attached on Application Form C78.

8.10.3　Enforcement orders

Either parent/party to the court case can make an application for an *enforcement order* if the warning notice to a contact order has been breached.

The relevant form is C79.

The court can order the parent in breach to do 40–200 hours of unpaid work (also known as community service).

The court must be satisfied beyond reasonable doubt that there is no reasonable excuse for non-compliance with the contact order.

The court will look at the same factors as for CAD/CAC, and also the welfare of the child – but this is not paramount.

CAFCASS will be sent a copy of the application and it will make checks as to reported non-compliance and provide any other relevant information.

8.10.4　Compensation for financial loss

This is a very welcome new rule, as it is very often the case that one parent loses out financially owing to the 'unreasonableness' of the primary carer, and they can never get their money back. This happens, for example, where one parent has booked tickets to go somewhere in anticipation of having contact with the child at that time, and then the other parent refuses to let the child go for contact.

A party may make an application for compensation for loss caused by the other party's non-compliance with terms of the order. The welfare of the child is considered by the court.

The court can request information from CAFCASS as to the effect on the welfare of the child of one party paying compensation.

8.11　INHERENT JURISDICTION OF THE COURT IN RELATION TO CHILDREN

8.11.1　Wardship

Since the enactment of various statutes, including CA 1989 and the Child Abduction Act 1984, the use and scope of wardship has declined sharply. Now it is utilised only where the court feels that it has inadequate power to protect the child under other legislation, such as in matters of publicity.

The effect of becoming a ward of court was encapsulated in the phrase that 'no major step' may be taken in that child's life without leave of the court. The court and the judge are in effect *in loco parentis*. Such major or important step will cover such matters as education, medical treatment and change of name of the child.

The application is to the High Court by way of originating summons supported by affidavit.

8.11.2 Child abduction

There are two different reactions to child abduction, each depending on the country to which the child has been taken. The first question to ask is whether the relevant jurisdiction is a signatory to the Hague Convention on the Civil Aspects of International Child Abduction 1980.

If the children have been wrongfully retained in a country which is a signatory of the Hague Convention, an application can be activated via the International Child Abduction and Contact Unit, which is the Central Authority in England and Wales for the Hague Convention. The matter is heard in the court of the child's last habitual residence, even though the child is not physically present in that jurisdiction. This is on the basis that summary return is sought to the original member state.

An application under the Hague Convention can only be made by someone who has 'rights of custody' within the meaning of the Convention. This means that the applicant must have parental responsibility, or has a case pending in the courts of the child's last habitual residence to determine parental responsibility or contact or residence.

If the relevant country is not a signatory, the procedure is not so simple. Some jurisdictions, such as Egypt and Pakistan, have established protocols for dealing with these situations.

8.12 TRANSPARENCY AND CONFIDENTIALITY

Previously proceedings involving children were generally heard in private, although the Family Proceedings Court was always open to the press, the media being barred from the county court and the Family Division. The Court of Appeal sits in open court when hearing children cases. Children's identities are concealed in anonymised judgments.

At the end of April 2009, thousands of family courts were opened up to the media. For the first time, lawyers have to advise their clients that the media might be present at their hearings. However, just because the media can attend a hearing does not mean that they can report very much or have access to any court documents. A journalist must apply to the judge for permission to publish information about the case. If they publish without that, they risk being in contempt of court.

The attendance and reporting rules for members of the press are quite restrictive. The media are allowed in to all hearings concerning children and financial matters, but cannot report anything which might lead to the identification of a child.

The press cannot come into court hearings at which any negotiation or conciliation takes place, which covers most children hearings.

In addition, the judge can exclude the media if he or she wishes, or in response to a request from one of the people involved in the case.

PUBLIC PROCEEDINGS

8.13   LOCAL AUTHORITY INVOLVEMENT WITH CHILDREN

Parts III, IV and V of CA 1989 are the main parts of the statute dealing with local authority involvement with children. Part III sets out the duties and powers that a local authority has in relation to provision of services for children in need and their families, provision of accommodation for children and the duties owed to children who are 'looked after'. Part IV deals with care and supervision proceedings: collectively these are known as public law Children Act proceedings, noting the state's role (in the guise of the local authority) in such court proceedings. Part V discusses other aspects of child protection, related orders and the powers at the disposal of the local authority. Various orders can be applied for and these are set out in the statute. The key orders are explained in this chapter. Some orders such as child assessments orders and education supervision orders are infrequently used and are not discussed here.

8.14   CHILD PROTECTION

If a referral is made to the local authority, the matter will become the responsibility of its children's services department. Any referral should be given proper attention. An initial assessment may be carried out before further action is considered and it may be the case that it is decided that no further action is deemed necessary.

8.14.1   Section 47 investigations

A local authority has a duty to commence a s.47 investigation in certain circumstances. If the test is satisfied the local authority 'shall make, or cause to be made, such enquiries as they consider necessary to enable them to decide whether they should take any action to safeguard or promote the child's welfare'. The circumstances in which the local authority should commence the investigation are where they:

(a) are informed that a child who lives, or is found, in their area –

    (i) is the subject of an emergency protection order; or
    (ii) is in police protection; or
    (iii) has contravened a ban imposed by a curfew notice within the meaning of Chapter I of Part I of the Crime and Disorder Act 1998; or

(b) have reasonable cause to suspect that a child who lives, or is found, in their area is suffering, or is likely to suffer, significant harm.

Where the local authority has obtained an emergency protection order in relation to a child there are additional requirements, which require consideration as part of the investigation.

Section 53(3) of the Children Act 2004 places a new duty on the local authority when conducting an investigation under CA 1989, s.47. Section 47(5A) (as amended) holds that for the purpose of making a determination under the section as to any action to be taken in respect of a child, the local authority shall 'so far as reasonably practicable and consistent with the child's welfare' ascertain the child's wishes and feelings about the action to be taken in relation to him or her and give due consideration (having regard to the child's age and understanding) to the wishes and feelings that have been ascertained.

The assessment carried out as part of the investigation is known as a core assessment.

The possible outcomes of the s.47 investigation are:

- no further action is considered necessary;
- the possibility of significant harm is believed to exist but no real evidence has been found and so careful monitoring is required;
- the concerns are substantiated but it is judged that there is no subsisting risk of significant harm in which case a plan might be able to be agreed between the closest agencies involved and the family and child; or
- there is a continuing risk of harm and so a child protection case conference should be initiated.

8.14.2 Initial child protection conference

The purpose of the child protection conference (CPC) (sometimes called the child protection case conference) is 'to bring together and analyse in an inter-agency setting the information which has been obtained about the child's developmental needs, and the parents' or carers' capacity to respond to these needs to ensure the child's safety and promote the child's health and development within the context of their wider family and environment' (*Working Together to Safeguard Children*, HM Government, 2006, p.123). It will also consider the evidence and make judgements as to the likelihood of a child suffering significant harm in the future and any continuing risk of significant harm to the child.

The CPC is multi-disciplinary. It will normally include the parents, any other persons with PR and any person acting in an official capacity in relation to the child. This can include the family GP, school nurse, teachers, social workers and wider family members. Parents are permitted to bring an advocate, friend or supporter. A parent's lawyer can attend but only in the role of supporter. If lawyers are to attend, it is wise that they clarify the remit of their role with the Chair of the CPC in advance.

8.14.3   Child protection plan

An outline child protection plan (CPP) will be agreed at the CPC itself as will the identification of members for a core group who will develop and implement the CPP. The core group should meet within 10 working days of the CPC. At that meeting the main aim will be to further develop the (outline) CPP already formulated.

8.14.4   Child protection review conference

The composition and format of the child protection review conference (CPRC) is similar to the initial CPC and must be held within three months of the initial CPC; however, further CPRCs should be held, at the very least, at six-monthly intervals. Such CPRCs will be held until the child is no longer the subject of a CPP, i.e. when the test of 'continuing risk of significant' harm cannot be satisfied. The CPRC is charged with asking the question and determining whether the risk continues. If it does not then the child should no longer be the subject of a CPP.

A CPRC may find itself reaching this conclusion for one or more of the following reasons:

- the likelihood of harm is reduced owing to the effective intervention and change identified in the CPP;
- a reassessment of the child and family demonstrates that a CPP is not needed; or
- the child's and the family's circumstances change.

8.15   EMERGENCY PROTECTION ORDERS

Emergency protection orders (EPOs) are the province of CA 1989, s.44. An application for an EPO can be made by any person but will usually be made by a local authority.

8.15.1 Effect of an emergency protection order (section 44(4))

If an EPO is granted, it:

(a) directs any person (who can do so) to comply with any request to produce the child;

(b) allows the applicant to remove the child at any time to accommodation provided by or on behalf of the applicant and to keep the child there; and

(c) authorises the prevention of the child being removed from any hospital or other place of accommodation immediately before the making of the EPO.

An EPO gives the successful applicant parental responsibility for the child but that parental responsibility can only be used reasonably and in pursuit of safeguarding or promoting the welfare of the child (with regard to the duration of the order). Any exercise of parental responsibility must therefore be proportionate and carefully considered.

An EPO will last eight days but where the eighth day lands on a public holiday or a Sunday the court may state a period which ends at noon on the first subsequent day which is not a public holiday. An application for extension of the EPO can be made and if granted it will not exceed a further seven days. The court must have 'reasonable cause to believe that the child concerned is likely to suffer significant harm' were it not to grant the extension (s.45(4), (5)).

8.15.2 Grounds for granting an emergency protection order

The court must be satisfied that the test for granting an EPO is satisfied. The test is set out at s.44(1):

(a) there is reasonable cause to believe that the child is likely to suffer significant harm if –

    (i) he is not removed to accommodation provided by or on behalf of the applicant; or

    (ii) he does not remain in the place in which he is then being accommodated;

(b) in the case of an application made by a local authority –

    (i) enquiries are being made with respect to the child under section 47(1)(b); and

    (ii) those enquiries are being frustrated by access to the child being unreasonably refused to a person authorised to seek access and that the applicant has reasonable cause to believe that access to the child is required as a matter of urgency; or

(c) in the case of an application made by an authorised person –

    (i) the applicant has reasonable cause to suspect that a child is suffering, or is likely to suffer, significant harm;

    (ii) the applicant is making enquiries with respect to the child's welfare; and

    (iii) those enquiries are being frustrated by access to the child being unreasonably refused to a person authorised to seek access and the applicant has reasonable cause to believe that access to the child is required as a matter of urgency.

An 'authorised person' is defined at s.31(9) as the NSPCC and any person authorised by order of the Secretary of State to bring proceedings under s.31 (care proceedings).

8.15.3 Ancillary directions (section 44(6))

On making an EPO, the court can also give directions as it considers appropriate in relation to contact between the child and any named person: that is to say, direct that contact should take place or prohibit contact. Subject to any direction given as to contact, the applicant is required to allow the child reasonable contact with various persons. The duty itself and categories of persons are set out at s.44(13).

The court may also give directions in respect of any medical or psychiatric examination or assessment of the child and indeed it may give a direction that there is to be no examination or assessment at all or not until further order. Section 44(7) states that where the child is of sufficient understanding to make an informed decision, the child may refuse to submit to an examination (medical or psychiatric) which has been directed.

Directions under s.44(6) may be made at the time of making the EPO or at any point while it is in force and can be varied at any time.

8.15.4 Exclusion requirements (sections 44A, 44B)

Where the court makes an EPO it may include an exclusion requirement compelling a particular person to be excluded from the home in which the child lives.

Where however, the applicant for the EPO has removed the child (for a continuous period of over 24 hours) from the home from which the person subject to the exclusion requirement is so excluded, the order insofar as the exclusion requirement is concerned ceases.

Section 44B deals with the court's ability to accept undertakings from a particular person as an alternative to making an exclusion requirement. An undertaking will have the same effect as the requirement save that a power of arrest cannot be attached to it.

8.15.5 Procedure

1. Applications are made in the Family Proceedings Court.
2. Applications are made by the local authority on Forms C1 and C11.
3. The respondents will be the child, all persons with parental responsibility, and those persons believed to have had parental responsibility immediately prior to the making of any care order, if the child is in care.

142

4. Others to whom notice must be given are all persons believed by the applicant to be a parent, any local authority providing accommodation to the child and any person with whom the child is living or who is providing refuge.
5. Service of application must be one day before the hearing of the application.
6. Applications can be made without notice: see the 14-point guidance in *X Council* v. *B* [2004] EWHC 2015 (Fam), [2005] 1 FLR 341. This was endorsed by McFarlane J in *Re X Emergency Protection Order* [2006] EWHC 510 (Fam), save for two supplements: (1) that the EPO application should be tape recorded and if that is not possible then a dedicated note-taker in addition to the clerk should attend to take a verbatim note; and (2) extending the duty to give information when parents asked for this, McFarlane J stated that 'unless there is very good reason to the contrary, the parents should always be given a full account of the material submitted to the court, the evidence given at the hearing, the submissions made to support the application and the justices reasons whether they ask for this information or not' (para.65(b)).

Section 30 of the Children and Young Persons Act 2008 removes the 72-hour moratorium on the court's powers to hear an application to discharge an EPO by repealing s.45(9) of CA 1989.

8.15.6 Pre-proceedings

Local authorities must attempt to avoid having to issue applications under s.31 of CA 1989 by first seeking to resolve issues of concern under pre-proceedings stages. This will only be possible where the child can be adequately safeguarded without the need for a court order. Naturally, there will be cases where concerns are so compelling that a local authority will take the view that there is no window of opportunity to work with the family to resolve issues and therefore an application for an EPO or an interim care order must be made immediately. Where there is such a 'window', the local authority, having held a legal planning meeting between relevant personnel from children's services and its lawyers, and having taken a decision that the concerns (in its view) meet the threshold for the making an application to the court, must send a letter before proceedings to the parents and those with parental responsibility for the child. The letter before proceedings will be tailored to the facts of the particular child's case but must set out, *inter alia*, what the local authority's concerns are, a statement of what the local authority has done to work with the family, and information about what must now change in order to prevent the local authority from applying to the court. A template letter before proceedings features at Annex A to the (revised) *Children Act 1989: Guidance and Regulations*, vol. 1, Court Orders (2008). The letter ends by inviting the recipients of the letter (together or separately) to a pre-proceedings meeting with the local authority.

Although the pre-proceedings meeting is convened by the local authority and cannot bind any party to the meeting, lawyers for both the local authority and the parents or those with parental responsibility are invited to attend, participate and advocate for their respective clients. The Legal Services Commission introduced a new level of service, Family Help Lower, to fund legal advice and assistance to those who receive a letter before proceedings which permits the lawyer for the parent or person with parental responsibility to attend the pre-proceedings meeting.

The local authority will hope that through negotiations at the pre-proceedings meeting an agreement can be reached with the parents or persons with parental responsibility to ensure the child is safeguarded without the need for an application for a care order or supervision order to be made. Agreements should be in writing and supported by a child protection plan, child in need plan or looked-after child plan. Pre-proceedings stages allow the local authority to be creative in planning for the child with the co-operation of the family. A child may, for example be placed with an alternative carer under a voluntary, s.20 agreement whilst assessments and further planning are undertaken.

Ultimately, if a pre-proceedings meeting does not resolve matters or if agreements that have been made subsequently break down, the local authority will have to initiate court proceedings. As a result of work at the pre-proceedings stages it is hoped that even if the court's intervention is sought, the local authority will at least have made its intentions clear and will have sought to work with the family to avoid the need for the court's involvement. Another aim of the pre-proceedings stages is that some of the issues in contention will have been agreed through the pre-proceedings meeting so that only the live and significant issues of concern have to be raised within court proceedings.

8.16 CARE ORDERS

An application for a care order will be made by the local authority. The purpose of the application is for the local authority to be granted responsibility by the court for the child. If the order is granted the local authority will acquire parental responsibility for the child and has the power to determine the extent to which a parent, guardian, special guardian or step-parent with parental responsibility may meet their responsibility towards the child.

A care order may not be made once a child is 17 or over, or 16 if the child is married. A care order will last until the child reaches the age of 18 or, if the order is discharged, before that date. It cannot be made until after a child is actually born. In the unusual case of *Bury MBC* v. *D* [2009] EWHC 446 (Fam), the local authority sought anticipatory declaratory relief from the court that its plan to remove the child immediately upon birth from the mother without informing her of that plan was lawful. In that case the child had not yet been born. The declaration was made.

Although the court cannot make a care order or supervision order without an application having been made for one, it can make an interim care or supervision order if it makes a direction under s.37 to the local authority that it should investigate.

8.16.1   Grounds

The court must be satisfied that the local authority's case has met what are called the threshold criteria. The relevant standard of proof is the civil standard, i.e. the balance of probabilities. This was confirmed again in *Re B (Children)* [2008] UKHL 35. The threshold which must be crossed is:

(a)   that the child concerned is suffering, or is likely to suffer, significant harm; and
(b)   that the harm, or likelihood of harm, is attributable to –
  (i)   the care given to the child, or likely to be given to him if the order were not made, not being what it would be reasonable to expect a parent to give to him; or
  (ii)   the child's being beyond parental control.

(CA 1989, s.31(2))

Harm

At s.31(9), CA 1989 states that '"harm" means ill-treatment or the impairment of health or development including, for example, impairment suffered from seeing or hearing the ill-treatment of another'. 'Health' means physical or mental health and 'development' means physical, intellectual, emotional, social or behavioural development.

Findings of fact

In some cases it may be necessary to establish facts which go to the heart of the threshold. For that purpose, a split hearing may be directed so that facts can be established as soon as possible. The court may then be better positioned to manage the rest of the case on the basis of decided facts.

8.16.2   Post-threshold considerations

If the court does not find that the threshold criteria have been met, the local authority's application will be unsuccessful and a care order will not be made. If the court finds the threshold is met, it must go on to consider what order to make.

Principles

The welfare principle and checklist are dealt with at **8.2.1** and feature here when the court considers an application for a care order, as do the 'no delay' and 'no order' principles (see **8.2.2** and **8.2.3**).

145

8.16.3 Care plan

Of relevance to the court's decision-making will be what the local authority proposes in relation to the care of the child both in the interim as well as at the final hearing. The local authority will do this by producing a care plan to support its application for an interim/final care order, and the plan will be usually be updated during the course of the proceedings. The court will not be able to decide whether an order is in the child's best interests unless it is fully informed of what the local authority planning for the child is. Therefore, a final order cannot be made by the court until the court has scrutinised the care plan.

8.16.4 Assessments

Core assessment

The local authority will need to have conducted a core assessment which will have included interviews with parents, other significant persons in the child's life and also an account of the child's wishes and feelings. The assessment is comprehensive and will also include details of the family's background and histories.

8.16.5 Interim care order

If granted, an interim care order will last for up to eight weeks. After that the court can make further interim care orders, each lasting for up to one month. The effect of the interim care order is the same as the care order in that the local authority obtains parental responsibility and can limit the exercise of other persons' parental responsibility. The threshold criteria do not have to be satisfied to the same degree as in the case of final care orders. The local authority needs only to show that there are reasonable grounds for believing that the threshold conditions are met (s.38(2)).

Exclusion requirements

On the making of an interim care order, s.38A permits the court to impose an exclusion requirement on a person if the exclusion of that person will remove an element of risk thereby allowing the child to remain in the home.

A power of arrest can be attached to the requirement. An undertaking can be accepted by the relevant person in place of making an exclusion requirement. Such an undertaking can only be accepted where the court has the power to make an exclusion requirement. No power of arrest can attach to an undertaking.

Assessment of the child

On the making of an interim care order, the court can give a direction for assessment of the child under s.38(6).

8.16.6   Contact

Whether making an interim care order or a final care order the court must consider arrangements for contact between the child and other persons. The local authority will have set out its proposals for contact in the (interim) care plan. The court must invite the parties to comment on such proposals. Section 34(1) imposes a duty on the local authority to allow the child reasonable contact with his or her parents and other persons specified (s.34(1)(b)–(d)). The local authority can refuse contact if satisfied that such action is necessary to safeguard or promote the child's welfare and the action is either urgent or does not last for more than seven days. If the refusal is for more than seven days the local authority should make an application under s.34(4) asking the court to make an order authorising the local authority to refuse contact. The court itself does not actually order the refusal of contact.

8.16.7   Protocol for procedure

The Public Law Outline was introduced in May 2008 to replace the previous Protocol for Judicial Case Management in Public Law Children Act Cases of 2003. It introduces new stages in the proceedings which follow on from the pre-proceedings stage where the local authority will have sought to work with the family to avoid the need for court proceedings. The four new stages are:

1. Issue and the first appointment.
2. Case management conference.
3. Issues resolutions hearing.
4. Final hearing.

The Public Law Outline also introduces new case management tools and forms. It contains an overriding objective of enabling the court to deal with cases justly. Comprehensive consideration of procedure is outside the scope of this text and one of the detailed practitioner works should be consulted.

8.16.8   Children's guardian

The child will (together with any person with parental responsibility) be an automatic respondent to an application for a care order or supervision order. The court will appoint a children's guardian to represent the child in the proceedings unless it finds that it is not necessary to do this to safeguard the child's interests. Allocation of the children's guardian is usually undertaken by CAFCASS, which will identify a suitably experienced officer of its service to that role. The children's guardian will be independent of the local authority and any of the other parties. A solicitor will also be appointed to represent the child and will usually take instructions from the children's guardian.

8.17 SUPERVISION ORDERS

Where the local authority has met the threshold criteria under s.31(2) the court will consider whether to make any order. The local authority may have applied for a care order or supervision order and it is for the court to decide which, if either, it wishes to make. It matters not which of the two orders was the subject of the local authority's originating application.

A supervision order will last for a year but can be extended on an application by the supervisor to last up to three years from the date of the making of the original supervision order. However, an order of three years' duration cannot be made at the outset (*T(A Child)* v. *Wakefield MDC* [2008] EWCA Civ 199). Unlike a care order, parental responsibility does not attach to an supervision order. As such the supervisor will not have authority to remove the child and instead will need to apply for an EPO or interim care order accordingly. The exclusion requirements which can attach to an interim care order cannot be applied to a supervision order.

8.17.1 Effect

If made, the supervision order places duties on the supervisor:

(a) to advise, assist and befriend the supervised child;
(b) to take such steps as are reasonably necessary to give effect to the order; and
(c) where –
  (i)   the order is not wholly complied with; or
  (ii) the supervisor considers that the order may no longer be necessary,

to consider whether or not to apply to the court for its variation or discharge.
(CA 1989, s.35(1))

Various powers which attach to a supervision order include (CA 1989, Sched.3, Part I):

(a) requiring the child to comply with directions given by the supervisor to live at a particular place for a particular period;
(b) requiring the child to present himself or herself to a person(s) specified at a certain place and time; or
(c) requiring the child to participate in specified activities.

Obligations can also be imposed by the supervisor on responsible people: that is any person with parental responsibility and any person with whom the child is living. Those obligations, which can only be made with the consent of the responsible person, are that the responsible person should:

(a) take reasonable steps to ensure that the child complies with directions given by the supervisor (as above);
(b) take reasonable steps to ensure that the child complies with requirements in the supervision order itself relating to psychiatric or medical examinations or treatment; and

(c) comply with any direction by the supervisor requiring attendance at a particular place and time for taking part in a specified activity and to attend with the child if so directed.

Psychiatric and medical examinations and treatment of the child can be made requirements of the supervision order. Where such a requirement relates to the child being a resident patient at a hospital or care home, it can only be made by the court if the court is satisfied of its need, having considered evidence of a registered medical practitioner that the child may be suffering from a physical or mental condition that requires treatment and may be treatable and that a period as a resident patient is necessary for the purpose of the examination. If the child is of sufficient understanding to make an informed decision, the court can only make the requirement if it is satisfied that the child consents. The court should also satisfy itself of the arrangements for the examination. Similar provisions apply for psychiatric or medical treatment.

8.17.2   Other orders

On making a supervision order, the court can make any other s.8 order in conjunction. In *M (A Child)* [2006] EWCA Civ 404, Wall LJ stated that 'the mere fact that the threshold criteria for an interim care order are met does not mean that the court has to make an interim care order'.

8.17.3   Care or supervision order

The cases have enveloped the concept of proportionality and encouraged the principle that the intervention granted by the courts must be proportionate to the risk posed to the child. It is not the case that a care order should be made just because it can be. Proper consideration must be given to the less draconian supervision order, if it is appropriate. Two cases of relevance to the principle are *Re EC Child* (2001) (Lawtel) and *Re O (A Child)* [2001] EWCA Civ 16, [2001] 1 FLR 923, in which Hale LJ said of the decision as to whether to make a care order or supervision order that it 'has to be considered in the light of the Human Rights Act and Article 8 of the European Convention on Human Rights' (para.27). She reaffirmed her earlier decision of *Re C and B (Children) (Care Order: Future Harm)* [2000] 2 FCR 614, in which she commented on the state's intervention being proportionate to the legitimate aim which it pursues. In *Re T (A Child)* [2009] EWCA Civ 121 the president held that where the parties were agreed on which order was most appropriate, yet the judge takes a different view, cogent reasons must be supplied to support that decision.

8.18   PLACEMENT ORDERS

A placement order is made under the Adoption and Children Act 2002, s.21. It is made on the application by a local authority to place a child for adoption with any prospective adopters who may be chosen by the authority. A placement order can only be made if the child is the subject of a care order, the court is satisfied that the threshold criteria of CA 1989, s.31(2) are satisfied or the child has no parent or guardian. Finally, the placement order can only be made if the court is satisfied that each parent or guardian has consented to the child being placed for adoption and has not withdrawn that consent, or that the parent or guardian's consent should be dispensed with.

A placement order will remain in force until it is revoked, an adoption order is made, or the child reaches the age of 18 or marries. Once a placement order is made, an application can be made by any person to revoke it. Save for an application being made by the child or the local authority, any person wishing to make an application for revocation needs to have obtained leave of the court and the local authority must not have actually placed the child for adoption. Leave will only be granted if the circumstances have changed since the placement order was made.

8.19   ADOPTION ORDERS

An adoption order will formally sever the relationship between the birth family and the child. Parental responsibility of the parents and any other person is extinguished and the adoptive parent(s) acquire parental responsibility of the child. Effectively the adoptive parent(s) are deemed the legitimate parents.

8.20   SPECIAL GUARDIANSHIP ORDERS

Special guardianship orders (SGOs) are made under the Adoption and Children Act 2002 which inserted ss.14A–14G into CA 1989. The purpose of the order is to provide long-term security and stability for the child where other orders are not entirely suitable. It is recognised that long-term fostering is not ideal and does not afford the permanency which is desired for children.

8.20.1   Effect

An SGO confers parental responsibility on the special guardian. It also allows the special guardian to exercise his or her parental responsibility to the exclusion of any other person with parental responsibility (apart from another special guardian). It is this provision which gives the SGO teeth over and above that of a residence order. The power to exercise parental responsibility to the exclusion of others is subject to:

(a) any other CA 1989 order in force in respect of the child;
(b) the operation of any statute or rule of law which requires the consent of more than one person with parental responsibility in relation to a matter concerning the child, for example removal of the child from the jurisdiction (but see below) or change of the child's name; and
(c) the rights which a parent of the child has in relation to the child's adoption or placement for adoption.

Like a residence order, the SGO is subject to the restrictions (s.14C(3)) that whilst the order is in force, no person shall cause the child to be known by a new surname, or remove the child from the UK without either the written consent of every person with parental responsibility or the leave of the court. The special guardian can remove the child from the UK for a period of less than three months without leave or consent: this is more generous than powers afforded under a residence order.

An SGO can only be varied or discharged on the application of the persons described at s.14D(1) or the court may vary or discharge it within family proceedings where the question of the child's welfare is raised if the court considers that the order should so be varied or discharged. The persons listed at s.14D(3) need to obtain leave of the court before they can make an application for variation or discharge. The test for leave being granted to those persons is whether the court is satisfied that there has been a significant change in circumstances since the making of the SGO.

8.20.2 Requirements

The applicant(s) must be aged 18 or over, not be a parent of the child to whom the application relates, and be a person entitled to make an application for an SGO or one who has obtained leave of the court to make the application.

The court can make an SGO even if no application has been made if the court considers that an SGO should be made. It can only make the 'own motion order' in family proceedings in which a question arises with respect to the welfare of the child.

Three months' written notice must be given to the local authority by the proposed applicant of the intention to make an application. The relevant local authority will be the one with 'looked after' responsibility for the child, and if the child is not looked after then the relevant local authority is the one in which the prospective applicant normally resides. If the court proposes making an SGO of its own motion, there is no need for the notice period to have been complied with as no application has actually been made. Once it receives notice, the local authority must then investigate and prepare a report to the court. The report must address the suitability of the applicant to be a special guardian, other matters the local authority considers relevant and the list of matters prescribed by reg.21 of the Special Guardianship Regulations 2005, SI 2005/1109 which are set out in the Schedule to the regulations.

8.20.3 Support services

Section 14F of CA 1989 and Part 2 of the Special Guardianship Regulations 2005 deal with special guardian support services. Section 14F places a duty on local authorities to make arrangements for the provision of services. A child who is the subject of an SGO, a special guardian, a parent or any other person who falls within a 'prescribed description' can make a request for an assessment of needs for support services and the local authority may assess. Only in the case of persons who fall within the prescribed description must the local authority carry out an assessment of that person's need for support services. The persons falling within the prescribed description comprise: a child who is looked after by the local authority or was looked after immediately prior to the making of any SGO, the special guardian or prospective special guardian of any such child, or a parent of any such child.

Following an assessment and if support services are to be provided a plan should normally be produced. Any plan must be compiled in accordance with the regulations. In addition the former Department for Education and Skills published guidance to local authorities, Special Guardianship Guidance, 2005. Like most local authority guidance, it is not binding in the way that statute is but only exceptional reasons will justify departure from it.

CHAPTER 9

Domestic abuse

Jane Wilson

Domestic abuse occurs across our society regardless of social class or race. Twenty-six per cent of women and 17 per cent of men have experienced at least one incident of domestic violence since they were 16. In one in three cases of child abuse the mother is also being abused. Yet almost a third of abused women and nearly two-thirds of abused men tell no one of the worst incidents. The greatest risk from domestic abuse is at separation. Family lawyers need to be aware of the frequency and sensitivity of the issue and the dynamics of abusive relationships. Domestic abuse sufferers often experience loss of self-esteem. This makes it difficult for them to take and follow through the steps necessary to leave an abusive relationship. It is harmful for a child to see or hear domestic abuse being inflicted upon another and in 90 per cent of cases where the parties have children a child will be within sight or earshot of the abusive behaviour. Perpetrators frequently minimise or deny the abuse and blame the sufferer for causing the situation.

9.1 PUBLIC FUNDING

9.1.1 Public funding for the applicant

Financial eligibility for Legal Help and Full Representation is extended for domestic abuse sufferers. The upper income limit, gross income cap and disposable capital limit are waived. Any contribution will not be waived. An emergency grant of Legal Representation can be made where the applicant or a relevant child is in imminent danger of significant harm. The conduct complained of must have taken place within the last three weeks and prospects of success must be at least borderline. If the conduct complained of is trivial its cumulative effect can be taken into account.

A warning letter must be sent to the respondent first unless its receipt may trigger further violence, the threat to the applicant is serious and imminent, or the parties are still under the same roof.

Where the incident constitutes an assault or other crime, public funding will not be granted unless the sufferer has notified the police and given them opportunity to deal with the perpetrator, unless involving the police might jeopardise the long-term financial or other interests of the family.

It is not normally appropriate to apply for an injunction where a restraining order is likely to be imposed or when the perpetrator is in custody or there are bail conditions (unless they are likely to finish shortly).

Legal Representation to apply for an occupation order is most likely to be granted when the applicant is in a refuge or other temporary accommodation having recently been excluded from a property or where there is significant likelihood of risk in remaining in or returning to the property.

9.1.2 Public funding for the respondent

A respondent will not be granted public funding to defend a non-molestation application unless there are very serious allegations, which are denied wholly or in part, but the impact on contact or other related family proceedings will be taken into account. Help at Court may be used where the issue is whether to give an undertaking or where the main issue is whether a power of arrest should be attached. Public funding will be granted to defend an application for an occupation order where the respondent has reasonable prospects of success.

9.1.3 Enforcement proceedings

Cover for both the applicant and respondent extends to representation when a civil court considers a breach following the exercise of a power of arrest.

It is unlikely Legal Representation will be granted for committal proceedings for breach of a non-molestation order where criminal proceedings have already been instigated by the police. Where criminal proceedings have not already been instigated, the breach must be reported to the police and they must be given the opportunity to deal with it by a criminal charge, unless the considerations refered to in **9.1.1** apply.

A warning letter must first be sent to the respondent.

When deciding whether to grant funding for a committal application in respect of breach of a non-molestation or occupation order, the seriousness of the applicant's allegations, all the other circumstances and the likely benefit to the client are looked at. Legal Representation will usually be justified for the perpetrator.

9.1.4 Protection from Harassment Act 1997 and other injunctions

When the behaviour complained of arises out of a family relationship the same considerations apply as for non-molestation injunctions.

9.2 CRIMINAL OFFENCES AND CIVIL ORDERS UNDER THE PROTECTION FROM HARASSMENT ACT 1997

9.2.1 Criminal remedies

The police can charge a perpetrator who pursues a course of conduct which amounts to harassment of another, and which he knows or ought to know amounts to harassment of the other (Protection from Harassment Act 1997 (PHA 1997), s.1).

Breach of s.1 is an offence rendering the perpetrator liable on summary conviction to imprisonment for a term not exceeding six months, or a fine or both (PHA 1997, s.2).

A perpetrator whose course of conduct causes another to fear, on at least two occasions, that violence will be used against him or her is guilty of an offence if the perpetrator knows or ought to know that his or her course of conduct will cause the other so to fear on each of those occasions. The perpetrator is liable on conviction on indictment to imprisonment for a term not exceeding five years, or a fine, or both or on summary conviction to imprisonment for a term not exceeding six months, or a fine, or both (PHA 1997, s.4).

References to harassing a person include alarming the person or causing the person distress and 'conduct' includes speech (PHA 1997, s.7). The Act is intended to protect the sufferer from being in a state of alarm or distress.

9.2.2 Civil restraining order imposed by criminal court on conviction

The criminal court sentencing or otherwise dealing with a person convicted of an offence under PHA 1997, ss.2 or 4 may also make a restraining order for the purpose of protecting the victim of the offence, or any other person mentioned in the order, from further conduct which:

(a)   amounts to harassment, or
(b)   will cause fear of violence.

The order may prohibit the defendant from doing anything described in the order (PHA 1997, s.5), and may have effect for a specified period or until further order. The prosecutor, the defendant or any other person mentioned in the order may apply to the court which made the order for it to be varied or discharged by a further order.

If without reasonable excuse, the defendant does anything which he or she is prohibited from doing by an order the defendant is guilty of an offence and is liable on conviction on indictment to imprisonment for a term not exceeding five years, or a fine, or both, or on summary conviction, to imprisonment for a term not exceeding six months, or a fine not exceeding the statutory maximum or both.

Section 12 of the Domestic Violence, Crime and Victims Act 2004 was implemented on 30 September 2009. It extended the power to impose a restraining order under PHA 1997. A criminal court can impose a restraining order when convicting a perpetrator of any offence. A restraining order can also be made on acquittal, if necessary to protect a person from harassment by the accused. The victim has the right to be heard on any application to vary or discharge the order.

Sentencing for breach of a restraining order

The court has to consider:

- whether the offence was harassment contrary to PHA 1997, s.2 or causing fear of violence contrary to s.4;
- any history of disobedience to court orders in the past, and whether these were orders under PHA 1997 or civil orders;
- the seriousness of the defendant's conduct (e.g. actual violence or direct contact is likely to be more serious than letters or other forms of indirect contact);
- whether the misconduct was persistent, or a single incident;
- the physical and psychological effect of breach on the victim and whether the victim required protection;
- the level of risk posed by the defendant;
- the mental health of the defendant and whether he is willing to undergo treatment or accept help from the probation service; and
- whether the defendant pleaded guilty and was remorseful.

For a first offence, a short, sharp sentence may be appropriate, though much will depend on the factors of repetition, breach of court orders and the nature of the misconduct. For a second offence, a sentence of about 15 months on a plea of guilty is an appropriate starting point: see *R* v. *Liddle; R* v. *Hayes* [1999] 3 All ER 816.

Sentencing guidelines have been issued for breach of protective orders. Additional aggravating features to be taken into account include impact on children, using contact arrangements with a child to instigate an offence, forcing the victim to leave home and breach shortly after the order (see **9.5.9**).

9.2.3 Injunction application to civil court

A victim of an actual or apprehended course of conduct of harassment can bring a claim in the county court in civil proceedings. Where the court grants an injunction for the purpose of restraining the defendant from pursuing any conduct which amounts to harassment, and the plaintiff considers that the defendant has done anything which he or she is prohibited from doing by the injunction, the plaintiff may apply for the issue of a warrant for the arrest of the defendant (PHA 1997, s.3).

Where the defendant does anything which he or she is prohibited from doing by the injunction the defendant is guilty of an offence. Breach can be punished either as contempt of court or as an offence, but not both.

The person guilty of an offence is liable on conviction on indictment to imprisonment for a term not exceeding five years or a fine or both, or on summary conviction, to imprisonment for a term not exceeding six months, or a fine not exceeding the statutory maximum, or both.

Unlike anti-social behaviour orders under the Crime and Disorder Act 1998, s.1, to which the criminal standard of proof applies, the civil standard of proof is to be applied to injunction applications under PHA 1997, s.3. Injunctions are designed to protect the rights of individuals rather than to restrain defendants for the benefit of the community (*Hipgrave and Another* v. *Jones* [2005] 2 FLR 174, QB).

9.3   INJUNCTION ORDERS UNDER THE FAMILY LAW ACT 1996, PART IV

Application can be made by a domestic abuse sufferer for orders designed to protect the applicant and/or any relevant child from molestation by an 'associated person' (as defined by the Family Law Act 1996 (FLA 1996), s.62(3)) and to regulate the occupation of a family home.

Most applications are 'free standing', but applications can be made within other family proceedings. The court may make a non-molestation order in other family proceedings whether or not a formal application has been made and of its own motion.

Application can be made in the Family Proceedings Court, the county court or the High Court.

Respondents must understand that an order has been made forbidding them to do certain things and that if they do them they will be punished: see *P* v. *P (Contempt of Court: Mental Capacity)* [1999] 2 FLR 898, CA. In that case the husband was deaf and dumb, had tunnel vision and an average IQ, but was not suffering from a mental health difficulty. The judge found that the husband knew he should not go to the matrimonial home and would be liable to go to prison if he did so. The fact of disability, whether a mental disability or because a person is under 18, does not of itself prevent an injunction order being made or provide a defence to a charge of contempt; the issue is whether the respondent is able to understand the order and its consequences (*Wookey* v. *Wookey* [1991] 2 FLR 319, CA).

9.3.1   Non-molestation orders

'Molestation' is not defined in FLA 1996; however, it:

> ... implies some quite deliberate conduct which is aimed at a high degree of harassment of the other party so as to justify the intervention of the Court. It does

not include enforcing an invasion of privacy per se; there has to be some conduct which clearly harasses and affects the Applicant to such a degree that the intervention of the Court is called for . . .

(C v. C [1998] 1 FLR 554, Sir Stephen Brown)

Under previous case law molestation has been held to include harassment falling short of violence or threatened violence such as where a husband had been handing his wife threatening letters and intercepting her on the way to the station (Horner v. Horner [1983] 4 FLR 50). Molestation also includes pestering as in the case of a husband who pestered his ex-wife to go out with him, see him and speak to him and called on her at home early in the morning and late at night and at work making a nuisance of himself (Vaughan v. Vaughan [1973] 3 All ER 449).

The standard wordings available for non-molestation orders are:

1. The Respondent is forbidden to use or threaten violence against the Applicant [and must not instruct, encourage or in any way suggest that any other person should do so] and/or
2. The Respondent is forbidden to intimidate, harass or pester [or *specify*] the Applicant [and must not instruct, encourage or in any way suggest that any other person should do so] and/or
3. The Respondent is forbidden to use or threaten violence against the relevant children [*insert names and dates of birth*] [and must not instruct, encourage or in any way suggest that any other person should do so] and/or
4. The Respondent is forbidden to intimidate, harass or pester [or *specify*] the relevant children [*specify names and dates of birth*] [and must not instruct, encourage, or in any way suggest that any other person should do so].

Now that breach of a non-molestation order is a criminal offence the order needs to be in terms which are readily understandable by the respondent if a successful prosecution is going to be possible following breach of the order. It was said in *Manchester City Council* v. *Lee* [2004] EWCA Civ 1256 that 'An injunction which leaves doubt as to what can or cannot be done is not a proper basis for committal proceedings.' The injunction order in that case followed precisely the wording of s.152 of the Housing Act 1996 under which it was made, but was not specific enough.

A non-molestation order should therefore specify the acts of harassment prohibited, e.g. 'the Respondent is prohibited to continue to harass the Applicant by sending threatening or abusive text messages'.

It is no longer possible to attach a power of arrest to a non-molestation order. Breach of a non-molestation order is a criminal offence.

Undertakings

Section 46 provides that in any case where the court has power to make a non-molestation order the court may accept an undertaking from any party to the proceedings. However, s.46(3A) states that:

> The court shall not accept an undertaking ... instead of making a non-molestation order in any case where it appears to the court that –
>
> (a) the respondent has used or threatened violence against the applicant or a relevant child; and
> (b) for the protection of the applicant or child it is necessary to make a non-molestation order so that any breach may be punishable under section 42A.

Associated person

The applicant must be a 'person who is associated with the respondent' (s.42(2)(a)). 'Associated persons' are defined in FLA 1996, s.62(3):

1. They are or have been married to each other or are civil partners of each other.
2. They are cohabitants or former cohabitants (defined as two persons who, although not married to each other, are living together as husband and wife or as if they were civil partners).
3. They live or have lived in the same household, otherwise than merely by reason of one of them being the other's employee, tenant, lodger or boarder.
4. They are relatives (defined as father, mother, step-father, step-mother, son, daughter, step-son, step-daughter, grandmother, grandfather, grandson or granddaughter) of the applicant or of the applicant's spouse or former spouse or brother, sister, uncle, aunt, niece or nephew (whether of the full blood or of the half blood or by affinity) of the applicant or of the applicant's spouse or former spouse, civil partner or former civil partner or cohabitant or former cohabitant.
5. They have agreed to marry one another or enter into a civil partnership agreement (whether or not that agreement has been terminated) (but not later than three years after termination).
6. In relation to any child, they are both persons falling within FLA 1996, s.62(4) (i.e. parents, or have, or have had, parental responsibility).
7. They are parties to the same family proceedings (other than proceedings under FLA 1996, Part IV).
8. Two persons who have or have had an intimate personal relationship with each other which is or was of significant duration.

Duration of non-molestation orders

Under FLA 1996, s.42(7) a non-molestation order may be made for a specified period or until further order.

The usual practice is for the court to make initial orders of three or six months in duration. However, a longer order may be appropriate, for example where the respondent persists in molesting the applicant after the initial order is made. An indefinite order can be made if appropriate in the circumstances (*Re B-J (Power of Arrest)* [2000] 2 FLR 443).

9.3.2 Occupation orders

An application can be made for an occupation order against an associated person in respect of a dwelling house in which they cohabit or cohabited or, if one or both has a right of occupation, in which they intended to cohabit. The type of occupation order that can be made and the criteria for granting the order depend on the relationship between the parties and the legal rights that either of them has to occupy the home.

Section 33 – applicant has legal right to occupy or home rights

Occupation orders under FLA 1996, s.33 are available to:

1. A person who has a legal right to occupy the family home, against any associated person (including cases where both parties are in occupation and both have a legal right of occupation).
2. A spouse or civil partner in occupation but with no legal right of occupation, as against the other spouse or civil partner who has a right of occupation (applicant has home rights).
3. A spouse or civil partner who is not in occupation and has no legal right of occupation against the spouse or civil partner in occupation who has a right of occupation (i.e. applicant has contingent home rights).

ORDERS THAT CAN BE MADE UNDER SECTION 33

A declaration that:

- the applicant is entitled to occupy (address) as his/her home; or
- the applicant has home rights in (address); and/or
- the applicant's home rights shall not end when the respondent dies or their marriage or civil partnership is terminated and shall continue until (date) or further order.

An order that:

- the respondent shall allow the applicant to occupy (address); or
- the respondent shall allow the applicant to occupy part of (address) namely: (specify part);
- the respondent shall not obstruct, harass or interfere with the applicant's peaceful occupation of (address);
- the respondent shall not occupy (address);

- the respondent shall not occupy (address) from (date) until (date); or
- the respondent shall not occupy (part of address); and/or
- the respondent shall not occupy (address or part of address) between (specify dates or times);
- the respondent shall leave (address or part of address) (forthwith) (within ___ hours/days of service on him/her of the order); and/or
- having left (address or part of address) the respondent shall not return to, enter or attempt to enter (or go within (specify distance) of) it.

CRITERIA FOR AN OOCUPATION ORDER UNDER SECTION 33

There is a presumption that an order should be made if it appears to the court that the applicant or any relevant child is likely to suffer significant harm attributable to the conduct of the respondent if an order under s.33 containing one or more of the provisions mentioned in subsection (3) is not made.

If the court decides that likelihood of significant harm has been established then it shall make the order unless it appears to it that:

(a)   the respondent or any relevant child is likely to suffer significant harm if the order is made; and

(a)   the harm likely to be suffered by the respondent or child in that event is as great as, or greater than, the harm attributable to conduct of the respondent which is likely to be suffered by the applicant or child if the order is not made.

This is referred to as the balance of harm test and is set out in FLA 1996, s.33(7).

Harm means ill-treatment or impairment of health and in relation to a child also includes impairment of development and seeing or hearing harm being inflicted upon another.

If the first criterion of significant harm is not passed there is still discretion to make an order under FLA 1996, s.33(6) but as an occupation order is of a draconian nature affecting property rights it should be restricted to exceptional cases (*Chalmers* v. *Johns* [1999] 1 FLR 392). The court shall have regard to all the circumstances including (s.33(6)):

(a)   the housing needs and housing resources of each of the parties and of any relevant child;

(b)   the financial resources of each of the parties;

(c)   the likely effect of any order, or of any decision by the court not to exercise its powers under subsection (3), on the health, safety or well-being of the parties and of any relevant child; and

(d)   the conduct of the parties in relation to each other and otherwise.

To meet the test under s.33(6) there must be more than the heightened tensions that any family has to live with whilst the process of divorce and separation is current (*G* v. *G* (*Occupation Order: Conduct*) [2000] 2 FLR 36).

DURATION OF SECTION 33 ORDERS

An order may be for a defined period, until the occurrence of a specified event or until further order.

Section 35 – applicant with no right of occupation and respondent is former spouse or civil partner with right of occupation

A former spouse or civil partner, who has no right of occupation against the former spouse of civil partner who has a right of occupation, can make an application. The orders that can be made are:

- the applicant has the right to occupy (address) and the respondent shall allow the applicant to do so; and
- the respondent shall not evict or exclude the applicant from (address) or any part of it namely (specify part); and
- the respondent shall not occupy (address); or
- the respondent shall not occupy (address) from (date) until (date); or
- the respondent shall not occupy (specify part of address); or
- the respondent shall leave (address) (forthwith) (within ___ hours/days of service on him/her of the order); and/or
- having left (address or part of address) the respondent shall not return to, enter or attempt to enter (or go within ___ (specify distance) of) it.

CRITERIA FOR A SECTION 35 ORDER

These are set out in FLA 1996, s.35(6) as 'all the circumstances including':

(a) the housing needs and housing resources of each of the parties and of any relevant child;
(b) the financial resources of each of the parties;
(c) the likely effect of any order, or of any decision by the court not to exercise its powers under subsection (3) or (4), on the health, safety or well-being of the parties and of any relevant child;
(d) the conduct of the parties in relation to each other and otherwise;
(e) the length of time that has elapsed since the parties ceased to live together;
(f) the length of time that has elapsed since the marriage or civil partnership was dissolved or annulled; and
(g) the existence of any pending proceedings between the parties –

    (i) for an order under section 23A or 24 of the Matrimonial Causes Act 1973 (property adjustment orders in connection with divorce proceedings etc.);
    (ia) for a property adjustment order under Part 2 of Schedule 5 to the Civil Partnership Act 2004;
    (ii) for an order under paragraph 1(2)(d) or (e) of Schedule 1 to the Children Act 1989 (orders for financial relief against parents); or
    (iii) relating to the legal or beneficial ownership of the dwelling-house.

If the court does decide to grant a s.35 order and the applicant or a relevant child is likely to suffer significant harm if an order excluding the respondent from all or part of the property is not made then the court must make such an order unless after applying the balance of harm test (see above, s.33 orders) the harm likely to be suffered by the respondent or a relevant child is as great or greater.

DURATION OF SECTION 35 ORDERS

A s.35 order must be limited to a specified period not exceeding six months, but it may be extended on one or more occasions for a further specified period not exceeding six months.

Section 36 – one cohabitant or former cohabitant with no existing right to occupy

Orders under FLA 1996, s.36 are available to a person who is a cohabitant or former cohabitant in a situation where only one of them has a right of occupation in the property. (Note that if both cohabitants have a right of occupation, then the application should be made under s.33.)

The orders that can be made under s.36 are as follows:

- the applicant has the right to occupy (address) and the respondent shall allow the applicant to do so; or
- the respondent shall not evict or exclude the applicant from (address) or any part of it namely (specify part); and/or
- the respondent shall not occupy (address); or
- the respondent shall not occupy (address) from (specify date) until (specify date); or
- the respondent shall not occupy (specify part of address); or
- the respondent shall leave (address or part of address) (forthwith) (within ___ hours/days of service on him/her of the order); and/or
- having left (address or part of address) the respondent shall not return to, enter or attempt to enter (or go within ___ (specify distance) of) it.

CRITERIA FOR SECTION 36 ORDERS

Section 36 orders are discretionary.

When deciding whether to make an order the court must consider 'all the circumstances including' (s.36(6)):

(a) the housing needs and housing resources of each of the parties and of any relevant child;

(b) the financial resources of each of the parties;

(c) the likely effect of any order, or of any decision by the court not to exercise its powers under subsection (3) or (4), on the health, safety or well-being of the parties and of any relevant child;

(d) the conduct of the parties in relation to each other and otherwise;

(e) the nature of the parties' relationship and in particular the level of commitment involved in it;

(f) the length of time during which they have cohabited;

(g) whether there are or have been any children who are children of both parties or for whom both parties have or have had parental responsibility;

(h) the length of time that has elapsed since the parties ceased to live together; and

(i) the existence of any pending proceedings between the parties –

> (i) for an order under paragraph 1(2)(d) or (e) of Schedule 1 to the Children Act 1989 (orders for financial relief against parents); or
>
> (ii) relating to the legal or beneficial ownership of the dwelling-house.

When deciding whether to exclude the respondent from all or part of the property the court also needs to consider:

- the housing needs and housing resources of each of the parties and of any relevant child;
- the financial resources of each of the parties;
- the likely effect of any order, or of any decision by the court not to exercise its powers under subsection (3) or (4), on the health, safety or wellbeing of the parties and of any relevant child;
- the conduct of the parties in relation to each other and otherwise.

When deciding whether to make an order regulating the occupation of the home by the respondent the court must also apply the balance of harm test.

DURATION OF SECTION 36 ORDERS

A s.36 order must be limited to a specified period not exceeding six months, but may be extended on one or more occasions for a further specified period not exceeding six months.

Section 37 – neither spouse nor civil partner entitled to occupy

Occupation orders under FLA 1996, s.37 are available to a spouse or civil partner in occupation against the other spouse or civil partner also in occupation where neither has a right of occupation.

Possible orders that can be made are:

- the respondent shall allow the applicant to occupy (address) or part of it namely: (specify part); and/or
- the respondent shall not obstruct, harass or interfere with the applicant's peaceful occupation of (address); and/or
- the respondent shall not occupy (address or part of address) between (specify dates or times);
- the respondent shall leave (address or part of address) (forthwith) (within ___ hours/days of service on him/her of the order); and/or

- having left (address or part of address), the respondent may not return to, enter or attempt to enter (or go within ___ (specify distance) of) it.

CRITERIA FOR A SECTION 37 ORDER

These are exactly the same as the criteria for a s.33 order (see above), including a presumption that an order should be made where the applicant or a relevant child is likely to suffer significant harm and the application of the balance of harm test.

DURATION OF SECTION 37 ORDERS

A s.37 order must be limited to a specified period not exceeding six months, but may be extended on one or more occasions for a further specified period not exceeding six months.

Section 38 – neither cohabitant or former cohabitant entitled to occupy

An occupation order under FLA 1996, s.38 is available where a person is a cohabitant or former cohabitant where both parties are in occupation but neither has a right of occupation.

The range of orders that can be made is precisely the same as for s.37 orders (see above).

CRITERIA FOR A SECTION 38 ORDER

When considering a s.38 order the court must have regard to all the circumstances including (s.38(4)):

(a) the housing needs and housing resources of each of the parties and of any relevant child;
(b) the financial resources of each of the parties;
(c) the likely effect of any order, or of any decision by the court not to exercise its powers under subsection (3), on the health, safety or well-being of the parties and of any relevant child;
(d) the conduct of the parties in relation to each other and otherwise; . . .

When deciding whether to make an order the court must apply the balance of harm test (see above under s.33).

DURATION OF SECTION 38 ORDERS

An order under s.38 must be limited to a specified period not exceeding six months, but may be extended on one occasion for a further specified period not exceeding six months.

Checklist for Family Law Act injunction orders

Parties associated	NO	No orders
Parties associated	YES	Non-molestation order
Occupied/intended to occupy joint home	NO	No occupation order

Parties associated and occupied/intended to occupy joint home as follows:

	Criteria	Orders	Duration
Section 33 Applicant with right to occupy or home rights.	Presumption of order where risk of significant harm. Discretion to make order considering: – housing needs; – financial resources; – effect of order; – conduct of parties; – balance of harm test.	Orders that **may** be made: – Applicant entitled to remain. – Respondent to permit applicant to enter and remain. – Regulating occupation. – Restricting respondent's right to occupy/home rights. – Require respondent to leave. – Exclude respondent from defined area. – Applicant's home rights to continue after decree absolute or respondent's death.	For specified period or until event/further order.
Section 35 Former spouse or civil partner with no right to occupy.	Presumption of order where risk of significant harm. Discretion to make order considering: – housing needs; – financial resources; – effect of order; – conduct of parties; – length of time since separated; – length of time since decree absolute; – existence of other proceedings; – balance of harm test.	Orders that **must** be made: – Applicant not to be evicted/excluded by respondent. – Applicant has right to enter and occupy. – Respondent to permit applicant to enter and remain. Orders that **may** be made: – Regulating occupation. – Restricting respondent's right to occupy. – Require respondent to leave. – Exclude respondent from defined area.	Up to six months with extension for periods up to six months.

Section 36
Cohabitant or
ex-cohabitant with
no right to occupy.
	Discretion to make
	order considering:
	
	– housing needs;
	– financial resources;
	– effect of order;
	– conduct of parties;
	– length of time since
	  separated;
	– length of time
	  cohabited;
	– any children;
	– existence of other
	  proceedings;
	– nature of
	  relationship;
	– balance of harm
	  test.
		Orders that **must** be made:
		
		– Applicant not to be
		  evicted/excluded by
		  respondent.
		– Applicant has right to
		  enter and occupy.
		– Respondent to permit
		  applicant to enter and
		  remain.
		
		Orders that **may** be made:
		
		– Regulating occupation.
		– Restricting
		  respondent's
		  right to occupy.
		– Require respondent to
		  leave.
		– Exclude respondent
		  from defined area.
			Up to six
			months, with
			extensions for
			one period up
			to six months.

Section 37
Neither spouse/
civil partner
entitled to occupy.
	Presumption of order
	where risk of
	significant harm.
	
	Discretion to make
	order considering:
	
	– housing needs;
	– financial resources;
	– effect of order;
	– conduct of parties;
	– balance of harm
	  test.
		Orders that **may** be made:
		
		– Respondent to permit
		  applicant to enter and
		  remain.
		– Regulating occupation.
		– Require respondent to
		  leave.
		– Exclude respondent
		  from defined area.
			Up to six
			months, with
			extensions for
			periods up to
			six months.

Section 38
Neither cohabitant
or ex-cohabitant
entitled to occupy.
	Discretion to make
	order considering:
	
	– housing needs;
	– financial resources;
	– effect of order;
	– conduct of parties;
	– balance of harm
	  test.
		Orders that **may** be made:
		
		– Respondent to permit
		  applicant to enter and
		  remain.
		– Regulating occupation.
		– Require respondent to
		  leave.
		– Exclude respondent
		  from defined area.
			Up to six
			months, with
			extensions for
			one period up
			to six months.

9.3.3 Power of arrest

A power of arrest must be attached to one or more provisions of an occupation order which is granted at a hearing on notice to the respondent where 'it appears to the court that the respondent has used or threatened violence against the applicant or a relevant child' (FLA 1996, s.47(2)(b)), unless the court is 'satisfied that in all the circumstances of the case the applicant or child will be adequately protected without such a power of arrest' (FLA 1996, s.47(2)).

Where an occupation order is granted without notice, a power of arrest may be attached to one or more provisions of the order if it appears to the court that:

- the respondent has used or threatened violence against the applicant or a relevant child; and
- there is a risk of significant harm to the applicant or child, attributable to the conduct of the respondent, if the power of arrest is not attached to those provisions immediately.

Undertakings

An undertaking shall not be accepted by the court where a power of arrest would be attached if an occupation order was made (FLA 1996, s.46(3)).

9.3.4 Supplementary orders

The following orders can be made, under FLA 1996, s.40, when the court makes an order under ss.33, 34 or 35:

- the applicant/respondent shall maintain and repair (address); and/or
- the applicant/respondent shall pay the rent for (address); or
- the applicant/respondent shall pay the mortgage payments on (address); or
- the applicant/respondent shall pay the following for (address): (specify outgoings as bullet points);
- the (party in occupation) shall pay to the (other party) £_____ each (week/month, etc.) for (address);
- the (party in occupation) shall keep and use the (furniture) (contents) (specify if necessary) of (address) and the applicant/respondent shall return to the (party in occupation) the (furniture/contents/specify if necessary) no later than (date/time);
- the (party in occupation) shall take reasonable care of the (furniture/contents/specify if necessary) of (address);
- the (party in occupation) shall take all reasonable steps to keep secure (address) and the furniture or other contents (specify if necessary).

However, a s.40 order cannot be enforced by committal (*Nwogbe* v. *Nwogbe* [2000] 2 FLR 744, CA), and there seems to be no obvious way in which such an order can be enforced.

9.4 PROCEDURE UNDER PART IV

9.4.1 Procedure for application without notice

1. File application in Form FL401 and statement or affidavit in support. Evidence in support must state why the application is begun without notice.
2. Applicant attends court with any witnesses.
3. Obtain leave of court to produce oral evidence (unless written statement filed). Applicant hands court draft order.
4. Court makes order.
5. Court issues non-molestation order in Form FL404a, any occupation order in Form FL404 and if power of arrest has been attached also issues Form FL406 for delivery to police.
6. Applicant serves order, application and statement together with notice of hearing of inter-partes application on respondent personally.
7. Deliver a copy of Form FL404a to the police and any Form FL404 and FL406 plus a statement of service.

9.4.2 Application on notice

1. File with the court application Form FL401, a written statement (Family Proceedings Court) or a sworn statement (county court and High Court).
2. Court fixes date and time for hearing, returns papers to applicant for service.
3. Serve respondent with Form FL401, copy statement or affidavit and FL402 (notice of hearing) at least two clear days before the hearing – personal service required.
4. If application includes application for an occupation order under ss.33, 35 or 36, also requirement to serve copy of Form FL401 on mortgagee or landlord by first class post with notice in Form FL416 informing them of their right to make representations at the hearing.
5. File statement in Form FL415 confirming details of service.
6. If application opposed, directions will be given for the filing and service of evidence.
7. Applicant attends court with any witnesses, whose evidence is contained in a statement.
8. Court makes order.
9. Non-molestation order issued to applicant in Form FL404a and occupation order in Form FL404. If power of arrest is attached to the occupation order, court issues Form FL406.
10. Serve order on respondent personally, and deliver non-molestation order to police and occupation order and power of arrest if one is attached.

11. If an occupation order is made under ss.33, 35 or 36, a copy of the order must be served by the applicant on the mortgagee or landlord by first class post.

12. If the court accepts an undertaking rather than granting an order, then the court will deliver a copy in Form FL422 to the respondent at the hearing.

The hearing is adversarial. Lawyers should establish at an early stage what they have to seek to establish or cast doubt on and by what means and what evidence they could best do so. Full statements by both parties will establish what facts are in issue and therefore require proof and what are accepted. Where first-hand evidence is available in either documentary or witness form it should be presented. If a witness is unable to give a statement, hearsay evidence should be recorded in a statement from the applicant rather than drawn out in oral evidence. Evidence that corroborates or gives doubt about important allegations should be obtained where possible, such as police records of domestic violence incidents and medical evidence (*A (A Child) (Contact: Risk of Violence)* [2006] 1 FLR 283).

9.5 ENFORCEMENT FOLLOWING BREACH OF AN INJUNCTION ORDER UNDER FAMILY LAW ACT 1996

9.5.1 Breach of non-molestation order is a criminal offence

Since 1 July 2007 a person who without reasonable excuse does anything that he or she is prohibited from doing under a non-molestation order is guilty of an offence (FLA 1996, s.42A). On conviction on indictment the sanction is imprisonment for a term not exceeding five years, or a fine or both. On summary conviction he or she will be liable to a term not exceeding 12 months, or a fine, or both. Attendance on a domestic violence perpetrator programme is also a possible sentence. Breach of the non-molestation order is an arrestable offence and the breach is dealt with as a crime in the criminal court.

A person can only be guilty of an offence under s.42A in respect of conduct engaged in at a time when he or she was aware of the existence of the order. However, the respondent must either be served with the order or informed of its terms (whether by being present when the order was made or by telephone or otherwise).

Where a person is convicted of an offence under s.42A in respect of any conduct, that conduct is not punishable as contempt of court.

9.5.2 Proceedings for breach in the civil court

A person cannot be convicted of an offence under s.42A in respect of any conduct that has been punished as contempt of court. It is still possible for breach of a non-molestation order to be dealt with in the civil court – provided that the respondent has not already been punished for the breach in the criminal court.

Since s.42A has been implemented, breach of a non-molestation order can be dealt with in the civil court or as a criminal offence.

Breach of an occupation order continues to be dealt with in the civil court by way of committal proceedings.

9.5.3 Service

The undertaking or occupation order must be endorsed with a penal notice. A non-molestation order must contain a warning that if, without reasonable excuse, the respondent does anything which is forbidden by the order, he will be committing a criminal offence and liable on conviction to a term of imprisonment not exceeding five years or to a fine or to both.

The undertaking or order need not be served if the respondent was in court when the undertaking was given or the order was made or has actual notice by some other means, e.g. telephone or telegram informing him of the contents (*Hussain* v. *Hussain* [1986] Fam 134, CA). However, it is highly desirable that undertaking or order is served. The safest way is if the respondent is given a sealed copy after the undertaking is given or the order is made.

If the respondent is seeking to evade service an order for substituted service can be made. Otherwise there must be personal service. A statement of service on the respondent should be filed in court.

A non-molestation order and an occupation order with a power of arrest attached and a statement of service by the person who served the respondent with the order must be served on the officer in charge of the applicant's local police station.

9.5.4 Arrest

Warrant for arrest

Where there is no power of arrest or a power of arrest is only attached to certain provisions of the order, if the applicant considers that the respondent has failed to comply with the order, the applicant may apply for the issue of a warrant for the arrest of the respondent (FLA 1996, s.47(8)(b)).

The application must be substantiated on oath and show reasonable grounds for believing that the respondent has failed to comply with the order.

Following arrest the civil court may remand the respondent in custody or on bail.

Power of arrest

If a power of arrest is attached to certain provisions of an occupation order, a constable may arrest without warrant a person whom the constable has reasonable cause for suspecting to be in breach of any such provision (FLA 1996, s.47(6)).

The respondent must have been brought before the relevant judicial authority within 24 hours of arrest. If the matter is not then disposed of forthwith, the respondent may be remanded.

In reckoning the period of 24 hours no account is to be taken of Christmas Day, Good Friday or any Sunday.

9.5.5   Remand

Remand in custody

Remand in custody can be:

1.   For a maximum of eight days (unless for a medical report).
2.   If it is justified, e.g. for the reasonable protection of the applicant.
3.   To secure the respondent's attendance at court.

Remand for medical examination and report (FLA 1996, s.48)

1.   Remand to enable a medical examination and report to be made.
2.   If in custody – adjournment for no more than three weeks at a time.
3.   Otherwise, for no more than four weeks at a time.

If there is reason to suspect that a person arrested under a warrant or a power of arrest is suffering from mental illness or severe mental impairment there is power to remand for a report under s.35 of the Mental Health Act 1983.

Remand on bail (FLA 1996, Schedule 5)

1.   Remand on bail can be with or without sureties (Sched.5, para.2(1)(b)).
2.   It may be on condition to appear before court at the end of the period of remand, or every time the hearing is adjourned.
3.   There can be further remands on bail.

9.5.6   Application for committal

Where the alleged contemnor has not been arrested under a power of arrest or a warrant there must be an application to commit. The application is:

- in the county court, a notice to show good reason why the respondent should not be committed to prison in Form N78;
- in the magistrates' court, a complaint in Form FLA418.

The Form N78 should be signed by the applicant or the applicant's solicitors. It should be addressed to the respondent, specify the breaches alleged and call on the respondent to show cause why he or she should not be committed to prison. The respondent must be given reasonable notice of the hearing (*Williams* v. *Fawcett* [1985] 1 All ER 787, CA).

The application must be supported by an affidavit. It is not sufficient to particularise the breaches in the affidavit in support only. The notice must recite the relevant terms of the order or undertaking which it is alleged have been breached.

The notice must require the contemnor to attend at the hearing to show good cause why he or she should not be committed to prison. There must be personal service giving two clear days' notice.

9.5.7 The hearing

Contempt applications must normally be heard in public and preferably robed in the county court.

Ex parte (without notice) committal orders

Service of a copy of the notice to show cause can be dispensed with if the court thinks it is just to do so, but the circumstances in which it will do so are wholly exceptional, e.g. a threat to remove a child from the jurisdiction. A better approach is to activate the power of arrest or apply for a warrant for arrest.

Adjournments

If a notice is in any way defective the judge can determine whether to grant an adjournment to allow for preparation of an amended notice. The judge should also decide whether the respondent needs additional time to prepare his or her case.

Where the respondent has been arrested under a power of arrest, the charge should be put in writing and read over to the respondent at the outset of the hearing, so that the respondent knows the case he or she has to answer in order to comply with Art.6(3)(a), (b) of the European Convention on Human Rights.

A defendant must have adequate time and facilities to prepare his or her defence and seek legal advice (Art.6(3)(b)). The defendant must be offered the chance of legal representation and if necessary to apply for public funding (*King* v. *Read and Slack* [1999] 1 FLR 425). An adjournment may be necessary where the defendant has only recently been granted a funding certificate or Legal Help.

The hearing should not be adjourned pending the outcome of any criminal proceedings. Notice of any adjournment should be personally served if the alleged contemnor was not in court or did not hear the date.

Procedure at the hearing

The applicant for the injunction order is entitled to call evidence and make submissions. Although the proceedings remain civil the criminal standard of proof applies – proof beyond reasonable doubt.

The alleged contemnor must have had the capacity to understand what the order prohibited and that he or she would be punished for breach (*P* v. *P* *(Contempt of Court: Mental Capacity)* [1999] 2 FLR 898, CA).

Findings will be made in respect of each allegation and reasons given for the decisions. Once any contempt has been proved the respondent must have opportunity to mitigate and apologise before the court imposes any penalty.

9.5.8 The committal order

1. The order must particularise the breaches that have been proved.
2. There must be a separate identifiable punishment for each breach.
3. Sentences can be concurrent or consecutive.

9.5.9 The sentence

In *Hale* v. *Tanner* [2000] 2 FLR 879 the court gave guidelines as to sentence.

1. Imprisonment is not the automatic consequence of the breach of an order.
2. The court should consider the alternatives – adjournment, a fine, requisition of assets or a mental health order, particularly where no actual violence was involved. If a fine is considered to be the appropriate penalty, imprisonment should not be considered just because a fine cannot be afforded.
3. If imprisonment is appropriate the length of the committal should be decided without reference to whether or not it is to be suspended.
4. The seriousness of what had taken place is to be viewed not only for its intrinsic gravity but also to mark the court's disapproval of the disobedience to its order and to secure compliance in the future.
5. The length of the committal should relate to the maximum available, i.e. two years.
6. Suspension is possible in a wider range of circumstances than in criminal cases, and is usually the first way of attempting to secure compliance with the order.
7. The court has to consider whether the context was mitigating or aggravating in particular where there was a breach of an intimate relationship and/or children were involved.
8. The court should consider any concurrent proceedings in another court, and should explain to the contemnor the nature of the order and the consequence of breach.

Hale v. *Tanner* concerned a female respondent who had used violence towards the applicant. After they parted, she bombarded him with abusive and threatening phone calls. He obtained a non-molestation order. She continued to telephone him and an application was made to commit. She had admitted the allegations straightaway, this was the first breach and she was the mother of a young child. Her sentence was 28 days suspended for 12 months from the date of the original non-molestation order.

Parliament and society generally now regard domestic violence as demanding more condign deterrent punishment. There is more awareness of the impact of the violence on both adult and child victims. The fact that breaches took place in the context of a father seeking contact with a child is an aggravating not a mitigating factor (*H* v. *O* (*Contempt of Court: Sentencing*) [2005] 2 FLR 329). There had been serious violence and disobedient conduct but it did not warrant a sentence in the criminal court approaching the statutory maximum for contempt. The sentence was reduced to nine months, which marked the court's disapproval of the behaviour.

Following these judgments eight months' concurrent sentences were imposed for each breach where a defendant had visited the claimant's home and sent her two threatening and abusive text messages. The non-molestation order had been imposed after he had exhibited violent and abusive behaviour towards her and he had already been sentenced to four months' imprisonment for an earlier breach (*Murray* v. *Robinson* [2006] 1 FLR 365).

The sentence can be suspended. For example a three-month suspended sentence was imposed where the defendant, in breach of an injunction, got his nephew to deliver a note to his children saying he wished to see them (*Harris* v. *Sharpe* [1995] CL 2367, CA). The suspension will usually be until the expiry of the injunction order – even if expressed to last until 'further order of the court' (*Griffin* v. *Griffin* [2000] 2 FLR 44).

A sentence can be increased or reduced on appeal. A 14-day sentence for a 'vicious' attack outside a solicitor's office, which was admitted by the perpetrator, was increased on appeal to three months (*Wilson* v. *Webster* [1998] 1 FLR 1097).

The sentencing guidelines for breach of a non-molestation order charged as a separate offence in the criminal court are for a community order where there was no/minimal direct contact. A single breach involving violence or psychological harm would attract a three–six month sentence, six–nine months for more than one breach and more than 12 months for breach involving significant violence and significant physical and psychological harm to the victim. Aggravating factors are:

- a particularly vulnerable victim or impact on children;
- a proven history of violence or threats by offender;
- using contact arrangement with a child to instigate violence;
- that the victim is forced to leave home;

- that there have been earlier breach proceedings;
- that the offender has a history of disobedience to court orders;
- that the breach was committed immediately/shortly after the order was made.

9.5.10 Application to purge contempt

Application is made in writing, attested by the Governor of the prison, showing the applicant has purged or wishes to purge his contempt.

The party who applied for the committal is to be served with the application not less than one day before the hearing.

The outcome of the application can be 'yes', 'no', or 'not yet': i.e. to release the applicant, refuse the application or order release on a specified date. There is no jurisdiction to release on terms that the remaining part of the sentence is suspended (*Harris* v. *Harris (No.2)* [2001] 1 All ER 185).

9.6 FORCED MARRIAGE PROTECTION ORDERS UNDER THE FAMILY LAW ACT 1996, PART 4A

The Forced Marriage (Civil Protection) Act 2007 inserted Part 4A into FLA 1996 to make provision for protecting individuals from being forced to enter into marriage without their free and full consent or individuals who have been forced to enter into marriage without such consent.

9.6.1 Forced marriage protection orders

A forced marriage protection order can be made by the High Court or the county court to protect a person:

(a) from being forced into a marriage;
(b) who has been forced into a marriage.

'Force' includes coercing by threats or other psychological means (FLA 1996, s.63A(6)).

The conduct forcing the person to enter into a marriage can be directed against the person or against another person.

When considering whether to grant a forced marriage protection order the court must have regard to all the circumstances, including:

(a) the need to secure the health, safety and wellbeing of the person;
(b) the person's wishes and feelings (as far as they are reasonably ascertainable), in the light of their age and understanding (FLA 1996, s.63C(4)).

9.6.2   Terms of a forced marriage protection order

A forced marriage protection order may contain:

(a)   such prohibitions, restrictions or requirements; and
(b)   such other terms

as the court considers appropriate.

Terms may relate to:

(a)   conduct within and outside England and Wales (FLA 1996, s.63B(2)(a));
(b)   respondents who force or may become involved in an attempt to force a person to enter into a marriage (s.63B).

9.6.3   Procedure

An order can be made on application:

(a)   by the person to be protected;
(b)   by a relevant third party.

The application is in Form FL401A.
An order can also be made in other family proceedings (FLA 1996, s.63C).
An application can be made without notice, where the court considers it just and convenient, where:

(a)   there is risk of significant harm if an order is not made immediately;
(b)   it is likely the applicant will be deterred or prevented from making the application if the order is not made immediately; or
(c)   the respondent is deliberately evading service.

9.6.4   Undertakings

The court can accept an undertaking instead of making a forced marriage protection order (FLA 1996, s.63E).

9.6.5   Power of arrest

Breach of a forced marriage protection order is not a criminal offence. The court must attach a power of arrest to one or more of the provisions of the order when the respondent has used or threatened violence, unless it considers there will be adequate protection without a power of arrest (FLA 1996, s.63H).
Where there is a power of arrest a person arrested must be brought before the judge in the civil court within 24 hours. There will then be committal proceedings in the civil court for contempt. There are similar provisions to FLA 1996 Part IV in respect of warrants for arrest (s.63J), remand and bail.

9.7 ANTI-SOCIAL BEHAVIOUR INJUNCTION UNDER THE HOUSING ACT 1996

9.7.1 Injunctions under the Housing Act 1996

Social landlords can use the provisions of the Housing Act 1996 to provide protection for a domestic abuse sufferer who occupies premises they own or manage.

9.7.2 Conduct capable of causing nuisance or annoyance to a person with a right to occupy housing accommodation

A local housing authority, housing action trust or registered social landlord can apply for an anti-social behaviour injunction where a defendant is engaging, has engaged or threatens to engage in conduct capable of causing nuisance or annoyance to a person with a right (of whatever description) to reside in or occupy housing accommodation owned or managed by the landlord or other housing accommodation in the neighbourhood (Housing Act 1996, s.153A). It is immaterial where the conduct occurs and a complaint from the sufferer is not essential. The court can consider other evidence and take a view as to whether the conduct would have been capable of causing nuisance or annoyance.

9.7.3 Breach of a tenancy agreement by conduct capable of causing nuisance or annoyance

A landlord can apply for an injunction against a tenant in respect of a breach or anticipated breach of a tenancy agreement on the grounds that the tenant is engaging or threatening to engage in conduct capable of causing nuisance or annoyance to any person or allowing, inciting or encouraging any other person to do so (Housing Act 1996, s.153D).

9.7.4 Power of arrest

Where there is use or threat of violence or a significant risk of emotional or physical harm then a power of arrest can be attached to any provision of an order made under Housing Act 1996, ss.153C or 153D and the defendant can be excluded from any premises specified in the order or a specified area.

9.7.5 Without notice applications

The application can be made without notice if the court thinks it just and convenient (Housing Act 1996, s.153E(4)).

9.7.6 Enforcement on breach

Copies of an injunction with power of arrest attached must be delivered to the police after the defendant has been served. The Housing Act 1996, s.155 contains provisions covering breach of an anti-social behaviour injunction. They are similar to the provisions for breach of an injunction under FLA 1996.

CHAPTER 10

Cohabitation

Jacqui Jackson

10.1 INTRODUCTION

It is now an accepted part of society that a large number of heterosexual couples live together without marrying and a large number of same-sex couples live together without entering into a civil partnership. However, there is little protection for the vulnerable cohabitant.

The Law Commission published a consultation paper 'Cohabitation: The Financial Consequences of Relationship Breakdown' (Consultation Paper No. 179) which proposed law reform to provide financial relief for cohabitants with children and, possibly, for those who have lived together for over a minimum period of time. Such relief would be subject to proof of economic advantage or disadvantage as a result of the relationship. The government has chosen not to progress this proposal saying that it wishes to review the effect of the Scottish Cohabitation Act once it has been in force for a while.

Until there is such reform, in the absence of an enforceable cohabitation contract, cohabitants must rely on an array of statutes, some of which are very old and based on trust law, when they separate or one dies without making a will.

There are still a number of myths around – like the myth that there is such a thing as a 'common law marriage', which has not been possible since 1753; or the myth that if you live together for say six months or two years you will automatically be entitled to a share of your partner's property on separation. Lawyers need to take every opportunity to advise those in this situation of how vulnerable they are, what measures can be taken to protect themselves and the implications of marriage whilst keeping the often short-term nature of cohabitation in perspective.

This chapter will look at three different situations: first, when a couple is just setting up home together and the protective measures which can be taken; secondly, when a couple is separating and the remedies available for resolving disputes; and thirdly, what happens when one partner dies.

10.2 PUTTING PROPERTY INTO JOINT NAMES

10.2.1 Advising

As a solicitor, although you may not do any conveyancing yourself, you will still need to know what the conveyancer should do so that you can talk to your conveyancing colleagues about their approach and so that you know what to look for in the deeds or conveyancing file on a separation.

The conveyancer should clarify who the client is. A couple may make an appointment using the same surname but may not be married.

The conveyancer should keep attendance notes or confirm the advice given and the instructions received by letter. This does not always happen but it is important in order to avoid potential negligence claims. The conveyancer should be crystal clear with any explanations, limiting the use of legal jargon and taking particular care when explaining joint tenancies and tenancies in common.

The conveyancer should find out as much information as possible about the parties' circumstances:

- How is the money being provided? In what proportions? Is there a mortgage?
- Have they been married before? If so, has there been a clean break?
- Are there any children from previous relationships?

In *Taylor & Harmon* v. *Warners* (unreported, 1987) the solicitor was found negligent because he knew the background of one of the clients and was aware that she had children. Although he explained the legal difference between a joint tenancy and a tenancy in common he did not explain the effect of a joint tenancy – that it would disinherit her children.

The conveyancer should consider whether the parties should have separate legal advice. A solicitor must not continue to act where there is a conflict or potential conflict of interest and this is quite likely if the parties are contributing different amounts or where one party has children from a previous relationship. If solicitors believe that a client is giving instructions as a result of duress or undue influence, they should either see the client alone to satisfy themselves that the instructions are freely given or refuse to act.

When their circumstances have been clarified, the clients will have to be asked to decide, with the benefit of legal advice, how to hold the legal and beneficial title. The legal title is always held as joint tenants. The beneficial title can be held as joint tenants or as tenants in common.

10.2.2 Tenancies in common

It is possible to hold the beneficial title as tenants in common in fixed percentages; for example, the parties hold in the proportions in which they contributed to the purchase price or they agree to hold in equal shares. The advantage is that at all times their shares are easily calculable, but the disadvantage is that this does not take account of changing circumstances. It is possible to have a supplemental declaration of trust but once the arrangement is completed the parties rarely revisit it.

One alternative is to hold as tenants in common in flexible or floating shares, where the shares are not calculated until sale and then take account of every contribution made. The advantage is that this does take account of changing circumstances but the parties will have to keep meticulous records of every contribution they make and have it agreed with their partners to avoid any dispute.

Another alternative is to preserve the benefit of the initial investment, for example:

- one may pay a large part of the deposit and wish to preserve that initial investment;
- one may have been the original owner of the property and wish to preserve the value of the equity;
- one may have been a council house tenant who has bought the property from the council at a substantial discount and wishes to preserve that benefit;
- one may have inherited a property and sold it to a member of the family at less than market value who wishes to preserve that benefit.

Solicitors may be asked to draw up an agreement preventing an incoming partner from ever acquiring any interest in a property. In this situation, the incoming partner could be giving up valuable rights and so must have independent legal advice. Lack of legal advice, unequal bargaining power or fraud could vitiate such an agreement and it would be necessary to satisfy the court that the agreement represented the true intentions of the parties.

The conveyancer should point out that if the parties marry and then divorce, the court will decide how the property is dealt with in accordance with the criteria set down in MCA 1973, s.25 irrespective of how they have expressed their beneficial interests.

10.2.3   Drafting

It is important expressly to declare the beneficial interests. If a conveyance simply says '. . . to A and B as joint tenants' it will be possible to override the assumption that the parties hold the beneficial interests as joint tenants in equal shares by providing evidence that they were to hold in different shares.

It used to be thought that severing any joint tenancy would produce two equal shares. That view was criticised in *Goodman* v. *Gallant* [1986] 2 WLR 236 where the court held that if the beneficial interests are expressly defined in

181

a conveyance as being held as joint tenants the severance will produce two equal shares but if there is no express declaration, then severance will produce two shares but they will not necessarily be equal.

In *Kinch* v. *Ballard* [1999] Fam Law 738 notice of severance was sent to the joint owner's address. He was taken ill so the sender had second thoughts, retrieved it and destroyed it but the court held that under the Law of Property Act 1925, s.196(3) notice is sufficiently served if it is left at the last known address even if the addressee does not actually receive it. The sender's change of mind was irrelevant.

10.2.4 Standard Land Registry transfer

The transfer form used to cause a lot of problems because it did not ask for the beneficial interests to be expressly declared. It simply asked whether the survivor could give a valid receipt.

In *Harwood* v. *Harwood* [1991] 2 FLR 274 the husband was in business with a third party. The business paid a large part of the deposit and for improvements to the property bought in the couple's joint names with the survivor giving valid receipt. The wife argued that it must mean that they held in equal shares. The husband argued that they held the legal estate on trust for the partnership. The Court of Appeal agreed with him, saying:

> the form of declaration inserted in the transfer, though entirely consistent with the existence of a beneficial joint tenancy, was no less consistent with the husband and wife holding the property as trustees for a single third party.

Huntingford v. *Hobbs* [1992] Fam Law 437 concerned an unmarried couple where the woman contributed the proceeds of sale of the house she retained from her divorce settlement and the man assumed liability for the mortgage. The transfer form said the survivor could give a valid receipt. The woman said *Harwood* v. *Harwood* was distinguishable on its facts because in that case there was a possibility that a third party might have a beneficial interest in the property. The court held:

> that was a distinction without any material difference. For the purpose of deciding whether or not the declaration in the transfer constituted a declaration of trust, the meaning of the words used was alone material. Extrinsic evidence as to the presence or absence of third parties was neither relevant nor admissible for the purpose of determining the answer to that question.

The standard Land Registry transfer form was altered in 1997 and now provides that the parties hold on trust for themselves as joint tenants or as tenants in common and, if they are to hold as tenants in common in anything other than equal shares, what those shares are. Solicitors may still be consulted by a client who bought a property before the forms changed, in which case it is important to remember that registration of a restriction will mean a tenancy in common but if the beneficial interests have not been expressly defined there is room for argument.

In *Stack* v. *Dowden* [2007] UKHL 17 the parties purchased in 1993, there was no discussion about the shares and the transfer said the survivor could give a valid receipt. The parties did not understand what that meant. The court held that in cases where there was no declaration of trust of the beneficial interests the starting point was that equity followed the law. The burden of proof was on the person wanting to show that the beneficial ownership was different from the legal ownership. The court had to ascertain the parties' actual common intention regarding their respective shares in the light of the whole course of dealing between them. Differing views were expressed by their Lordships on what evidence would be taken into account but they decided that this was an unusual case justifying a finding that the parties intended to hold the beneficial interest in unequal shares because the parties had largely maintained their financial independence.

10.2.5   Trusts of Land and Appointment of Trustees Act 1996, section 15

If an application has to be made under TLATA 1996 the court has to consider the purpose of the trust. It can be helpful to set out in the declaration of trust the purpose for which the property is held as this could avoid expensive argument.

10.3   COHABITATION CONTRACTS

10.3.1   Introduction

Back in 1979 the Law Commission said that 'it might be appropriate to reform the law governing contracts between couples living together'. Despite a Private Members Bill in 1991 and, more recently, Lord Lester's Bill in the House of Lords which provided for cohabitants to opt out of the proposed legislation, no progress has been made on this. Cohabitants wishing to enter into a private agreement must rely on the principles of contract law for enforcement. In *Sutton* v. *Mishcon de Reya and Gawor & Co.* [2004] 1 FLR 837 Hart J made it clear that a cohabitation contract is valid and enforceable so long as the parties manifest an intention to create legal relations, there is no reference to payment for sexual services and no uncertainty, duress, undue influence or misrepresentation.

10.3.2   Functions

Cohabitation contracts may be useful in a number of situations, for example:

* couples living together as husband and wife who are not free to marry or where one does not (or both do not) wish to marry;

- couples of the same sex living together who are not free to enter into a civil partnership or where one does not (or both do not) wish to do so;
- families where an older relative is living with a younger relative and has provided money for a 'granny annex' or for a large property for them to share; and
- friends and relatives deciding to buy property together, perhaps because they cannot afford to buy alone and so they decide to pool their resources.

Framework on break up

Married couples are covered by MCA 1973 and registered civil partners are covered by CPA 2004 if the relationship comes to an end. Unmarried couples and unregistered civil partners are not and so to avoid being faced with lengthy costly court proceedings, they need to provide their own framework.

Record of intentions

If upon break up there is a dispute, the court may have to decide what the intentions of the parties were at the time. Once the relationship has broken down it can be very difficult to determine what those intentions were because each party will remember those intentions to suit their own case. Recording them at the time can avoid this problem.

Providing certainty

Discussing the terms to be included in a cohabitation contract can help to provide certainty to both parties during the relationship so that they know where they stand. A lot of relationships break down because couples do not talk openly about things. They may make assumptions and the uncertainty or misunderstandings can fester and grow and spoil a relationship.

Focusing minds

Again, discussing the terms to be included can help the parties to focus on the implications of what they are doing and the potential problems. If they pool resources or buy items together (perhaps on credit) how easy will it be to separate things out if the relationship ends?

10.3.3 Validity and enforceability

Most people want to know if cohabitation contracts are enforceable and without any statutory policy we are dependent on basic principles of contract law.

Are they legal?

At one time, the courts refused to enforce cohabitation contracts on the ground that they were illegal by reason of sexual immorality (*Fender* v. *Mildmay* [1938] AC 1). However, a number of cases in the 1970s reduced the effect of that bar, e.g. *Cooke* v. *Head* [1972] 1 WLR 518; *Eves* v. *Eves* [1975] 1 WLR 1338; *Tanner* v. *Tanner* [1975] 1 WLR 1346; *Horrocks* v. *Forray* [1976] 1 WLR 230.

Major contract law and family law academics and academic publications, such as Professor Atiyah, *Cheshire, Fifoot & Furmston's Law of Contract*, *Anson's Law of Contract*, Treitel, *The Law of Contract*, *Bromley's Family Law* and *Cretney's Family Law* all support the view that sexual immorality is now less likely to be a bar.

Recommendation R(88)3 of EC Council of Ministers says that member states should not preclude cohabitation contracts dealing with property and money on the ground that the parties are not married to each other.

So all in all, it is unlikely that the court would invoke the sexual immorality bar unless the arrangements explicitly involved payment solely in return for sexual services.

Is there an intention to create legal relations?

There is always a question in family or quasi-family relationships whether the parties intend to create a legally binding contract. Bromley points out that a contract between cohabitants is less likely to fail on this ground than a contract between a married couple because contract is the only way they can give legal effect to their relationship.

The more general and less precise the language the more difficult it is to infer the intention to create legal relations. In *Layton* v. *Martin* [1986] 2 FLR 227 the man wrote to the woman offering her financial security during his life and on his death but this was found to be too vague. The inference is that if one uses precise language, preferably in a recital in a formal written contract, the question will not arise.

Is there any consideration?

The consideration could be money changing hands or one person acting to his or her detriment, so it will depend on the circumstances of the case. It would be sensible to prepare cohabitation contracts as deeds so as to avoid this problem.

Have the parties had the benefit of independent legal advice?

If not, there is a chance that one party could try to argue subsequently that he or she was subject to undue influence or duress and that the contract should be set aside. It would be sensible to record in a recital to a written contract that the parties had had, or at least, had been advised to have, independent legal advice.

Has there been full and frank disclosure?

There could be a question over enforceability if full disclosure is not given. Again one party could argue that he or she would not have entered into the agreement if he or she had known the full extent of the other party's financial position. A summary of each party's financial position could be annexed to the contract so that it is clear on what basis the agreement was entered into.

What are the implications on marriage or civil partnership registration?

Upon divorce or dissolution of a civil partnership the court will apply the criteria set down in MCA 1973, s.25 or CPA 2004, Sched.5, Part 5. It might consider the contents of a cohabitation contract, but the court will have the final say in each case.

10.3.4 Contents of contract

Property

The contract could set out how the parties are to hold the beneficial interests in the property. It could deal with the shares in which major repairs would be paid for and what effect one party reducing capital outstanding on mortgage, paying for improvements or making non-monetary contributions would have on the size of their shares. It could also deal with what would happen if one party was unable to pay towards the mortgage or if there was a negative equity on sale.

Outgoings

The contract could provide that the household bills are to be paid in equal shares or percentages or that one person will pay them all. Some couples organise their finances so that one pays the mortgage and the other pays the bills, and they may want to make it clear that this is just a convenient financial arrangement and is not to affect their shares in the property.

Maintenance

There is no legal obligation to maintain but there is no reason why couples should not agree for the payment of maintenance. In *Horrocks* v. *Forray* [1976] 1 WLR 230 (a case about contractual licences) Scarman LJ said:

There is certainly nothing contrary to public policy in the parents coming to an agreement which they intend to be binding in law, for the maintenance of the child and the mother.

Contents

So far as items brought to the relationship are concerned it can be helpful to make it clear, perhaps by attaching lists as schedules to the contract, who has brought what with them at the beginning so as to avoid arguments on the breakdown of the relationship.

Once the parties are together, it will depend on whether they are pooling resources or keeping their finances separate. If pooling resources and buying items from joint monies they will have to decide who would take what item on separation.

Items bought on credit

Often items are bought on joint credit, and upon break up one wants to keep the item but the other does not see why he or she should continue to pay for it. The parties rarely appreciate the niceties of joint and several liability. Alternatively, the item may have been bought in one partner's sole name but the other wants to keep it. Credit agreements cannot normally be assigned. The contract can record how they will deal with division of such items and responsibility for payment, and provide for one to indemnify the other against any claims by the finance company. This will not affect their position vis-à-vis the finance company but helps to focus the parties' minds on what they are doing.

Car

The registration document may be in one person's name although the other partner paid for the vehicle, or it may be that the loan for the car is in one name but the other person uses it all the time and pays for it. Again finance agreements cannot normally be assigned but the contract could provide for how the parties would deal with this.

Credit cards

Credit cards are often used for a multitude of purchases, e.g. food, petrol, family holidays, and so it is important for couples to agree on how liability is to be borne between them.

Family loans

A large number of young couples receive loans from one or other parent to help them, but almost invariably no record is kept of any agreement about repayments. It would be sensible for the couple to acknowledge at least to each other (even if there is no formal agreement with the parent) whether they are jointly responsible for repayments or not and what would happen on separation.

Other assets

If the couple has joint bank or building society accounts check how they regard the ownership of those accounts. Banks often freeze the account if there is any dispute, which can cause cash flow problems, so it is important to agree and record the agreement in the contract or by letter to the bank or building society. If there are other assets such as caravans, boats or shares it would be sensible to record their agreement on ownership.

Children

If taking maternity (or paternity) leave or giving up work to look after the children is going to affect one party's ability to contribute to the mortgage or other outgoings, the couple should plan for this and agree on what should happen. If one party has a liability to maintain a child or children from a previous relationship, it would be sensible to establish whether this should come out of the joint account or from the parent alone. Talking about these issues can help to avoid problems.

Disputes

The parties can agree that any disputes would be referred to mediation or collaborative lawyers.

Events giving rise to termination

The contract should set out the events which would give rise to termination such as the death of either party, the marriage of the parties to each other, one giving notice in writing to the other, or the parties mutually agreeing that the relationship is over.

Provisions taking effect on termination

THE HOUSE

If either party wants to stay in the property, that person could agree to be given a set period of time to buy the other out. If they both want to stay, first option could be given to the person with care of the children or to the original owner. If that person then cannot raise the necessary funds, the other person could be given a set period of time to buy the other out. If no preference is given or exercised and both want to stay, the first to provide evidence that the necessary funds are available could buy the other out. If all else fails, the property would be sold and the proceeds divided in accordance with their beneficial shares.

It would be sensible to say what would happen if they could not agree on the value of shares, e.g. they would accept the valuation of a valuer appointed by the President of the Royal Institution of Chartered Surveyors.

MORTGAGE AND OUTGOINGS

The contract should provide for who would be responsible for paying the mortgage until transfer or sale and who would be responsible for the outgoings.

CONTENTS AND OTHER ASSETS

The contract should provide for how the contents and joint accounts and other assets are to be dealt with.

DEBTS

Termination of joint credit cards or other finance agreements should be agreed as should the ongoing responsibility for payment of any loans from family.

COSTS

The contract could set out who is responsible for the costs of preparing it.

For useful precedents see Resolution cohabitation precedents (available from Resolution central office – see **Appendix 2** for address).

10.4   OTHER PROTECTIVE MEASURES

10.4.1   Wills

It is particularly important for cohabitants to make wills because they have no entitlement to inherit under the intestacy rules. Contrast the cost and uncertainty of making an application to court with the simplicity and certainty of inheriting under a will.

Even matters such as burial or cremation can become an issue if there is no will. The family of the deceased may be less likely to go along with the wishes of a cohabitant than those of a spouse and this can result in distressing disputes about the place and manner of the funeral. It is helpful to record the testator's wishes.

Personal and household items do not automatically pass to the survivor as they do between spouses and registered civil partners and the family of the deceased may dispute ownership. Each partner could make an outright gift of all the personal and household items to the other so as to avoid such problems.

10.4.2   Life insurance and pensions

Life insurance is useful to cover at least the mortgage and large debts so that if the survivor has a share of the proceeds of sale it will be a reasonable sum. It is also useful for providing for other obligations such as those to children by a previous marriage.

Cohabitants do not have an insurable interest in each other's lives unless there is a direct financial risk. It may be necessary to take out own life cover and assign the benefit of the policy.

Dependants' benefits under company pension schemes do not automatically form part of the deceased's estate and may not be payable to surviving cohabitants. However, it is possible to complete a nomination form notifying the trustees of one's wishes in the event of death.

10.4.3   Parental responsibility agreements

Since 1 December 2003 unmarried fathers automatically acquire parental responsibility upon registering as father on the birth certificate. Unmarried fathers of children registered before that date do not have parental responsibility whether or not their details are on the birth certificate unless they enter into a parental responsibility agreement with the mother or acquire it by court order. Unmarried fathers of children registered after that date whose details are not on the birth certificate do not have parental responsibility unless they enter into an agreement with the mother or acquire it by court order. The agreement must be in the prescribed form recording the child's name, the names of the child's parents and must be signed and witnessed by a Justice of the Peace, justices' clerk or officer of the court. The agreement only takes effect once it is filed with the Principal Registry and then a copy is sent to each parent.

10.5   OCCUPATION RIGHTS

If the relationship has come to an end in an acrimonious way, it may be necessary to consider an application for an occupation order under FLA 1996 – see **Chapter 9**.

10.5.1 Licences

Bare licences

The most likely situation with cohabitants is that the owner has simply given the other party permission to stay. This is a bare licence which is a personal right giving no interest in the land. It can be revoked at any time upon giving reasonable notice to quit. What is reasonable depends on the circumstances of each case, e.g. whether there are children or the housing conditions in the area, but 28 days is the benchmark.

Contractual licences

These are less common with cohabitants because of the need to show an intention to create legal relations and consideration. Again they give a personal right but no interest in the land. Contractual licences can only be revoked in accordance with the terms of the contract and the licensor is liable in damages if the revocation is in breach. If no period of notice has been agreed, reasonable notice must be given and, again, 28 days is the benchmark.

In *Tanner* v. *Tanner* [1975] 1 WLR 1346 the claimant had given consideration for the agreement to live in the property by giving up the tenancy of a rent controlled flat and so the court found there was a contractual licence. In *Horrocks* v. *Forray* [1976] 1 WLR 230 there was no consideration.

Possession proceedings

If the other party remains in occupation after expiry of the notice to quit, it may be necessary to consider negotiation, mediation or collaborative law. If that is not successful possession proceedings could be instigated. However, solicitors should be alert to the possibility of the other party defending on the basis that they should be granted an equitable licence (see below), or that they have a beneficial interest in the property (see **10.6**).

Equitable licences

The court can grant a party an equitable licence if satisfied that all the elements of proprietary estoppel have been established, i.e. the legal owner has induced the claimant to believe that the claimant has a right to occupy, the claimant has acted to his or her detriment relying on that assurance and it would be unconscionable to deny the claimant the right to stay (see *Greasley* v. *Cooke* [1980] 3 All ER 710).

10.5.2 Tenancies

If the client has been sharing rented accommodation with the other party, it will be necessary to establish what type of tenancy agreement is involved, whether it is in joint names, private or public sector and whether there is any statutory protection. If both cohabitants sign a tenancy agreement or move in under a joint oral tenancy they each have an equal right to occupy. Neither can exclude the other except by court order.

Rent Act tenancies

If the tenancy agreement does not contain a covenant against assignment or allows assignment with the landlord's consent, then assignment should be possible. The assignment should be in writing and in the form of a deed.

If one joint tenant wants to leave and avoid any ongoing liability to pay rent, the tenancy will have to be terminated. One joint tenant cannot surrender a joint tenancy but can serve a notice to quit, without the knowledge or consent of the other tenant, if the tenancy is a periodic one.

If the tenancy is a Rent Act protected tenancy, the notice will convert the contractual tenancy into a statutory tenancy provided the remaining tenant is in occupation. So the remaining tenant will be able to stay unless there is some ground for possession. The notice must comply with the requirements of the Protection from Eviction Act 1977, s.5 by giving a minimum of four weeks' notice.

Where the tenancy is in one person's sole name and that person wants to leave, vacant possession must be given as part of any agreement to surrender. If the tenancy is already statutory, the departure of the tenant will bring the right of occupation to an end and the remaining cohabitant will be in a vulnerable position.

Assured tenancies

The Housing Act 1985, s.15 implies a term into every periodic tenancy that there must be no assignment without the landlord's consent. Usually the provision that such consent cannot be unreasonably withheld is excluded so that no reason has to be given for refusing. A fixed-term tenancy can be assigned provided there is nothing in the agreement to the contrary. Notice to quit by one joint tenant will terminate the joint tenancy and provide a ground for possession against all the occupants. A fixed-term assured shorthold tenancy cannot be brought to an end before the term has expired unless there is a break clause.

Secure tenancies

The Housing Act 1985, s.91 limits the assignment of periodic or fixed-term tenancies to exchanges with another secure tenant with the written consent of his landlord or to a person who could succeed to the tenancy had the tenant died immediately before the assignment. Introductory tenancies cannot be assigned except by a court order or to a person who would be qualified to succeed on the death of the tenant (Housing Act 1996, s.134).

In *Hammersmith and Fulham LBC* v. *Monk* [1991] 3 WLR 1144 the local authority granted a Mrs Powell and a Mr Monk a weekly tenancy and they cohabited. The agreement provided that the tenancy was terminable on four weeks' notice. The relationship came to an end and Mrs Powell left. The local authority agreed to rehouse her if she terminated the tenancy. She did this without Mr Monk's knowledge. The local authority then notified Mr Monk and started possession proceedings. The House of Lords held:

> In the absence of any express term in the tenancy to the contrary, one joint tenant can unilaterally terminate a periodic joint tenancy by giving proper notice to quit.

Protecting rights of occupation

If it seems that a tenant is going to serve a notice to quit, solicitors could consider applying for an injunction to preserve the client's position as occupier. An injunction to prevent the disposal of property or an interest in property is possible under the inherent jurisdiction of the court but there must be a cause of action such as an application for transfer of tenancy under FLA 1996, s.53.

Family Law Act 1996, section 53 transfer of tenancies

The Family Law Act 1996, s.53 incorporates Sched.7 to that Act, and Part 1 of Sched.7 states that if one cohabitant is entitled, in his or her own right, or jointly with the other cohabitant, to occupy a house in which they lived together as husband and wife (amended to include same-sex couples) by virtue of a relevant tenancy, and the cohabitants cease to live together, the court can make a Part II order. The court shall have regard to all the circumstances including:

- the circumstances in which the tenancy was created;
- the matters mentioned in s.33(6)(a)–(c) and s.36(6)(e)–(h) (see **Chapter 9**); and
- the suitability of the parties as tenants.

Under Part II if the tenancy was a protected tenancy under the Rent Act 1977, a secure tenancy under the Housing Act 1985 or an assured tenancy or assured agricultural occupancy under Part I of the Housing Act 1988, the court may order that with effect from a date specified in the order the interest of one cohabitant be transferred and vested in the other cohabitant. If the tenancy was a statutory tenancy within the meaning of the Rent Act 1977 or the Rent (Agriculture) Act 1976 the court may order that with effect from a date to be specified in the order one cohabitant is to cease to be entitled to occupy and the other cohabitant is to be deemed to be the tenant.

Part III of Sched.7 provides that the court may order the cohabitant to whom the tenancy was transferred to pay compensation to the other cohabitant. Payment can be deferred until a specific date or event or paid by instalments if immediate payment would cause the transferee financial hardship. The court shall have regard to all the circumstances including:

- the financial loss that would otherwise be suffered by the transferor as a result of the order;
- the financial needs and resources of the parties; and
- the financial obligations of the parties.

If the court makes a Part II order it may direct that both cohabitants are to be jointly and severally liable to discharge any or all of the liabilities and obligations in respect of the house which have fallen due before the date of transfer and may direct either cohabitant to indemnify the other.

The landlord will have to be given the opportunity of being heard.

Children Act 1989, Schedule 1

It is possible to seek a transfer of a tenancy for the benefit of a child of the relationship but this will depend on the assignability of the tenancy. The welfare of the child is not paramount and the criteria set out in Children Act 1989, Sched.1, para.4 would apply. There is no formal way of doing it, so serving a copy of the order on the landlord should be enough.

10.6 ESTABLISHING AN INTEREST IN PROPERTY OR SEEKING AN ORDER FOR SALE

10.6.1 Practice and procedure

If the beneficial interests are not expressly declared or the property is in the other party's sole name, the solicitor will need to consider applying for a declaration of beneficial interests under TLATA 1996, s.14. The solicitor may also wish to seek an order for sale in order to realise the client's interest. The solicitor should consider severing any joint tenancy and registering a Form A restriction at the Land Registry using Form RX1.

Such applications are governed by CPR 1998 so be aware of the court's overriding objective and case management powers set out in CPR 1998, Part 1.

There is no specific pre-action protocol for TLATA 1996 applications under CPR 1998 but solicitors must comply with the Protocols Practice Direction. For useful guidance on procedure see *H* v. *M* (Property: Beneficial Interest) [1992] 1 FLR 229.

The Law Society's *Family Law Protocol* Part 5, para.5.5.4 states that solicitors should:

(1) Send an initial letter . . . setting out the following information in concise form:

    (a) a clear summary of uncontroversial facts;
    (b) the main allegations of fact, including where appropriate a summary of what was said by the parties at the time;
    (c) an indication of the exact financial claim;
    (d) indications as to witnesses and a summary of their evidence; and
    (e) disclosure of relevant documents.

    . . .

(2) If possible and appropriate, refrain from issuing proceedings for six weeks, during which time full disclosure should be given and negotiations commenced.
(3) Give a preliminary reply within two weeks of receiving the initial letter of claim.
(4) Give a full reply within four weeks of receiving the letter of claim.

The Protocol goes on to say that as preparation of the initial letter will involve a substantial financial commitment from clients, solicitors must give proper advice to ensure that the claim is framed in the correct way. Solicitors must explain that failure to comply with the Protocol may lead to an order for indemnity costs and other financial penalties. Solicitors must consider whether proceedings should be issued to protect assets. Finally, if matters are settled, the outcome should be recorded in a deed.

The county court has unlimited jurisdiction. Application can be made under CPR 1998, Part 7 where there is a dispute on the facts, or CPR 1998, Part 8 where there is no dispute on the facts but the court is asked to say how the law applies to those facts. It is possible to issue under CPR 1998, Part 8 if, immediately before CPR 1998 came in, it would have been possible to issue using an originating summons or application. As CPR 1998, Part 8 does not involve drafting a pleading solicitors may prefer to issue by claim form under CPR 1998, Part 8. In the county court, the application has to be to the court for the district in which the defendant lives or carries on business or the district in which the property is situated. In the High Court, application can be made to any District Registry. The claim form must state that CPR 1998, Part 8 applies, the remedy the claimant is seeking and the legal basis for the claim and that the claim is brought under TLATA 1996. The claim form should be accompanied by a witness statement setting out the facts on which the claimant relies in support of the application for a declaration of beneficial interests or order for sale having regard to the principles on which the court will decide that application set out at **10.6.2**.

The defendant must return the acknowledgement of service within 14 days of service saying whether the defendant intends to contest the claim. The district judge will then give directions or fix a case management conference at which directions will be given. Further directions may include the filing of statements of case, disclosure, filing witness statements and valuation evidence. If the claim is disputed, the judge may direct that it proceed under CPR 1998, Part 7 which will involve the preparation of pleadings. The case will be allocated to the multi-track and case management directions will be given leading to the hearing.

The court should usually be encouraged to use its extensive case management powers to list the matter for a case management conference (CMC) which should take a form similar to a financial dispute resolution (FDR) hearing. Note that there are material differences between an FDR and a CMC so care needs to be taken to ensure appropriate directions are given. Suggested appropriate directions might be:

1. The case be listed for a directions appointment for the purpose of assessing the parties' positions and for the purpose of discussion and negotiation.
2. The parties to serve signed witness statements in advance.
3. The parties to file:

    (a) details of all offers;
    (b) position statements;
    (c) an agreed statement of issues.

4. The parties shall personally attend.
5. The appointment be conducted on a without prejudice basis.
6. In the event that the proceedings are not settled at the hearing the district judge hearing the appointment should not make any order or directions other than by consent, except to direct that the case shall be listed for a case management conference.
7. A realistic time estimate should be allowed (at least an hour) and the parties ordered to arrive at court an hour before to narrow issues.

10.6.2 The principles on which court will determine beneficial interests

Implied trusts

A deed is required for a conveyance or creation of a legal estate in land (Law of Property Act 1925, s.52). Under s.53(1) no other interest in land can be created or transferred except in writing but s.53(2) exempts the creation of resulting implied or constructive trusts.

A resulting trust is where the court assumes the parties had a particular intention because of direct financial contributions to the purchase of a property, e.g. the property is conveyed into the name of one person yet paid for by another. The owner will be deemed to hold the property on trust for the person who paid and if they both paid part, then in proportion to their respective contributions. This is always subject to evidence to the contrary so if there is evidence that they intended to hold the beneficial interests in proportions different from those suggested by their contributions there will be an implied trust based on their common intention and not a resulting trust (see *Drake* v. *Whipp* [1996] 1 FLR 826). It is unlikely there would be any presumption of advancement, i.e. a presumption that the person providing the purchase money intended it as a gift, to displace the resulting trust. If the evidence establishes that the money was paid as a loan or as a gift then the non-owner will not acquire a beneficial interest. Tenants' discounts will qualify as contributions as will liability for the mortgage (see *Huntingford* v. *Hobbs* [1993] 1 FLR 736) but not lending one's name for a mortgage (see *Carlton* v. *Goodman* [2002] 2 FLR 259). Quantum is directly proportionate to the size of the contributions.

A constructive trust is where the court is satisfied that the parties had a common intention that they would share the beneficial interests and the claimant has acted to his or her detriment or that intention can be inferred from the claimant's direct financial contributions. See *Lloyds Bank* v. *Rosset* [1990] 1 All ER 1111 where the property was bought in the husband's sole name and the wife supervised the builders and did some decorating. There was no evidence of an agreement and the monetary value of the wife's actions was considered to be too trifling to amount to direct financial contributions.

Indirect contributions are only relevant if there is evidence of an agreement or understanding between the parties. In *Gissing* v. *Gissing* [1970] 2 All ER 780 payment of some of the household expenses was evidence of a common intention where the wife went out to work immediately after the property was purchased in order to be able to pay towards the household expenses.

Construction work can raise an inference of a common intention that the beneficial interest is to be shared. The amount of work must be substantial and must be referable to the acquisition of the property. In *Cooke* v. *Head* [1972] 1 WLR 518 and *Eves* v. *Eves* [1975] 1 WLR 1338 the court was willing to find a common intention from the amount of work done, such as knocking down walls with sledge hammers, hod carrying, etc.

Looking after the family is not enough to infer a common intention. In *Burns* v. *Burns* [1984] Ch 317 a couple lived together for 19 years. The woman had looked after the family and had bought some fixtures and fittings and done some decorating but only towards the end of the relationship was she able to go out to work and put money towards the housekeeping. The court was unhappy that it could not give her anything but said it was a matter for Parliament.

In *Oxley* v. *Hiscock* [2004] EWCA Civ 546 the Court of Appeal found that there had been a discussion about whose name should go on the title in the context of a possible claim by the claimant's husband and that was only explicable on the basis that they both intended they should each have a beneficial share. That made it a constructive trust case and, as there was no evidence of any discussion about the size of the shares (per Chadwick LJ):

> each is entitled to that share which the court considers fair having regard to the whole course of dealing between them and that includes the arrangements they make from time to time to meet the mortgage, council tax, utilities, repairs, insurance and housekeeping.

In *Stack* v. *Dowden* [2007] UKHL 17 the court dismissed the appeal by the cohabitee against the Court of Appeal's valuation of beneficial interest in a property bought jointly with his partner, and held that 'the state of the legal title will determine the right starting point'. The burden of proof was on the person wanting to show that the beneficial ownership was different from the legal ownership. See **10.2.4** for further discussion of this case.

Quantifying the shares

The size of the shares will depend on whether or not there was an expressed common intention about them. If so, that would be conclusive. If not, then since *Midland Bank* v. *Cooke* [1995] 2 FLR 915 shares will be quantified not just on the basis of direct contributions but taking into account all conduct. Diane Wragg in an article 'Constructive trusts and the unmarried couple' [1996] Fam Law 298 said:

> establishing a beneficial interest remains a narrow and difficult gateway through which a cohabitee must pass. Having done so however, she now enters a liberal green pasture in which she may de facto enjoy rights akin to MCA s24.

See also *Oxley* v. *Hiscock* above. The problem is that this makes it very difficult to advise on quantum. In *Cox* v. *Jones* [2004] EWHC 1486 (Ch), a case involving two barristers and a flat in London and a country property both in the defendant's name, the claimant was awarded 100 per cent of the flat, on the basis that the defendant had bought it as her nominee and held on constructive trust for her absolutely, and 25 per cent of the country property on the basis that this was fair taking into account the whole course of dealings between them and the defendant's considerable contributions.

Valuing the shares

The value is ascertained at the date the property is actually sold or the interest is purchased by the other person – not at the date of separation. If one person is left in possession and pays the whole of the mortgage instalments until the property is sold or the trust terminates, that person is given credit for the mortgage instalments of capital paid on behalf of the other party and no credit is given for payments of mortgage interest as this is regarded as equivalent to an occupation rent.

Proprietary estoppel

There are four requirements. The claimant must show:

1. That he has incurred expenditure or otherwise prejudiced himself or acted to his detriment.

2. That such action took place in the belief either that he had a sufficient interest in the property or that he would obtain such an interest.
3. That the belief was encouraged by the owner of the land or someone acting on his behalf.
4. That there is no bar to the equity.

The court must be able to find that it would be unconscionable for a party to be permitted to deny that which, knowingly or unknowingly, he has allowed or encouraged another to assume to his detriment.

In *Layton* v. *Martin* [1986] 2 FLR 227 Mrs Layton failed to establish proprietary estoppel because the court found she had not relied on any representation made to her. In *Pascoe* v. *Turner* [1979] 1 WLR 431 Mr Pascoe left and said 'The house is yours and everything in it'. He never conveyed it to her but assuming it was hers, Ms Turner spent money on repairs and improvements. He claimed possession and she argued the property was held on trust for her or she had a licence to occupy. The Court of Appeal invoked the doctrine of proprietary estoppel and ordered him to transfer the property outright to her. So acting to one's detriment can be carrying out improvements to a property which are more than normal repairs and maintenance.

Wayling v. *Jones* [1995] 2 FLR 1029 involved two men, one of whom was chauffeur and companion to the other, a businessman. The businessman died without making a will. The claimant said he had been promised a share in a hotel business and relying on that promise he had worked for very little pay. The court held that he was entitled to an interest in the business on the basis of proprietary estoppel. Balcombe LJ said that once the promises have been established, the burden of proof shifts to the defendant to prove that the claimant did not rely on those promises.

In *Lissimore* v. *Downing* [2003] 2 FLR 308 the claimant relied on representations such as 'I bet you never thought all this would be yours in a million years', that she was to be 'the Lady of the Manor' and that she 'would not want for anything'. The court held that any representations must relate to some specific property, that she had not relied on them anyway and that she had not suffered any real detriment because of the benefits she had received.

10.6.3 Criteria for making orders under the Trusts of Land and Appointment of Trustees Act 1996, section 14

Section 5 of TLATA 1996 sets out, in no order of preference, what the court has to consider on applications under s.14:

- the intention of person(s) who created the trust;
- the purposes for which property subject to trust is held;
- the welfare of any minor who occupies or might reasonably be expected to occupy any land subject to the trust as his or her home; and
- the interest of any secured creditor of any beneficiary.

In addition, s.13, which deals with applications to exclude or restrict a beneficiary's right to occupy, says the court must have regard to the circumstances and wishes of the beneficiary and in the case of any other application, the court must have regard to the circumstances and wishes of any beneficiary of full age entitled to an interest in possession or, where there is a dispute, the majority of the beneficiaries according to the value of their combined interest.

There is no duty to sell so the court can take a more flexible approach. This could allow more reference to issues like those considered under MCA 1973, s.25, such as financial needs and obligations, age, physical situation, perhaps even conduct.

In *TSB* v. *Marshall, Marshall & Rodgers* [1998] 2 FLR 769 the court granted the bank the order for sale saying the principles established under the Law of Property Act 1925, s.30 still apply and that TLATA 1996, s.14 allows the court as a matter of discretion to do what is just and fair in all the circumstances. Where there is a conflict between a chargee's interests and those of an innocent spouse the interests of a chargee will prevail except where there are exceptional circumstances. Where a collateral purpose of the trust is still subsisting, i.e. providing a home for children, the court should not defeat that purpose by ordering a sale. However, the interests of children are only relevant up to the age of majority.

In *Mortgage Corporation* v. *Shaire & Others* [2000] 1 FLR 973 Mr Justice Neuberger said that s.15 gives the court a wider discretion when deciding whether to order a sale at the suit of a chargee, as the interests of a chargee are just one of the four specified factors to be taken into account with no more importance to be given to that than the interests of children living in the house. The increased flexibility is to the benefit of families and to the detriment of banks and other chargees.

In *Bank of Ireland Home Mortgages Ltd* v. *Bell & Bell* [2001] 2 FLR 809 the Court of Appeal said that although s.15 has given the court scope to change its previous practice of considering that the creditor's interest should prevail over that of the spouse's family save in exceptional circumstances, nevertheless a powerful consideration was whether a creditor was receiving proper recompense for being kept out of his money of which payment was due.

In *Holman* v. *Howes* [2005] EWHC 2824 (Ch), in 1979 the parties both contributed to the purchase of a property which was transferred into the defendant's sole name. From 1980 to 2005 the claimant lived there and she claimed that the defendant had promised that the house was hers. He said it was a joint venture and was held on trust in equal shares and sought an order for sale. The court found there was a constructive trust in equal shares and weighing up the factors in TLATA 1996, s.15 it would not be right to order an immediate sale as that would be running plainly counter to the intentions of the parties when they purchased, as well as the purpose for which the property was currently held.

Lawrence v. *Bertram* [2004] Fam Law 323 confirmed that the court has jurisdiction to order one of the parties to purchase the other party's interest.

10.7 APPLICATIONS UNDER THE MARRIED WOMEN'S PROPERTY ACT 1882

Cohabitants who were engaged to be married could apply under the Married Women's Property Act 1882, s.17 within three years of the termination of the engagement. The court can only declare or enforce proprietary rights in property which they possessed or controlled at the time of the application. The court can order sale, return or restitution or payment of lump sum equivalent to the value of an assessed interest. Application is made to the local county court or the Family Division using Form M23 with an affidavit in support. The Family Proceedings Rules 1991 apply. The court will apply the trust principles set out above and if there is a question of selling a property it will consider whether the house is providing a home for any relevant children. Similar provisions apply for those who agreed to register a civil partnership – see CPA 2004, ss.74 and 65–67.

10.8 CLAIMS RELATING TO PERSONAL PROPERTY

For an express declaration of trust of land there must be some writing signed by the person able to declare such a trust (Law of Property Act 1925, s.53(1)(b)), i.e. letters, notes, memos, etc.

There is no such requirement in respect of personal chattels and *Rowe* v. *Prance* [1999] 2 FLR 787 concerned a yacht. The claimant, a widow, had had a relationship with the defendant, a married man of considerable private means, for 14 years. In 1993 he told her he would divorce his wife and use the proceeds of sale of the former marital home to buy a yacht for them to share and sail around the world. He duly bought a yacht for £172,000 and she gave up her rented house and put her furniture into store to base herself on the yacht. In June 1996 he wrote saying they would soon be together and the yacht would be theirs to share so that they could live together. He frequently referred to the yacht as 'ours'. Towards the end of 1996 the claimant lost patience and demanded her share of the yacht's value. The judge found that the defendant had expressly declared himself as trustee for her and him by all the times he had talked of 'our' boat. Applying the maxim 'equality is equity' it was appropriate to quantify the shares as equal. He also found that the facts established a common intention and detriment (giving up the tenancy and putting the furniture in store) to support a constructive trust but he felt unable to quantify the shares on that basis and preferred to base his decision on the express declaration of trust.

An isolated loose conversation will not give rise to a declaration of trust but the repetition of words by the owner, especially in the context of an intimate relationship, will be enough. The claimant becomes beneficially entitled irrespective of any contribution (financial or otherwise) towards the acquisition or subsequent improvement of the property. Oral declarations of trust are confined to claims for personal property.

10.9 CHILDREN

See the discussion of claims under the Children Act 1989, Sched.1 in **Chapter 7**.

See also parental responsibility orders and changing the child's name, discussed in **Chapter 8**.

10.10 RESOLVING CLAIMS ON DEATH

10.10.1 Introduction

Cohabitants are particularly vulnerable to problems if one of them dies, because if the deceased has not left a will then the survivor has no right to inherit on intestacy. If there are no relatives to inherit under the intestacy rules the estate will pass to the Crown. In this case the Treasury Solicitor has a discretion to make an ex gratia payment to anyone dependent on the deceased at the date of death and other persons for whom the intestate might reasonably have been expected to make provision (Administration of Estates Act 1925, s.461(1)(vi)).

It is sometimes found that even though the deceased has left a will, it is unsatisfactory from the survivor's point of view – perhaps because it was made before the start of the relationship. Cohabitation does not revoke an existing will in the way that marriage does.

10.10.2 Remedies

Donatio mortis causa

In *Sen* v. *Headley* [1991] 2 All ER 636 a man who was dying told his former cohabitant the house was hers, the deeds were in a steel box and the keys were in her handbag. He died three days later and the Court of Appeal held that the three conditions for gift of land by delivery of title deeds were satisfied:

- the gift was made in contemplation of death;
- the gift was made on condition that it was to be absolute and perfected only on the testator's death, being revocable until death; and
- there had been delivery of the subject matter or title to it.

Actions against the estate

APPLICATION FOR DECLARATION OF BENEFICIAL INTEREST

The survivor can apply for a declaration that he or she is entitled to a share or a greater share of property to which the survivor contributed financially on the same trust principles as set out above. See *Hyett* v. *Stanley* [2003] EWCA Civ 942 where the claimant agreed to become jointly liable on the mortgage and the owner believed this gave her a right to the property. The court found there was a common intention and she had acted to her detriment by assuming the risk. The executors failed to establish that her interest was not absolute or that she would have no interest after his death.

APPLICATION UNDER THE INHERITANCE (PROVISION FOR FAMILY AND DEPENDANTS) ACT 1975

Cohabitants have the right to apply under the Inheritance (Provision for Family and Dependants) Act 1975 (see *Re Estate of John Watson (Deceased)* [1999] 1 FLR 878, *Gully* v. *Dix* [2004] 1 FLR 918, *Churchill* v. *Roach* [2004] 2 FLR 989 and *Jessop* v. *Jessop* 1992] 1 FLR 591). See also **Chapter 5** for further discussion of this point.

POST-DEATH VARIATION

The survivor might be able to reach agreement with the beneficiaries of the deceased's estate to vary the devolution under the will or intestacy by a deed of variation or disclaimer. If done within two years of the date of death it is effective for inheritance tax purposes in that the transfer will be treated as made at the date of death and not by the beneficiaries. The agreement of all the beneficiaries will be needed, and if there are children under 18, the consent of the court will be needed.

TENANCIES

If the tenancy was in joint names it transfers automatically to the survivor. If it was in the deceased's sole name, then if it was a public sector tenancy the crucial question is whether the survivor lived with the deceased in the house in question throughout the period of 12 months before death as husband and wife or civil partners. If there are competing claims the local authority will decide.

If it was a private sector tenancy a surviving cohabitant may be treated as a spouse of the deceased tenant provided that the relationship was of sufficient stability and permanence to constitute living together as husband and wife or civil partners. The cohabitant must have been living with the deceased immediately before death but there is no set time period (Housing Act 1988, s.39 and Sched.4, Part 1).

In *Fitzpatrick* v. *Sterling Housing Association* [1999] 2 FLR 1027 Mr Fitzpatrick had lived with a Mr Thompson (who was the tenant), in a homosexual relationship from 1976 until Mr Thompson's death in 1994. Mr Fizpatrick had applied to take over the tenancy but the housing association refused on the basis that same-sex partners cannot be construed as living as husband and wife. The House of Lords held that a same-sex partner of a tenant is capable of being a member of the tenant's family so as to succeed to the tenancy on death. In *Ghaidan* v. *Mendoza* [2004] UKHL 30 the European Court found that that interpretation infringed Art.14 of the European Convention on Human Rights. There is no justification for the difference in treatment of unmarried heterosexual couples and unmarried homosexual couples. Same-sex partners are to be treated as living as if they were husband and wife.

Social security

Some people think that if they have been treated as a family unit for benefit purposes, the survivor will be entitled to a widow's pension when a cohabitant dies. However, they will not. The survivor would only be entitled if that person had been receiving a widow's pension before beginning to live with the deceased cohabitant. The widow's pension would have been suspended and the survivor can apply for it to be reinstated. In other respects the survivor will revert to being treated as a single person for all benefit purposes.

Company pensions

Lump sum payments and dependant's pensions under company pension schemes do not automatically form part of the deceased's estate. Payments are usually made at the discretion of the trustees of the pension fund within the limits of the fund rules. In practice, the trustees will often pay some or all of the available monies to a surviving cohabitant depending on the other obligations of the deceased.

HM Revenue and Customs has expanded its definition of what constitutes 'dependant' to include an unmarried partner of the same or opposite sex who is financially interdependent on the employee, e.g. where the partner relied on a second income to maintain a standard of living. More pension schemes are introducing survivor's benefits for dependent cohabitants.

CHAPTER 11

Civil partnership

Andrea Woelke

11.1 INTRODUCTION

The Civil Partnership Act 2004 (CPA 2004) received Royal Assent just before the end of the parliamentary year on 18 November 2004. It came into force on 5 December 2005 and the first registration took place that day under the special procedure for terminally ill people. Since then a number of issues have become clearer while others have been obscured and CPA 2004 has been supplemented by other legislation to further equality for lesbians, gay men and same-sex couples. This chapter will provide an outline of the law. For a more in-depth analysis, the reader is referred to Andrea Woelke, *Civil Partnership* (Law Society Publishing, 2006).

From 2005 to the end of 2008, 31,287 civil partnerships were registered in England and Wales. In addition there are couples living in this jurisdiction who have registered a relationship or married abroad in 'overseas relationships', which count as civil partnerships in the UK (see **11.3.2**). The number of new registrations has been decreasing since 2006, which is unsurprising as the first two years no doubt saw couples registering who had been living together for a long time and been waiting for the change in the law. Male civil partnership registrations outnumber female registrations by 58 per cent to 42 per cent, while in 2008 civil partnership dissolutions between women outnumber those between men by 63 per cent to 37 per cent (**www.statistics.gov.uk/statbase/Product.asp?vlnk=14675**).

Since the important parts of CPA 2004 mirror existing and familiar legislation for marriage, this chapter will not describe the Act in detail, but will instead concentrate on the major important points and highlight practical issues.

11.2 WHAT IS CIVIL PARTNERSHIP?

11.2.1 Definition

In everyday speech most people refer to 'marriage' and 'wedding', as do newspaper and magazine articles. From a legal point of view of course, the law is entirely separate, but is civil partnership really gay marriage in all but name? Civil partnership is defined in s.1 of the Act:

(1) A civil partnership is a relationship between two people of the same sex ('civil partners') –

    (a) which is formed when they register as civil partners of each other –

        (i) in England or Wales (under Part 2),

        (ii) in Scotland (under Part 3),

        (iii) in Northern Ireland (under Part 4), or

        (iv) outside the United Kingdom under an Order in Council made under Chapter 1 of Part 5 (registration at British consulates etc. or by armed forces personnel), or

    (b) which they are treated under Chapter 2 of Part 5 as having formed (at the time determined under that Chapter) by virtue of having registered an overseas relationship.

(2) Subsection (1) is subject to the provisions of this Act under or by virtue of which a civil partnership is void.

(3) A civil partnership ends only on death, dissolution or annulment.

Civil partnership is therefore a purely statutory creation which did not exist before the 2004 Act. Indeed the Grand Chamber of the European Court of Human Rights in *Burden and Burden* v. *UK* (Application no. 13378/05) [2007] 1 FCR 69 at 62–66 also makes the distinction through the registration process. Marriage by contrast is a concept in common law, defined by Lord Penzance in *Hyde* v. *Hyde* (1866) LR 1 P&D 130 at 133, as 'the voluntary union for life of one man and one woman to the exclusion of all others'.

Civil partnership is equally voluntary, monogamous (only two people can be in a civil partnership, not more) and there is a duty to maintain each other (the financial consequences mirror Part 2 of the Matrimonial Causes Act 1973 and other relevant legislation). In other aspects there are significant differences:

1. Although a civil partnership is contracted for an indeterminate duration and a dissolution procedure is necessary if it breaks down, which mirrors divorce, there is nothing to indicate that civil partnership is *for life*. The significance of this is that prenuptial agreements entered into by engaged couples of the opposite sex are still void for being against public policy if they make provision for the situation following a possible divorce, because this is said to undermine the concept of marriage being for life (*MacLeod* v. *MacLeod* [2008] UKPC 64, at 36). No such bar should, at least in theory, exist for pre-registration agreements for civil partners and they should therefore be looked at in the same light as separation or maintenance agreements (see *MacLeod* v. *MacLeod* [2008] UKPC 64).

2. There is no duty to cohabit. While a separation order mirrors judicial separation and arguably there is no longer a duty to cohabit in marriage, this may have consequences when looking at contested behaviour petitions or same-sex couples who are not civil partners (see below).

3. Sex is not part of the package. Although non-consensual sex within marriage can now amount to rape (*R* v. *R (Rape: Marital Exemption)* [1991] 4 All ER 481), a marriage can still be voidable for non-consummation or if the respondent suffered from venereal disease (Matrimonial Causes Act 1973 (MCA 1973), s.12). No equivalent of these grounds for nullity exists for civil partnership; nor is there an equivalent to the fact of 'adultery' in divorce for civil partnership dissolutions (see below at **11.4**).

It is important to bear in mind these conceptual differences.

11.2.2 Living together as if they were civil partners

Interestingly enough, while the House of Lords (in the context of Rent Act protected tenancies) in *Ghaidan* v. *Godin-Mendoza* [2004] 2 FLR 600 effectively extended the concept of living together as husband and wife to same-sex cohabitants, CPA 2004 updated numerous legislative provisions to define same-sex cohabitants as couples who are 'living together as if they were civil partners'. While there is a common law concept of marriage and a couple may fulfil all the criteria bar the actual wedding ceremony, civil partnership is wholly defined through the registration process, so that once that is missing, there seems nothing else left. In essence that makes this definition meaningless from the start. In *Baynes* v. *Hedger* [2008] EWHC 1587 (Ch) Mrs Margot Baynes made an application under s.1(1B) of the Inheritance (Provision for Family and Dependants) Act 1975 against the estate of the late Mary Spencer Watson. Other family members made competing claims. It seems that known only to a small inner circle of people the two had had an intimate relationship from the 1950s onwards, although they had maintained two households throughout and in the final years before Mary's death, Margot had suffered from Alzheimer's and they had not seen much of each other as Margot became housebound. While the claim may have failed on the question of cohabitation in the first place, Lewison J first of all doubted that s.1(1B) applied to periods before CPA 2004 came into force; but this was obiter, as he then found that he would apply the Act to same-sex couples anyway following *Ghaidan* v. *Godin-Mendoza* (at 122). He goes on to express (also obiter, at 150) that:

> the true nature of the relationship between Margot and Mary was unacknowledged and, indeed, hidden. Some close members of the family knew of their relationship and other people guessed. But there were many people, including people who knew Mary well, who had no inkling. It seems to me that it [is] not possible to establish that two persons have lived together as civil partners unless their relationship as a couple is an acknowledged one. Indeed it may be that an acknowledgement of the relationship is also an ingredient of living in the same household, which would only reinforce my conclusion that Mary and Margot did not live in the same household during the last two years of Mary's life.

Looking at the leading cases from social security law (*Crake* v. *Supplementary Benefits Commission* (1981) 2 FLR 264, *Kimber* v. *Kimber* [2000] 1 FLR 383) on the issue of living together as husband and wife, it is clear that public presentation as a couple is only one of the criteria and no single criterion is decisive. To make public presentation a crucial condition for same-sex couples is failing to acknowledge the very real and continuing discrimination against lesbians and gay men. This discrimination exists even now and was even stronger in the 1950s when Mary Spencer Watson and Margot Baynes started their relationship. The decision cannot therefore be used as guidance and the obiter remarks must be wrong. Whether the court would have found against 'living together' if one partner of a heterosexual couple had gone into a care home is something we will not know.

11.2.3   Residual discrimination

Several issues which had been left untouched by CPA 2004, notably discrimination on grounds of sexuality or civil partnership status in the provision of goods and services and paternity after assisted fertilisation and surrogacy have now been remedied by statute in the Equality Act (Sexual Orientation) Regulations 2007, SI 2007/1263 and the Human Fertilisation and Embryology Act 2008 (HFEA 2008) respectively, see also below at **11.6.3**).

The following issues remain outstanding as real and important discriminatory areas:

1. Practical difficulties: Since civil partnership is legally not marriage, civil partners may find a myriad of small annoying inconveniences in daily life. For instance, while opposite-sex couples can get married in the Palace of Westminster, same-sex couples cannot register a civil partnership there (as pointed out by Prime Minister Gordon Brown on 20 October 2009 at the Speaker's Conference). Those whose civil partnerships have broken down may need to travel quite some distance to find a court where they can dissolve it: there are only nine in England and there is only Cardiff County Court for the whole of Wales (FPR 1991, rule 1.2, see below at **11.4.2**). There is no indication that this will change any time soon (not least as even the staff at those courts still make mistakes with the forms).

2. Pensions: Public sector final salary pension schemes will pay dependants' pensions only for years of service after 1988, while certainly for most male members of these pension schemes their widows will receive pensions for a number of years before then. This can make a real difference to some surviving civil partners and means some will have to rely on state benefits when they would receive a full living pension if they were widows instead. Private sector pension schemes only have to provide dependants' benefits for years of service after 5 December 2005 even though most schemes probably do not discriminate. As a practical point, this should be

queried and asked for specifically as part of the pension disclosure on a dissolution. The basic state pension is hideously complicated, treats men and women unequally and (although this may not be a logical consequence to everyone) treats civil partners differently from married couples. National insurance contribution credits are, however, available for former civil partners as they are on divorce. However, some people, in particular women who were married before, may want to wait until after their retirement before registering a civil partnership as they will lose their former husband's or civil partner's NIC credits otherwise. For a detailed treatment of pensions for civil partners see Andrea Woelke, *Civil Partnership* (Law Society Publishing, 2006), chapter 9.

3. Civil partnership: The label is different, which makes it easy to recognise and distinguish (and discriminate against) same-sex couples. It will make them stick out in many areas in everyday life from the notice of the civil partnership registration, which is displayed at the local register office, to the myriad of forms one has to complete. They may, for example, have to out themselves as gay or lesbian on official and private forms. This probably prevents a lot of couples from registering because they do not want their sexuality to be part of numerous official government registers and private records. Only the introduction of same-sex marriage would be able to abolish this discrimination. Although the label may not matter to some, it does to others (*Wilkinson* v. *Kitzinger* [2006] EWHC 2022 (Fam), [2007] 1 FLR 295). Marriage is open to same-sex couples in Norway, Sweden, the Netherlands, Belgium, Spain, Canada, South Africa and several US states.

4. Internationally the concept of UK civil partnership has no status in itself. While some countries which have introduced similar same-sex registered partnership regimes or same-sex marriage may or may not have specific legislation to recognise UK civil partnership, this is not automatic. By way of example, although France has a form of partnership registration (the Pacs, which confers the same inheritance tax exemptions and rates as marriage) some English surviving civil partners living in France have lost their French home to French inheritance tax because France did not recognise civil partnership. Legislation has now been passed to remedy this, as a result of diplomatic lobbying from the UK government. Fortunately, this will be retrospective. By contrast, marriage is a universal concept and so at the very least same-sex marriage would be recognised fully in all other countries where this is recognised (and some others, e.g. Israel).

5. Future legal change may of course be made to give married couples privileges, rights and tax advantages, which will not be extended to civil partners, although this seems unlikely for the foreseeable future.

Civil partnership is a political creation by the Labour government at the beginning of the twenty-first century to almost achieve equality for same-sex couples without any real danger of having to force the hand of backbenchers or peers who may have opposed opening up marriage by the repeal of MCA 1973, s.11(c). As a result there is residual discrimination as well as conceptual difficulties, which may create interesting work for practitioners.

11.3 REGISTRATION

11.3.1 Registration under English law

Civil partnership registration for England and Wales is dealt with in Chapter 1 of Part 2 of CPA 2004 and follows civil marriage. There are corresponding provisions for prohibited degrees of relationship (s.3 and Part 1 of Sched.1), eligibility and consent (ss.3 and 4), parental consent for people between 16 and 18 (s.4, not required in Scotland, mirroring Scots law on marriage), housebound and detained and seriously ill people (ss.18, 19 and 21–27), prohibition of registration on religious premises or religious services during the registration (s.6 and s.2(5)) and notice to be given and the registration to be publicised 15 days in advance (ss.8, 10 and 11).

The main differences are that there is no alternative provision for religious registration in any form at all. While a couple become husband and wife through the exchange of vows, and the marriage certificate is only evidence of the solemnisation of the marriage, same-sex couples only become civil partners once both of them have signed the civil partnership document (s.2(1)). Although there is no prescribed form of words, most registrars will provide a suggested wording if the partners choose to have it. Whilst there is no offence corresponding to bigamy, it is an offence to give false information on the notice (s.80, maximum penalty seven years' imprisonment or a fine or both).

Of course registration in Scotland (which has no residence requirement so may be a way to avoid a public notice being displayed at the town hall where the parties live) and Northern Ireland is equally recognised.

Chapter 1 of Part 5 makes provision for registration in overseas diplomatic missions (s.210) if one of the partners is a UK national. Only a handful of diplomatic missions permit this as it is subject to a veto by the host country. The registration counts as if it took place in the part of the UK with which the couple has the closest connection, which may be difficult, but important, for example, for questions of validity as well as in countries such as South Africa, where the law governing the marriage or civil partnership seems to be the law of the place of marriage. Armed forces personnel abroad can register on ships and on land (s.211). Both these paths to registration are regulated by Order (the Civil Partnership (Registration Abroad and Certificates) Order 2005, SI 2005/2761 and the Civil Partnership (Armed Forces) Order 2005, SI 2005/3188 respectively).

11.3.2 Overseas relationships

Other countries have approached the issue of recognising same-sex relationships in different ways. Denmark started with registered partnership in a statute which simply defined it as being the same as marriage with some exceptions (adoption, religious weddings) and many other countries followed; others have introduced a registration scheme, sometimes for both opposite-sex and same-sex couples, with rights lesser to those of married couples (e.g. Germany, France) and more recently several countries have opened up marriage to same-sex couples. CPA 2004 aims to recognise a wide range of overseas relationships. Such relationships are thereby deemed to be civil partnerships so the English law of civil partnership applies, whether the couple registered in a regime which is almost only symbolic or whether they got married in a church. For some, this may provide obligations to each other that go far beyond what they ever agreed to; others feel short-changed (*Wilkinson* v. *Kitzinger* [2006] EWHC 2022 (Fam), [2007] 1 FLR 295).

Chapter 2 of Part 5 of the Act provides that overseas relationships are recognised if they either fulfil the 'general conditions' listed in s.214 or are listed in Sched.20 (s.213). In either case they must be (s.212(1)):

(b) ... registered ... with a responsible authority in a country or territory outside the United Kingdom, by two people –

    (i) who under the relevant law are of the same sex at the time when they do so, and

    (ii) neither of whom is already a civil partner or lawfully married.

This means that those regimes open to same-sex and opposite-sex couples (e.g. French Pacs) are recognised, but only for same-sex couples.

Schedule 20 was really meant to make this easier so that the government could check and approve foreign regimes. It was updated before the Act came into force (the Civil Partnership Act 2004 (Overseas Relationships and Consequential, etc. Amendments) Order 2005, SI 2005/3129 and the Civil Partnership Act 2004 (Overseas Relationships) Order 2005, SI 2005/3135) but it has not been updated in the last four years despite many countries having introduced same-sex partnership registration and marriage. The 'general conditions' are (s.214):

(a) that the relationship is of indeterminate duration;

(b) that the parties are treated as a couple generally or for specified purposes or as married; and

(c) that the process of entering into the relationship requires a registration with the authorities in that jurisdiction.

This means that any legal form of recognised relationship which can be entered into by merely living together for a certain time is not recognised, even if a couple can also enter it through registration (for example the 'stable unions' in Catalonia can be entered into either by registration or automatically after a period of cohabitation). For the practitioner, issues may arise as to whether someone who registered in a foreign regime is actually in a civil partnership as a result or not. If he or she is, they cannot register a civil partnership again here before dissolving the existing civil partnership. If an immigration issue is involved, time may be tight. If one of the partners is a British citizen, they may apply to the UK consulate, embassy or high commission under art.15 of the Civil Partnership (Registration Abroad and Certificates) Order 2005, SI 2005/2761 for transmission of the foreign certificate to the relevant Registrar General in the UK to prove that the foreign registration counts as a civil partnership here. For regimes not listed in Sched.20, evidence on the foreign law may need to be obtained. Since the foreign regime, if recognised, is recognised as a civil partnership, it can be dissolved here provided the English courts have jurisdiction (see below). There are special provisions for any couples who registered abroad before 5 December 2005, which would go beyond the scope of this chapter and reference should be made to Andrea Woelke, *Civil Partnership* (Law Society Publishing, 2006) chapter 8.

11.4   DISSOLUTION, SEPARATION ORDERS AND NULLITY

11.4.1   The law

The law on dissolution of civil partnership mirrors the law on divorce with a few differences. The law is set out in Chapter 2 of Part 2 of the Act and the practitioner will realise that the sections are arranged differently from those in the MCA 1973. The ground for dissolution is irretrievable breakdown of the civil partnership, which has to be shown by one of four facts. These correspond to the facts in MCA 1973, s.1 except adultery, namely (s.44(5)):

(a)   behaviour;
(b)   two years' separation and consent;
(c)   five years' separation; and
(d)   desertion.

The definition of adultery as extra*marital* makes it impossible to transpose it to civil partnership dissolution. Sexual infidelity can of course form the basis of a behaviour petition and nothing more needs to be said than the particulars one would usually find in an adultery petition. Although CPA 2004 talks about applications, FPR 1991 talk about petitions, being in line with the (outdated and eventually to be overhauled) procedural law on divorce. However, instead of decrees nisi and absolute, there are conditional and final orders respectively.

There is also provision for separation orders mirroring judicial separation (s.56), which seems to make little sense since there is no duty to cohabit, but which may in extreme circumstances allow the court to make capital financial provision in the first year of the civil partnership. The grounds for civil partnerships to be void mirror those for void marriages (s.49), while those making a civil partnership voidable mirror those in MCA 1973, s.12 except for non-consummation and venereal disease (s.12(a), (b) and (e)). There are provisions for presumption of death orders and declarations of validity.

11.4.2 Practical points

The petition looks very much the same as a divorce petition and needs to be accompanied by a certificate of reconciliation and a statement of arrangements for children. The requirement to confirm appropriate jurisdiction is not based on the EU Brussels II regulation (see below at **11.5**). Where in a divorce petition the petitioner needs to say whether the wife has had any other children, in civil partnership petitions, this must be stated for both parties. Note also that you can only apply to a limited number of courts, namely Birmingham, Brighton, Bristol, Cardiff, Chester, Exeter, Leeds, the Principal Registry in London, Manchester and Newcastle (Civil Courts (Amendment) Order 2005, SI 2005/2923).

11.5 JURISDICTION AND RECOGNITION OF OVERSEAS DISSOLUTION

11.5.1 Jurisdiction

The Civil Partnership (Jurisdiction and Recognition of Judgments) Regulations 2005, SI 2005/3334 made under powers conferred by s.219 make rules for jurisdiction following Brussels II (EU Regulation 2001/2003). These are supplemented by CPA 2004, s.221. Accordingly the English court has jurisdiction for dissolution, separation and nullity of civil partnerships as follows:

1. If any of the following grounds based on habitual residence apply (SI 2005/3334, reg.4):

   (a) both civil partners are habitually resident in England and Wales;
   (b) both civil partners were last habitually resident in England and Wales and one of the civil partners continues to reside there;
   (c) the respondent is habitually resident in England and Wales;
   (d) the petitioner is habitually resident in England and Wales and has resided there for at least one year immediately preceding the presentation of the petition; or
   (e) the petitioner is domiciled and habitually resident in England and Wales and has resided there for at least six months immediately preceding the presentation of the petition.

2. If the English courts do not have jurisdiction on the above grounds (neither Scots nor Northern Irish courts have jurisdiction under identical provisions), English courts have jurisdiction if:

   • one civil partner is domiciled in England and Wales (s.221(1)(b)); or

213

- the civil partnership was registered in England and Wales and 'it appears to the court to be in the interests of justice to assume jurisdiction' (s.221(1)(c)).

This last ground is novel and does not exist for divorce. It is important in such cases to set out the law when applying for directions for trial and include the details of why it is in the interests of justice for the court to assume jurisdiction. This could, for instance, be the case if the parties now live in a country where they cannot dissolve the civil partnership (e.g. two Italians who register as civil partners while living in England and both have moved back to Italy), or if the foreign court would need to have expert legal evidence on English civil partnership law to great cost and delay for the parties.

11.5.2   Recognition of overseas dissolutions

Sections 233 to 238 make provision for recognition of overseas dissolutions similar to Part II of the Family Law Act 1996. Both dissolutions 'by means of proceedings' and 'otherwise than by means of proceedings' will be recognised provided some minimum standards have been met. In individual cases practitioners will need to work their way through the legislation. A handy flow chart is provided in chapter 8 of Andrea Woelke, *Civil Partnership* (Law Society Publishing, 2006). The problem is that overseas relationships which are recognised as civil partnerships are so variously different that the rules for divorce do not do justice to them. It is, for example, possible in some countries for the registered partnership there to be dissolved by one party marrying someone of the opposite sex. This would not necessarily be recognised, however, under English law, leaving the two former partners in a limbo situation where according to English law they are civil partners while according to the foreign law one of them is married to someone else. This could result in a number of problems, including for example inheritance, let alone that the people involved are unlikely to realise their predicament.

The other potential problem is that dissolutions from other EU countries are recognised without questioning on which basis the court there had jurisdiction. This works for divorce because Brussels II binds other EU countries in the same way as it binds the courts here. Hence a divorce pronounced, for instance, by a Polish court is based on one of the Brussels II grounds of jurisdiction. There is no such rule for civil partnership dissolutions and conceivably an EU member state could become a 'quickie divorce' tourist destination for English couples as a result.

11.6   CHILDREN

Many same-sex couples are bringing up children. Many children growing up in same-sex couple families are the children of previous opposite-sex relationships

A growing number of same-sex couples choose to have their own children and there are various ways such couples go about having a family. For children from previous relationships issues may arise (and continue to do so in practice) about residence on separation. The Children Act 1989 was of course largely neutral and flexible from the start and residence orders can be made in favour of any-one, including the non-biological mother of the children in a same-sex couple (*Re G (Children) (FC)* [2006] UKHL 43). CPA 2004 was largely silent on the matter of children, but the Adoption and Children Act 2002 and HFEA 2008 have brought about change going a long way towards equality for the children and parents in families headed by same-sex couples.

11.6.1   Adoption

The Adoption and Children Act 2002 did not come into force until 30 December 2005, shortly after CPA 2004. Before this, only married couples and single people could adopt; since then civil partners and 'two people (whether of different sexes or the same sex) living as partners in an enduring family relationship' can also adopt (s.144(4)). So for the first time this allowed a child in England to have two mothers or two fathers. In addition step-parent adoption now no longer requires the biological parent to adopt their own child as it used to. This obviously makes it easier for a lot of same-sex couples to establish legal parentage of both parents for their children, although even in cases where the child was conceived through anonymous sperm donation at a UK licensed clinic and there is therefore no legal father, the scrutiny from social services is still as thorough as in cases where a child is adopted through an adoption agency. Of course in this situation an opposite-sex married cou-ple did not have to go through such a procedure because the husband was automatically the father of the child (Human Fertilisation and Embryology Act 1990, s.28(2)). Adoption is still the only option where children are brought into the relationship from a previous relationship and where HFEA 2008 does not make the partner a legal parent (see below).

11.6.2   Parental responsibility agreements

The Adoption and Children Act 2002 also introduced parental responsibility agreements for step-parents, including civil partners of one parent (Children Act 1989, s.4A). The form (PRA2) is similar to the one for unmarried fathers and can be downloaded from HM Courts Service's website (**www.hmcourts-service.gov.uk**). The explanation on the back of the form should make it easy for most people to deal with it without having to consult a solicitor. It is an easy, quick and cost-effective way for the civil partner of a parent to obtain parental responsibility and even in cases where the couple plan adoption (or surrogacy, see below), an agreement should be signed to ensure that the other parent has an immediate legal connection with the child. In cases where the

215

couple are not civil partners (or where the civil partnership has been dissolved) a joint (or shared) residence order would be the appropriate option (see *Re G (Children) (FC)* above and the lower courts' and previous decisions in this case). It is easy for the family practitioner to forget that parental responsibility is a concept of family law that simply determines issues while the child is a minor. It does not, however, make them children of the adult, which can of course be important for issues in later life, such as inheritance and succession rights. The only way to achieve a parent–child relationship where there is none by law is through adoption (or in surrogacy cases, parental order).

11.6.3   Fertility treatment, sperm donation etc.

For lesbians to conceive one option is to go to a fertility clinic. This is costly as most clinics still seem to require unsuccessful unprotected heterosexual intercourse before treating any woman on the NHS, which obviously is not (ordinarily) an option for a woman in a same-sex couple. Private arrangements between lesbians and (mainly) gay men therefore seem common in England although there do not seem to be reliable statistics on this. Some women seem to feel uncomfortable with not knowing who the sperm donor is; in the past others may have found that a clinic will not treat them. The Human Fertilisation and Embryology Act 1990 was focused on married couples and even provided that:

> A woman shall not be provided with treatment services [in a UK licensed fertility clinic] unless account has been taken of the welfare of any child who may be born as a result of the treatment (*including the need of that child for a father*), and of any other child who may be affected by the birth.
> (Human Fertilisation and Embryology Act 1990, s.13(5); emphasis added)

HFEA 2008 changed the law in this area and achieved equality for same-sex couples. Instead of the child's perceived need for a father the clinic now has to consider the child's need for 'supportive parenting' (HFEA 2008, s.14(2)(b)).

For deemed parentage the law provides as follows as of 6 April 2009:

If *a married woman or a woman in a civil partnership* has a child other than through intercourse (through the 'placing in her of the embryo or of the sperm and eggs or of her artificial insemination': HFEA 2008, ss.35 and 42), the husband or the civil partner of that woman is automatically the father or 'second parent' respectively of the child. The couple must be married or in a civil partnership at the time of conception (or rather the insemination, etc.). A later civil partnership registration does not remedy the situation (in the way an unmarried father can legitimate his children for example). Parentage here is not a presumption that could be rebutted through DNA testing, but a consequence of the law. The only exception is if the husband or civil partner did not consent, imaginable, for instance, in a case where the couple had separated and the husband or civil partner had no knowledge of the conception. This also therefore applies to cases of self-administered sperm donation. The information on the website of the Human Fertilisation and Embryology Authority is confusing here and it strongly recommends that everyone goes to a clinic. The wording of both ss.35 and 42 is, however, clear. At the time of writing, it is not clear how registrars will deal with the registration of the birth, although the General Register Office has assured the author that registrars will receive specialist training. (If clients do encounter problems, please feed this back to the author.)

If *a woman is not married or in a civil partnership*, only fertility treatment in a UK licensed clinic will provide automatic paternity for her partner (HFEA 2008, ss.36 and 43). If an opposite-sex or same-sex couple are treated together and sign the necessary forms, the woman's partner will be the father or the 'second parent' respectively of the child by operation of law. This does therefore not apply to treatment in clinics abroad and any DIY sperm donation. Lesbian couples who want to save money and go abroad for treatment (where it can be significantly cheaper) or want to arrange for a private donor without a clinic should therefore consider registering as civil partners before the conception.

In typical cases where a lesbian couple and a gay man agree to have children together without involving a UK licensed clinic, the new law reverses the legal situation entirely if the lesbian couple are civil partners at the time of conception. Previously (and if they are not civil partners), the man is legally the father of the child, can possibly enforce contact rights, but also runs the risk that he may have to pay maintenance through the CSA or the courts. By contrast if the lesbian couple are civil partners, and the intention is that the father has some involvement with the child, there is no legal basis for this and his position is at most comparable to that of a family friend or godfather. Whether this is the situation that is desired, depends on the people involved. However, contrary to the views of some potential clients there is no way to contract out of these rigid legal consequences and a child cannot have three or four parents, for instance. Residence orders and parental responsibility agreements can go some way to achieve what may be desired, but are not a satisfactory solution in most cases. In this last respect the law is possibly still lagging behind the real social situation of gay families in the UK in the twenty-first century.

In this context note, however, that in *Re B (Role of Biological Father)* [2008] 1 FLR 1015 (also *sub nom. TJ* v. *CV and S and BA*) in a case where the child was the biological child of one of the women in a same-sex couple and the brother of the other woman, the court ordered that the father's involvement should be limited to a minimum and compared the situation to that of a traditional nuclear family. Whether that was the intention is difficult to ascertain after the birth if the only evidence is the oral evidence from the parties. A written agreement, entered into before the conception, would therefore go a long way and have great evidential value for the parties should a dispute arise later on. Interestingly in this case the biological father claimed that he had had sexual intercourse with the mother while the mother denied this. The mother's partner had not been present during the insemination. Hedley J found that he did not have to decide on this question as it was irrelevant. However, if this situation arose now and the couple were civil partners at the time of conception, it would make all the difference whether intercourse took place or conception was by artificial insemination. It may be advisable to have a friend in the house who witnesses the handing over of the sample; although this may seem overkill, everything depends on it.

11.6.4 Surrogacy

Surrogacy is not illegal in England, although commercial surrogacy, i.e. taking part in negotiating a surrogacy arrangement for payment, is unlawful (see the detailed offences under the Surrogacy Arrangements Act 1985, s.2). As a result couples who have no other way of having children tend to go to the US, India, the Ukraine or similar countries and arrange commercial surrogacy there. Some agencies, especially in the US, target the UK gay market. If a child is born as a result of surrogacy, English law provides for a 'parental order' to be made, a form of fast-track adoption (Human Fertilisation and Embryology Act 1990, s.30). The main difference compared to adoption is that there is no requirement for a prior suitability assessment and the procedure is different. The consequences are the same and a new birth certificate is issued.

Until April 2010 only married couples may apply for a parental order. From April 2010 unmarried and same-sex couples and civil partners will also be able to apply (HFEA 2008, s.54). The application has to be made within six months from the birth. For couples other than married couples the law is retrospective, so that an application can be made within six months from April 2010 for an order even for older children. The time limit is short and cannot be extended under any circumstances. Therefore practitioners must ensure that the deadline is not missed. Parental order applications are subject to some stringent conditions and in many cases the payment made will be an issue (s.54(8)). Cases can be lengthy and costly. Family practitioners should also work closely together with immigration specialists. It would go beyond the remit of this chapter to elaborate on parental orders and in any possible case the practitioner should research this area of law further or refer to a specialist.

CHAPTER 12

Legal aid

Vicky Ling

12.1 INTRODUCTION

The number of family legal aid practices has suffered a marked decline from 4,500 in 2000 to 2,658 in 2008–09. Most family practitioners find that the remuneration is set at levels well below their private rates, and yet, in order to provide legal services to disadvantaged and vulnerable clients, they continue to do work funded under the scheme. This chapter provides an overview of the family scheme as at August 2009. It will probably be of most assistance to those who are not experienced legal aid practitioners, or to those returning after a career break.

However, all solicitors are under a professional duty to consider whether their client might be eligible for public funding (Solicitors' Code of Conduct 2007, rule 2.03). Eligibility can be checked using the LSC's calculator at **http://calculator.communitylegaladvice.org.uk/ecalc/questions.asp**.

12.1.1 Key information sources

Despite the LSC's declared attempts to simplify the legal aid scheme, it remains complex. All legal aid practices are required to have a copy of the LSC Manual, which is in three volumes: *Volume 1 – The Framework*, contains the legislation and regulations, as well as Specialist Quality Mark (see Quality Standards, below); *Volume 2 – Civil Contracting*, contains the Unified Contract standard terms and specification, costs assessment guidance and guidance on financial eligibility for some types of legal aid; *Volume 3 – The Funding Code*, sets out the applicable procedures and guidance as well as further guidance on financial eligibility and the standard wordings to be used under devolved powers (see below for more information). These documents are absolutely essential to any solicitor or caseworker providing publicly funded services. Unless they have ready access to them, fee earners are very likely to make mistakes which could cost their firms considerable sums of money.

The LSC website **www.legalservices.gov.uk** is a mine of useful information; but practitioners generally find it difficult to navigate. Some suggest that Google searches are more successful than the site's own search engine. Getting to grips with the website is essential as the LSC sends out much less in paper format and simply puts new information on to the site. Signing up for the LSC's newsletter, which emails updates, announcements and changes, is recommended. The newsletters provide a brief summary of the issue concerned, and links to further information. David Emmerson, Chair of Resolution's Legal Aid Committee, recommends Ling and Pugh, *Making Legal Aid Work* (Legal Action, 2009). He said 'This book is the most comprehensive guide to legal aid since the old fashioned *Legal Aid Handbook* . . . It is an essential reference book for all from the senior lawyer to the new paralegal.'

Resolution's Legal Aid Committee is heavily involved with the LSC when changes are proposed, to explain the likely impact of the LSC's reforms on both practitioners and their clients, and make positive suggestions for the benefit of all concerned with legal aid. Currently, the Committee is lobbying for public funding to be extended to cover collaborative law. Resolution provides a legal aid 'e-newsletter' and training to members. The Legal Aid Practitioners' Group is also a useful source of information, support and guidance.

12.1.2   The structure of legal aid

Legal aid is in general a means-tested benefit which provides free or low-cost legal services to people of limited means, (although some kinds of legal aid are available regardless of means or merits, see below). It is administered by the Legal Services Commission, which is an independent governmental agency sponsored by the Ministry of Justice. Services are delivered under contracts with the LSC by a network of solicitors in private practice, law centres, other charities such as Citizens Advice Bureaux, and a small number of commercial organisations. The overwhelming majority of contracts are for face-to-face services; but the Community Legal Advice telephone service, which includes family work, is growing in importance.

Expenditure on legal aid has regularly been the subject of reviews and reports, for example Lord Carter of Coles' review, which was completed in 2006. Historically, contracts were available to organisations as long as they met defined quality standards. Policy currently reflects his recommendations for a market-based approach, including competitive tendering. All civil and family contracts are due to come to an end in October 2010. The LSC is proposing that these will be tendered using selection criteria based on quality and service delivery. National price competitive tendering is not envisaged before 2013. It is not clear how organisations will enter the market between 2010 and 2013, although the LSC makes opportunities known through its website **www.legalservices.gov.uk/civil.asp** (Community Legal Service (CLS)).

12.1.3   Tenders

The LSC is endeavouring to allocate funding to geographical areas according to the likely need for publicly funded legal services, using a model devised by its research unit, known as 'indicative spend'. It is also developing fixed and graduated fee schemes in place of remuneration based on hourly rates (see below for more information). At the same time as these far-reaching reforms are being implemented, the budget for administering the scheme is being progressively reduced. It is fair to say that at times the LSC has struggled to deliver as planned, and this has caused disruption to the Commission and those it describes as its 'providers'.

12.2 GETTING A CONTRACT, QUALITY AND PERFORMANCE STANDARDS

12.2.1 Contracts from October 2010

The LSC intends that bids for contracts to start in October 2010 will be conducted online and this will be the first time that the LSC has used an online bidding process on such a large scale. England and Wales have been divided into 134 procurement areas, usually, but not invariably, aligned with top-tier local authority areas.

The first stage for bidding will be to register and complete a prequalification questionnaire. This will deal with basic standards that an organisation contracting with the LSC will have to meet, for example: professional standing with the Solicitors Regulation Authority; financial conduct, e.g. having up-to-date accounts, payments to HMRC for VAT and PAYE; compliance with key legislation, e.g. health and safety, equality and diversity, data protection legislation, insurance, etc. The second stage will require applicants to address the minimum requirements in the invitation to tender. These will cover some generic issues and some relevant to the category of law and/or the procurement area.

The element of competition will come into play if the bids submitted would require more 'new matter starts' (i.e. advice and assistance under Legal Help funding) than the LSC has available for the procurement area. The LSC will use selection criteria to choose between bids. The LSC states it will want to identify those organisations that are able to deliver the best services to clients, so it is likely that organisations already operating in a procurement area, with staff in place, would be preferred over those which would need to acquire offices and recruit personnel.

12.2.2 Specialist Quality Mark

Legal aid providers need to hold the Specialist Quality Mark (SQM), which is the LSC's organisational quality assurance standard. A firm needs to have standard operating procedures that are documented in an office manual, in order to apply. Applications can be submitted at the same time as a contract bid. Firms need to submit:

- Form QM1;
- SQM self-assessment checklist;
- supervisor self-declaration form;
- status enquiry forms; and
- a copy of the office manual.

The LSC will assess the documentation through a 'desk-top' audit at the LSC's offices and if it is satisfactory, a provisional Quality Mark will be granted to allow a successful firm to begin to operate under the contract. The LSC will later carry out an on-site audit, to ensure all the required procedures are in effective operation.

Information about how to apply for an SQM can be found on the LSC's website. The SQM is currently being updated, although changes are expected to be minor. Many requirements of the SQM are also found in Lexcel, which is the Law Society's accreditation scheme for its practice management standards. The LSC and the Law Society are working to ensure that the SQM and Lexcel are comparable, so that from 2010 Lexcel will be an acceptable alternative to the SQM.

12.2.3 Peer review

Peer review is the measure that the LSC uses to assess quality of advice. It has been developed over several years under the auspices of the Institute of Advanced Legal Studies. There are five possible scores: excellence (1), competence plus (2), threshold competence (3), below competence (4) and failure in performance (5). Threshold competence is the lowest acceptable level under the Unified Contract. At below competence level, the organisation is given six months to improve. If it does not achieve at least threshold competence at the next assessment, its contract is terminated. An organisation assessed at failure in performance has its contract terminated quickly because of the risk to clients. However, although the LSC originally intended that every legal aid practice would be reviewed every three years, this has not been possible, not least due to the cost of the process. The LSC says that in future assessments will be carried out according to a number of risk indicators, so it will be entirely possible to provide legal aid services without the quality of advice being assessed.

12.2.4 Key performance indicators

The LSC has included some 'key performance indicators' (KPIs) in its contracts. At the time of writing, there are no contract sanctions for failing to achieve a KPI. However, they are regarded as indicators of areas where performance needs explanation, and the firm's account manager or relationship manager may ask for an explanation of the reasons that a firm's or department's figures are 'out of profile'.

- Forty per cent of completed cases must have outcome codes that the LSC considers demonstrate a substantive benefit to clients.
- When exceptional cases are assessed (i.e. cases that escape the fixed or standard fees and are paid under hourly rates), the costs claimed must not be reduced by more than 10 per cent.
- The costs of licensed work cases must not be reduced by more than 10 per cent on assessment.
- Fixed fee margin – 20 per cent maximum. This KPI can only be met if the total cost of cases under fixed fees when calculated in minutes and items is at least 80 per cent of the appropriate fixed fees.
- Eighty-five per cent of the allocation of controlled work matter starts must be used.

It is very likely that achieving levels of KPI performance will be mandatory from 2010. All firms that have contracts with the LSC must have systems to monitor KPI performance and take corrective action where necessary.

12.3 HOW FAMILY LEGAL AID WORKS

12.3.1 Controlled work

Controlled work is granted by the solicitors according to rules under the Unified Contract. It is called 'controlled' because the LSC controls the number of matter starts which firms are allowed each year. The kinds of controlled work that are relevant to family practitioners are Legal Help (which developed from the old 'Green Form' scheme) and Family Help Lower (see below). Legal Help funds advice and assistance in relation to a specific matter, but does not cover issuing proceedings, advocacy, or the instruction of an advocate. Legal Help is also known as level 1 in the Family standard fees scheme and Family Help Lower is level 2.

The LSC wants to encourage clients to settle at the earliest opportunity, and has introduced incentives for both clients and their advisers to try and encourage this. In private family law, practitioners can claim settlement fees for cases that conclude at level 2 without the issue of proceedings (save to obtain a consent order in respect of finances).

12.3.2 Licensed work

Clients need a certificate, sometimes known as a full legal aid certificate or certificate of public funding to be represented in legal proceedings. This is called licensed work as the firm has a general licence to do such work, and numbers of matter starts are not limited. Certificates may be granted by the LSC, or, in urgent circumstances, granted under devolved powers by the firm.

The forms mentioned below can be downloaded from the LSC's website.

12.3.3 Controlled work procedures

The general rule is that the client must come to the adviser's office and sign the form personally (although there are exceptions, see below). The applicable form is the CW1. The assessment of means and client's details sections must be fully completed, and signed by the client, normally in the presence of someone from the firm, before legal work is started. The LSC has provided a useful eligibility calculator on its website at **www.legalservices.gov.uk/civil/guidance/ eligibility_calculator.asp**. This will carry out all the calculations required and provide a form ready for signing, as long as the 'print CW1' option is selected.

Exceptions

If there is a good reason, it is possible to:

- travel out of the office to visit a client (for example because they are detained);
- give telephone advice before the signature of the form;
- claim for outward travel before the signature of the form;
- accept an application sent by post; and
- accept an application from a child or patient or someone on their behalf (other than a member of the firm's staff).

Another general rule is that a client cannot be given further advice on the same problem within six months; but again there are exceptions, for example if the client is reasonably dissatisfied with the service, or has moved away from their initial adviser, or a conflict of interest or other good reason precludes the adviser from providing further advice.

If a client returns after the case has been closed, further advice may be provided if at least three months has elapsed since the claim for the first matter was submitted *and* there has been a material development or change in the client's instructions.

The reason must be justified in accordance with the relevant rule of the Contract Specification and recorded on the CW1 form.

Financial eligibility for controlled work

Except where a local authority has given written notice of potential s.31 care proceedings under the Children Act 1989 (Public Family Help Lower – form CW1PL), clients must be of limited means. Financial eligibility is assessed on three separate criteria, in relation to capital, gross income and disposable income. The limits are usually reviewed once a year, when benefit levels are up-rated. There is guidance in *Volume 2 Part F* of the LSC Manual. In the case of controlled work, the decision on whether the means test is met is delegated to the solicitor.

Clients directly or indirectly in receipt of income support, income-based jobseekers' allowance, the income-based element of employment and support allowance, or guaranteed state pension credit are automatically eligible for all types of legal aid without the need for further assessment of either capital or income. These benefits are referred to as passporting benefits.

Capital is 'every resource of a capital nature belonging to [the client] on the date on which the application is made' (Community Legal Service (Financial) Regulations 2000, SI 2000/516, reg.26). Where the client owns property, the value of the client's equity should be taken into account. At the controlled work level, where property is the subject matter of the dispute, the value of that property is disregarded from the calculation.

Evidence of means

The evidence must relate to the calendar month prior to the date the form is signed. The Unified Contract specification (rule 2.4) says that you must obtain evidence of a client's means *before* starting work. The LSC does allow work to start without evidence if it is 'not practicable to obtain it before commencing Controlled Work' (rule 2.5); but the practitioner needs to show that it was reasonable to do so. This should be recorded on the initial attendance note.

The LSC accepts that sometimes the client's circumstances will mean that you never get evidence (e.g. mental disability, age or homelessness); but it expects this to be very rare. In these circumstances, an explanation must be recorded on the CW1 form.

Clients are under a duty to report any change of financial circumstances which occurs after the original assessment, whether for controlled or licensed work. The LSC's guidance for Legal Help states that work must stop and the file be closed if a client's means change significantly and the matter is likely to run for three months or more.

Merits

The Legal Help merits test is known as the sufficient benefit test: 'Help may only be provided where there is sufficient benefit to the client, having regard to the circumstances of the matter, including the personal circumstances of the client, to justify work or further work being carried out.' (Funding Code, Criteria for Legal Help, 5.2.1).

The general approach to the test is set out in the guidance to the Funding Code. The question is whether a reasonable private paying client of moderate means would pay for the work. The LSC makes the point that it may well be worthwhile paying for initial advice, even if the case is not worth pursuing further. The more Legal Help is provided, the more relevant the cost/benefit test becomes. In purely financial matters, the cost of providing Legal Help should not exceed the amount in issue. Even when payment is a fixed fee, the costs for the test should be calculated at hourly rates.

Separate matters

All aspects of a client's problem should be dealt with under one Legal Help form. It is possible have more than one Legal Help matter open at the same time, but only if they relate to entirely separate family disputes.

Clients may only have two Family Help Lower cases open at the same time, one in respect of children issues and one in respect of finance. Only one CW1 form is signed although it is advisable to keep time recording for the two aspects separate, because of the way exceptional cases are calculated (see below).

Disbursements

Disbursements may be claimed in addition to fixed fees provided that they meet the LSC's criteria:

(a)   it is in the best interests of the client to incur the disbursement;
(b)   it is reasonable to incur the disbursement for the purpose of providing controlled work – i.e. necessary for the purpose of giving advice to the client or progressing the case;
(c)   the amount of the disbursement is reasonable; and
(d)   it is not a disbursement which is specifically prohibited.

The Contract Specification provides a non-exhaustive list of disbursements that may not be incurred in the provision of controlled work.

Ending a controlled work matter

A matter should be closed if:

- the client decides not to proceed, or indicates that they wish to take the matter forward themselves;
- the client fails to give instructions for three months (unless the matter is on hold, for example, because a third party is yet to do something, or a pause has been agreed with the client);
- funding is granted under Section C of the Funding Code procedures (unless further Legal Help is required on matters not covered by the certificate) or the matter begins to be funded outside the contract;
- the adviser considers that the matter is completed;
- the adviser considers that the provision of controlled work is no longer justified having regard to the applicable Funding Code Criteria;
- the adviser can no longer act through a conflict of interest or other reason of professional conduct.

It is not permitted to close a matter simply because the value of profit costs is equal to, or more than the fixed fee. However, if the time and item costs of a case exceed a threshold, the case becomes 'an exceptional case', and full costs and disbursements can be claimed. At the time of writing, the threshold was three times the controlled work fixed fee. In exceptional cases, the fixed fee is claimed in the usual way (see below) and an EC1 claim form is submitted with the file to the appropriate LSC office in order to be credited with the balance above the fixed fee.

Fixed fees must be claimed via online Consolidated Matter Reports within three months of the matter ending.

Fixed fee contract compliance audits

The LSC can assess all claims for controlled work costs. However, claims costs for fixed fee cases are simply submitted to the LSC online. The LSC needed some kind of audit to verify these claims, and a working group was set up to consider the process for contract compliance audits. It included representatives from the Law Society, and other groups representing solicitors, e.g. Resolution, the not-for-profit sector, and the National Audit Office. It was decided to assess these claims on a sampling basis. The criteria for civil files are as follows:

- Scope – the matter must be within scope of the Access to Justice Act 1999 (as amended).
- Financial eligibility – the client must meet the criteria.
- Evidence of means – this must be on the file (unless a permitted exception applies).
- Disbursements – these must be reasonable in amount and reasonably incurred.
- Sufficient benefit – the case must meet the test at the outset and throughout.
- Reporting – the case must have been reported using the correct codings.

Contract compliance audit sanctions

Since the criteria are fundamental to whether a case can be funded or not, there are only two outcomes of a contract compliance audit: either the file is paid in full, or it is nil assessed and nothing is payable. The LSC has agreed to take a graded approach to audit sanctions. At the lowest level of non-compliance, no sanctions are applied. After that, sanctions start with recoupment of fees on the actual files assessed and progress to a point where the result of that particular audit is extrapolated and applied to all claims made over the preceding year. In addition, contract notices may be served.

12.3.4 Licensed work procedures

A certificate for full Legal Representation or Public Funding authorises the conduct of litigation and the provision of advocacy and representation, and includes steps preliminary and incidental to proceedings, and steps to settle or avoid proceedings. In almost every case, a certificate is only granted subject to two limitations. First, to a particular step in the proceedings, and secondly in relation to costs, usually £2,500 plus VAT in the first instance.

Under the LSC's funding schemes, level 3 covers work from the issue of proceedings to a final hearing and level 4 covers a final hearing to the conclusion of the case. At the time of writing, private law family work at level 3 was remunerated under hourly rates, and public family law level 3 work under standard fees. The LSC was expected to issue new fixed and graduated fee schemes for private family law licensed work, and a new scheme of payment for advocacy, whether carried out by solicitors or counsel, to take effect from October 2010.

An issue of concern for Resolution is that the LSC's fixed and graduated fee schemes to date have not recognised the accredited quality provided by Resolution and Law Society panel membership, by way of financial uplifts.

Financial eligibility for licensed work

The capital and income rules generally apply as for controlled work, except in specified family proceedings. Where property is the subject matter of the dispute, there is a cap on the amount of capital which can be disregarded.

Where a client's main or only dwelling in which s/he resides is the subject matter of dispute, disregards are applied as follows:

1. Apply the mortgage disregard (actual mortgage or £100,000 whichever is the less) to the value of the property to establish the total amount of equity within the property; this figure is then multiplied by the client's percentage share of the property (normally 50 per cent unless there is evidence to the contrary).
2. Apply the subject matter of dispute disregard of £100,000 to the client's share of any equity within the property.
3. Apply the equity disregard of £100,000 to the remainder (if any) of the client's share of the equity within the main dwelling.

Example: The matrimonial home is worth £320,000 and the mortgage is £150,000.

Value of home	£320,000
Deduct mortgage up to limit	£100,000
Equity	£220,000
Client's share	£110,000

As this is the subject matter of the dispute, it can be disregarded up to the limit of £100,000, leaving the client with £10,000 of capital, which means that the client is eligible for licensed work after applying the equity disregard.

Also, see non-means/non-merits tested cases, below.

Clients who are not in receipt of a passporting benefit may have to pay contributions throughout the lifetime of the case. Should the amount paid in contributions exceed the final costs as assessed, the client is entitled to a refund of the difference. Eligibility on means for licensed work is determined by the LSC, not the solicitor, but the client must be advised in advance of submitting the application of his/her potential liability for a contribution. Clients who pay contributions have a financial interest in the costs of the case and must be supplied with costs estimates and regular costs updates. Changes in circumstances must be reported to the LSC. If a client is no longer eligible for funding the certificate will be discharged.

In an emergency, a client may be granted legal aid before there is time to carry out a detailed means test. If the client is subsequently found to be ineligible financially, fails to co-operate with the means assessment or does not accept an offer of a certificate because a contribution is required, the emergency certificate will be revoked. This means the certificate will be cancelled and the client treated as though he or she was never in receipt of legal aid.

The client will be responsible for the full costs of his or her representation and will not have the protection from opponents' costs provided by a certificate of public funding. If a certificate is revoked, the LSC will pursue the client for costs.

Merits tests – private law cases

These vary according to the type of case – see below. Cases must pass a 'prospects of success' test and a 'cost benefit or successful outcome' test.

In private law children cases (that is those concerning contact, residence, parental responsibility, financial provision for children, and other matters which are not special Children Act or other public law proceedings), the practitioner needs to show that a significant improvement in the arrangements for children is likely to be obtained. Representation will be refused if prospects of success are poor.

In financial provision and ancillary relief cases a significant improvement in financial or other arrangements must be likely. Representation will be refused if prospects of success are poor; or if they are borderline or unclear unless the case has overwhelming importance to the client (here, roof over his/her head).

In both children and financial provision cases, the likely benefits must justify the likely cost, such that the reasonable private paying client would be prepared to take or defend the proceedings in all the circumstances.

In domestic abuse cases, representation is available to apply for, or contest an application for, an injunction under Part IV of the Family Law Act 1996. Representation will be refused if prospects of success are poor; and likely benefits must justify likely costs, having regard to the prospects of success and all other circumstances.

229

Referral to mediation in private law cases

The LSC expects every effort to be made to resolve issues through mediation rather than through contested proceedings. Therefore, practitioners should encourage clients to consider mediation wherever possible. Clients must attend an intake assessment with a mediator, unless one of the following applies:

1. Family proceedings are already in existence and the client is a respondent/defendant who has been notified of a court date which is within eight weeks of the date of notification.
2. The client has a reasonable fear of domestic abuse from a partner or former partner (see below for more information).
3. The client or other party cannot see a mediator (examples given include where bail conditions prevent contact with an ex-partner, or where the client is in custody or hospitalised, or lives more than two hours away, etc.).
4. The other party is unwilling to attend mediation.
5. Emergency representation is required.

Legal aid for mediation

Legal aid is available for family mediation, for clients who are financially eligible. Mediators work under contract with the LSC and are paid direct by the LSC, rather than as a disbursement.

Means and merits tests – public law cases

Public law family proceedings are defined in section 2 of the Funding Code and mean special Children Act proceedings, related proceedings and other public law children cases. A CLS funding certificate in family public law can only be granted when the local authority issues proceedings, and is therefore usually granted initially as an emergency certificate under devolved powers. It authorises the conduct of litigation and the provision of advocacy and representation.

An application for funding in special Children Act cases is granted automatically, without reference to means or merits.

Certificates in other public law children cases are means tested and are subject to a limited merits test (Funding Code Criteria, 11.9). Representation will be refused if alternative funding is available (e.g. in adoption, where the child is placed by the local authority who consent to the adoption, it would be reasonable to expect them to bear the costs of the application), or if not necessary (for example, because of the involvement of other parties or a professional guardian), or it appears unreasonable for funding to be granted (e.g. where the client's interests are substantially the same as another party's, there is no need for them to be separately represented).

CLSAPP5 is used for special Children Act proceedings and CLSAPP3 for other cases.

Devolved powers

Certificates can be granted for full Legal Representation in urgent cases. Some limitations on substantive certificates can be amended in urgent circumstances. Guidance can be found in the LSC Manual, *Volume 3, Part C, Funding Code Decision Making Guidance*, section 24.

Firms need to have a Quality Mark and a contract in the relevant category to exercise devolved powers. The LSC monitors the use of devolved powers, and may suspend or terminate them, if they have been seriously misused. The LSC has issued guidelines in respect of the consequences that will follow if devolved powers are used incorrectly. They are graded to reflect the seriousness of the error (LSC Manual, *Volume 3, Part C, Funding Code Decision Making Guidance*, section 12.8 and 12.9).

Amendments to certificates – private and public family law

Requests for amendments to either scope or costs limitations are made to the LSC, using Form CLSAPP8. In making a request, the caseworker will be obliged to demonstrate that the case continues to satisfy both limitations of the merits test, and state what new scope or costs limitation is required. There must be merit in each step of the proceedings.

Prior authority for disbursements

In some cases, disbursements can be large, and there is a risk to the firm that they will not be allowed, or allowed in full, on assessment of the bill. The prior authority scheme allows an organisation to apply to the LSC for authority to incur a disbursement in advance, if it is above £100. The application is made using Form CLSAPP8, accompanied by a quote for the disbursement and reasons why it is necessary. The advantage of having authority is that no question as to the validity of the disbursement can be raised on assessment of the bill, unless and to the extent that it exceeds the amount or scope of the authority. Prior authority therefore gives a measure of reimbursement protection for expensive disbursements.

Payments on account

Up to 75 per cent profit costs can be claimed on account, three months after the issue of a CLS funding certificate. Thereafter, further applications can be made at six-monthly intervals (provided that no more than two applications can be made in any 12-month period). Applications can also be made in relation to significant disbursements. Applications are made using Form CLSPOA1.

Billing certificated cases

Once a case has concluded, the final bill should be submitted to the court or LSC for assessment, as appropriate (see below). It should be noted that both the LSC and the court require authority to assess the bill. The authority to assess is either a discharged certificate, or a final order requiring costs to be assessed. Therefore, if the final order makes no mention of costs, a discharge should be sought before submitting the bill.

In Family Proceedings Court cases, the LSC assesses all bills. In cases in the county court and above, if the case ends before proceedings have been issued, the LSC assesses the bill.

Where proceedings have been issued, the LSC assesses all bills up to £2,500 (excluding VAT). Bills in excess of £2,500 are assessed by the court. The exception to this is where there is an element of costs between the parties, where the bill is assessed by the court regardless of the size of the claim.

Claims to the LSC are made on Form CLSCLAIM1, which must be completed in full and accompanied by the certificate, fee notes and invoices, orders, and the full file of papers.

12.3.5 Costs protection

Historically, one of the main benefits of legal aid funding was that costs could not be awarded against a legally aided client if unsuccessful. However, in 2005, this protection was removed from clients in certain family proceedings. Clients therefore need to be advised of the risk of costs, for example if they conduct the litigation unreasonably.

12.3.6 Statutory charge

Legal aid is not necessarily free as far as a client is concerned. If property is recovered or preserved, it operates like a loan. The charge also catches payments made to a third party (for example if one partner offers to pay the other's debts). It also applies to the lump sum element of a pension. However, periodical payments are exempt. It is extremely important to inform clients about the statutory charge at the outset and remind them of it at six-monthly intervals when they are updated on costs liability.

The charge gives the LSC first call on any money or property. Any money must be paid to the solicitor, and if the statutory charge is not protected, the solicitor can be liable for any loss to the fund. The LSC can recover the statutory charge from the client through enforcement proceedings. Therefore, it is advisable to ensure that in cases involving property, an executed CLS Admin1 form (consent to postpone enforcement of the statutory charge) is completed as soon as possible and executed by all relevant parties.

The amount of the charge is calculated to compensate the LSC for funding the case, and includes solicitor's costs, disbursements, counsel's fees and VAT. In family cases, related certificates are also covered, so the charge would apply not just to ancillary relief proceedings but also to any related Children Act or injunction proceedings.

The statutory charge does not apply to cases completing under Legal Help (level 1).

The home is exempt from the charge in cases completing under Legal Help, Help at Court or Family Help Lower. However, even where a lump sum is paid, the statutory charge does not apply to standard fee cases. This is a powerful incentive to clients to settle at level 2 as in most cases, their legal aid will be free.

However, in exceptional cases, the charge applies, but only to costs above the exceptional case threshold (i.e. those costs over three times the standard fee).

At level 3 (certificated work), the charge applies in favour of the LSC and includes the fees at levels 1 and 2.

In certain circumstances, if the money is to be used to provide a home for the client and/or their dependants, the LSC may postpone enforcement of the charge, if it is satisfied that the property will provide sufficient security. Clients should be informed that it is an expensive form of finance as it attracts interest at 8 per cent per annum. Unfortunately, those in the most severe financial hardship are the ones who will have no alternative but to incur this liability until the home is sold.

12.4   FUTURE DEVELOPMENTS IN LEGAL AID

12.4.1   Electronic working

In December 2008, the LSC published 'Managing Legal Aid Cases in Partnership – Delivery Transformation: A Response to Consultation'. It can be downloaded from the LSC's website at: **www.legalservices.gov.uk/aboutus/ electronic_working.asp**.

The LSC anticipates that one of the key benefits will be the reduction of instances where data has to be entered more than once. The LSC has been careful not to pitch the technical requirements too high: all that will be needed is a computer, a web browser, an email address, a printer and dial up internet connection (but broadband is recommended). A scanner is recommended but the LSC says it will not be mandatory. Electronic payments have been in existence for some time but at some point in the future the LSC hopes that practitioners will be able to do the following online:

- make applications for civil certificates;
- conduct means assessments in straightforward cases;
- use devolved decision-making powers to grant certificates to a greater extent;

- use devolved powers to discharge certificates in straightforward cases;
- bill all civil cases, including certificated work.

12.4.2 Policy developments

In March 2007 the LSC published a strategy for family law called 'Making Legal Rights a Reality for Children and Families'. Priorities for funding were stated to be:

- Directing funding towards services for children and adults at risk of abuse and parents whose children are the subject of care proceedings.
- Providing further incentives for parents in private law proceedings to resolve cases without going to court.
- Increasing access to services for those at risk of domestic abuse.
- Piloting specialist family advice through the CLS telephone service intended to include both advice and full legal representation.
- Reviewing the operation of the Funding Code to reflect funding priorities.
- Purchasing integrated family and social welfare law services.
- A rational allocation of regional budgets based on an analysis of eligible clients.

As can be seen in this chapter, the LSC has been implementing these policies through new fee schemes and commissioning exercises. It is likely that these priorities will continue to inform funding decisions in an increasingly harsh public spending environment. Legal aid for divorce, ancillary relief and child contact cases could come under severe pressure.

CHAPTER 13

Alternative dispute resolution

Emma Harte

13.1 DEFINITION OF ALTERNATIVE DISPUTE RESOLUTION

'Alternative dispute resolution' (ADR) consists of a range of procedures which are used as alternatives to the adjudicatory procedures of litigation and arbitration for the resolution of disputes, commonly, although not necessarily, involving the assistance of a neutral third party who helps to facilitate such resolution.

Arbitration was originally an alternative procedure although it is now normally regarded as being closer to litigation in its approach and is therefore generally part of mainstream practice, leaving ADR to refer mainly to consensual, rather than to adjudicatory, processes.

13.2 WHY CHOOSE ADR OVER LITIGATION?

References sometimes made to the 'ADR movement' in both the UK and the US might suggest that there is one single school of thought guiding the development of ADR processes. However, this is questionable as, in practice, supporters of ADR have varying philosophies, cultures and practices. As can be seen later, there are different models used within the various ADR processes.

Motivations for ADR are sometimes said to include the empowerment of individuals using it; the increased responsibility given to the parties; the possibilities for co-operative problem solving; the preservation of relationships and better communication (so important in family matters where children are involved); the scope for better and more acceptable outcomes; the informality of the process; confidentiality; and the reduction of cost and delay. These are all valid aims but there can be no guarantee that all (or indeed any) of these benefits will arise in any given case.

ADR complements litigation and other adjudicatory forms, providing processes which can either stand in their own right or be used in addition to adjudication in the hope that an overall resolution can be agreed before any costly hearings, etc. are needed (with the exception of collaborative law which can only be used where there are no court applications on foot, see **13.5**). This allows practitioners to select the processes and procedures appropriate to individual disputes.

As outlined above, ADR:

- allows parties greater control in resolving the issues between them;
- encourages problem-solving approaches;
- provides for more effective and tailored settlements (appropriate for those particular parties – as opposed to a resolution imposed by the court which realistically cannot embody all the needs and concerns of the parties involved);
- enhances co-operation and enables better communication, conducive to the preservation of relationships;
- often includes effective neutral third party involvement which can assist in overcoming blocks to settlement; and
- generally expedites and facilitates resolution, thereby potentially saving costs and avoiding the delays and risks of litigation.

It is very important to bear in mind, however, that ADR processes, like adjudicatory procedures, have advantages and disadvantages which make them suitable for some cases but not for others.

13.3 DISPUTE RESOLUTION PROCEDURES

Essentially, all dispute resolution processes (traditional and alternative) can be divided into three main categories:

- negotiation;
- adjudication; and
- mediation.

13.3.1 Negotiation

Negotiation stands firmly in its own right in addition to falling into the traditional framework as part of most cases started by adjudication and being an inherent part of mediation, collaborative law and all other ADR processes.

Negotiation tends to be a practical skill learned by personal experience. However, there are various theories of negotiation as well as many different styles and approaches.

13.3.2 Adjudication

Adjudication is a dispute resolution process in which a neutral person has and exercises the authority to hear the respective positions put forward by the parties in dispute and to make a decision on their dispute which will be binding on them. This may occur through litigation; arbitration (where the neutral person is chosen privately and/or the procedure follows the rules of arbitration); administrative or statutory tribunals; expert determination (in which the parties appoint an expert to consider their issues and to make a binding decision without necessarily having to conduct an enquiry following adjudicatory rules); or private judging (in which, in those jurisdictions which have adopted this procedure, but not yet within the UK, the court refers the case to a referee chosen by the parties to decide some or all of the issues, or to establish any specific facts).

13.3.3   Mediation or conciliation

Mediation is a process by which disputing parties enlist the assistance of a neutral third party to act as a facilitating intermediary (i.e. mediator) who has no authority to make any binding decisions but who uses various procedures, techniques and skills to help the parties to resolve their dispute by negotiated agreement without adjudication.

The term 'conciliation' is sometimes used with 'mediation'. Mediation is often used to describe a more proactive mediator role, while conciliation may be used to describe a more facilitative mediator role.

13.3.4   Hybrid processes

Each main process (litigation, arbitration or mediation) can be used in its own right. In addition, by drawing elements from these main processes and 'tailoring' them, an ADR practitioner can create a mixture of procedures and approaches which fit all the nuances of the parties' needs and circumstances without being constrained by prescribed rules. For instance, the practitioner might have informal discussions with the parties, arrange for certain facts or technical issues to be investigated, and then allow each of the parties to present their respective cases informally to one another before resuming further attempts at settlement. This and any other 'mixture' can be met by creating a sequence of procedures specifically designed for that dispute and those parties.

Certain common combinations of the main processes have developed like this and have become known as 'hybrid processes'. The most widely used processes are described below.

The mini trial

This is a form of evaluative mediation or a condensed non-binding arbitration, followed by negotiation and/or mediation.

Med-arb (mediation-arbitration)

This involves starting with the mediation process and if that does not result in the dispute being resolved, continuing with a binding arbitration.

The neutral fact-finding expert

This involves an investigation by a neutral expert into certain specific issues of fact, technicality and/or law with, if necessary, a mediatory role, and eventually participation in an adjudicatory process if required.

Early neutral evaluation

This requires a neutral evaluator to meet parties at an early stage of a case to make a confidential assessment of the dispute, partly to help them to narrow and define the issues, and partly to promote efforts to arrive at a settlement.

Court-annexed arbitration

This requires statutory introduction into the court system and, depending on the model adopted, may be binding or initially non-binding. It may or may not provide for a rehearing by a judge under certain circumstances.

Mediation and hybrid processes often provide a framework of informal procedures in which a neutral party assists the disputing parties with information gathering; clarifying and narrowing issues; facilitating discussions and negotiation; ironing out personal conflicts; identifying options; testing the reality of options; risk assessment; impasse resolution; and, in some cases, non-binding evaluation as an aid to reaching agreement.

Alternative dispute resolution is used in the civil and commercial spheres and in the area of family law. However it is fair to say that in the area of family law, there are only really two forms of ADR currently being used in the UK, i.e. mediation and collaborative law. This chapter will focus on both. Arbitration in family law matters, however, is likely to be an option in the near future.

13.4   FAMILY MEDIATION

13.4.1   What is family mediation?

Family mediation is a process in which a couple or family members, whether or not they are legally represented, at any time, whether or not there are or have been any legal proceedings, agree to the appointment of a neutral third party (the mediator). The mediator is impartial and has no authority to make any decisions with regard to separation, divorce, children issues, property and finances or any other issues that may be raised. A mediator should help them reach their own informed decisions by negotiation and without adjudication.

13.4.2 Fundamental principles of mediation

Notwithstanding the different models of mediation, there are some fundamental principles that run through all mediation. These are as follows.

The use of a mediator

There cannot be mediation without a mediator. Mediation requires a third party to intervene impartially between the parties. It is this element of neutral third party intercession that gives mediation its unique quality.

The mediator's impartiality

This is essential. Impartiality or even-handedness implies being able to move one way or the other but always fairly and without overall favour.

The mediator's authority to determine the issues

A mediator cannot decide any issues for the parties. The mediator's job is to help the parties reach their own decisions (including the power to manage the process). A neutral third party who makes decisions may be an arbitrator, or perhaps an expert undertaking expert determination, but this is not the function of a mediator.

Consensual resolution

The objective of mediation is that the parties themselves should agree on the outcome. The issues can only be said to be resolved when the parties have reached an agreement. If at the end of a mediation, the parties cannot agree, the mediation will end without any resolution (although often the issues will have been narrowed and the parties may be close to achieving an overall resolution) and the parties will be free to use another process.

Secure negotiation

All forms of mediation will normally provide a secure environment in which the mediation is conducted (i.e. secure in terms of the physical conditions and secure in terms of the mediation being confidential), with ground rules laid down to enable the parties to communicate freely to aid resolution.

13.4.3 The role of the mediator

The mediator has different roles within the process, for example:

- facilitator – facilitating discussions;
- manager – managing the process;
- information gatherer – gathering all the financial disclosure where financial aspects need to be resolved;
- information provider – providing legal information and for example details about the CSA and its formula for calculating child maintenance;
- reality tester – testing whether or not particular options are achievable in real life;
- note taker – making sure there is a note of the various options discussed and the issues raised and dealt with.

13.4.4 The basic stages of mediation

What does the mediator do when faced with an enquiry from a couple who potentially wish to take part in mediation? There are essentially five stages involved in the mediation process.

Stage 1 – engaging the parties in the process

1. Have even-handed dealings on the telephone with both parties beforehand.
2. Inform both parties about the process and ground rules and that meetings normally take place with the mediator and the parties in the same room around the same table.
3. Discuss the process, procedure, costs and timing – not the merits.
4. Ensure there is no misunderstanding about the mediator's role.
5. Obtain names, addresses and contact numbers.
6. Check the urgency of the matter and the timetable involved.
7. Arrange a mediation appointment if required.
8. Send written information about the mediation process including the preliminary information form and the agreement to mediate.

Stage 2 – obtaining commitment and agreeing rules (usually at first session)

1. Make sure the room and seating are appropriate (for example, check that the mediator is seated at the same distance from each party).
2. Use the form of agreement to mediate.
3. Check all aspects of the agreement to mediate are understood and agreed, especially the confidentiality and privilege section. Note that it is clearly stated within the agreement to mediate that all financial information is

provided on an open basis which means that it can be used in court, but that discussions about possible terms of financial settlement are conducted on a 'without prejudice' basis. Provisions about confidentiality and privilege will not apply, however, if any child or other person is suffering or likely to suffer significant harm.

4. Make sure the parties understand that substantive decisions are not binding until all parties have the opportunity to take advice from their solicitors.
5. Ask the parties to sign an agreement to mediate at the first session.
6. Consider the agenda, following receipt of the preliminary information form and further discussion.

Stage 3 – information gathering

Information is gathered by:

(a) use of initial information from discussion (use preliminary information form);
(b) mediation financial statement (Form E) where financial issues are involved, together with supporting documents;
(c) probing and appropriate use of a flipchart to ensure that the information is shared.

Stage 4 – facilitating discussions and negotiations

In order to facilitate discussions and negotiations between the parties, it is necessary for the mediator to:

- establish and develop a working agenda;
- help the couple to adopt a problem-solving approach;
- maintain future focus where possible;
- help the couple to consider the children and family;
- provide legal and other information but on an even-handed basis;
- identify, generate and list options, i.e. brainstorm with the couple;
- help the couple to explore, consider and prioritise options;
- assist the couple in testing the reality of different options and ideas;
- help the couple to communicate with each other;
- if necessary, help parties to hear one another;
- allow ventilation of emotions to a degree but then bring the couple back to the issues;
- help the couple with their decision making, perhaps by suggesting short-term solutions where appropriate;
- assist sensible creativity and flexibility;
- maintain empathy and impartiality; and
- manage the process fairly and effectively but always be prepared to be firm where necessary.

Stage 5 – concluding the mediation

The mediation will come to an end when:

- issues are completely or partially resolved;
- either or both parties wish to terminate the mediation;
- the mediator wishes to terminate the process.

In most circumstances, thereafter, the mediator will prepare a summary (a 'Memorandum of Understanding') which the parties can then take to their respective solicitors for advice. The mediator's role may be built into a post-termination phase, however, so that the parties can revert as necessary on either the children or finance issues, depending on whether or not an agreement is reached.

13.4.5 Mediation skills

There are a number of skills which the mediator must develop and use:

- effective listening;
- observing non-verbal communication, i.e. body language;
- helping the parties to hear one another;
- questioning (in order to obtain facts, find out about parties' concerns and see what needs to happen for those concerns to be addressed);
- summarising;
- acknowledging;
- neutralising (to maintain impartiality);
- normalising (if appropriate, explaining that it is common for the parties to feel or behave in this way in this situation);
- re-framing (to make issues sound more palatable and not so personal to enable parties to move forward);
- managing conflict and venting of emotion;
- managing the process (the mediator must keep control of the mediation);
- lateral thinking (making alternative suggestions where appropriate); and
- encouraging a problem-solving mode – essential for making progress.

13.4.6 Dealing with emotions in mediation

It is very common for parties, both male and female, to show emotion, by way of tears, anger or otherwise and so the mediator should make this clear, i.e. 'normalise'. The mediator should consider referring the couple to counselling if that is not already in place; while the mediator is to manage the process, he or she should be aware of his or her own limitations.

Ventilating of emotions is fine as long as it is controlled and is not abusive. The mediator should remind the parties of the ground rules agreed at the outset, however, and try to bring the parties back to focus on the central issues as soon as possible.

13.4.7 Power imbalances

Redress

Concern is sometimes expressed as to whether and how power imbalances between parties can effectively be redressed in mediation. These concerns are probably more prevalent in relation to family mediation, which may be perceived as benefiting the more powerful partner to the prejudice of the more vulnerable one. Although in fact either partner may be more powerful than the other, it is probably fair to say that a common stereotype in referring to these power imbalances is that of a powerful husband using mediation to dominate a weaker wife.

The nature and form of power

How does power manifest itself in the relationship between a couple? An exhaustive list cannot be given but, for example, it may be the respective education and qualifications of each partner; the social standing of each partner; the financial standing of each of the partners and whether either is independent or dependent on the other, etc.; control or influence over financial affairs or children of the family; power exerted through threats; and the power of irrationality, i.e. the possibility that one will act unpredictably and irrationally with certain effects and consequences if a particular result is not achieved.

Dealing with power imbalances

It is not the mediator's function to try to change the power relationship between the parties for the future. However, an effective family mediation could have some impact on the power relationship between the parties.

It can be empowering for the less dominant party if the mediator helps the couple to communicate with one another more effectively so that they can address any issues which they may not have been able to express by themselves, and deal in an orderly way with those issues. For example, it can be empowering for one person to be heard properly and have his or her views taken seriously, or for financial information to be shared in a way that may never have happened during the course of the relationship.

The mediator's responsibility is to ensure therefore that any power disparity that exists does not impact on the process in such a way as to make it unworkable and unfair. However, if an imbalance of power is impacting to the extent that it is making the process unfair, it will be necessary to terminate the mediation. Mediation is not appropriate for all couples by any means and the mediator needs to be constantly alert as to whether it would be fair to continue the process in each case on a session-by-session basis.

Potential violence or harm

Where power imbalance involves potential violence or harm, mediators must take particular care to establish whether mediation can take place at all, and if it can, under what circumstances and conditions. Cases of potential violence and harm should be identified as soon as possible – usually from the initial telephone calls to each party and from their completed preliminary information forms.

If mediation is to take place in a situation where one party is thought to be at any risk of harm by the other party, the mediator must take steps to try to ensure that both parties and the mediator are safe in the mediation. This should, for example, be addressed by appropriate arrangements for reception on arrival and for departure after the mediation, and by any other arrangements or conditions that the mediator may consider to be suitable.

Discussion of imbalances and establishing ground rules

By way of clarification, if a particular form of imbalance persists and it is impacting on the process, the mediator might decide to discuss this with the parties with a view to seeking some agreed formula for overcoming the problem, i.e. bring it into the open so that a way can be found to overcome it.

As a manager of the process, the mediator can stipulate ground rules to deal with any problems which may obstruct progress. It is a matter for the mediator whether this should be done by virtue of his or her authority or discussed and implemented by agreement with the parties.

If, for example, one party displays a tendency to interrupt and speak over the other, the mediator might make a specific rule to prevent this from happening. Alternatively, the mediator might discuss this with the parties, explaining that it is inhibiting progress and ask for authority from both of them to intervene should this occur again. Once both parties have given the mediator that specific authority, it becomes more difficult for an offending party to persist in the unhelpful conduct.

Other methods of reducing power imbalance

Power imbalances do not always have to be specifically discussed with the parties. For example, if one person has a greater control over the financial information than the other, this will be redressed by the procedures for providing and sharing relevant information.

It is generally accepted that having lawyers representing each party, as in the traditional process, helps to redress any power imbalances that exist between the parties. This is of course true in the main but many of the other power imbalances will remain.

13.4.8 Solicitor's role in mediation

In some models of family mediation, solicitors are not generally brought into the mediation process. Similarly, in the Resolution model, mediation is conducted by and large without solicitors in attendance but there is a readiness to involve the parties' solicitors within the mediation process where this is appropriate and both the parties desire. There is also scope for flexibility and the ability to deal with matters in the way in which civil/commercial mediations proceed, i.e. through caucusing sessions (where the mediator meets separately with each party) in which information disclosed is confidential unless authority is given for it to be disclosed to the other party. This can be extremely useful when trying to get to the root of a problem and to achieve a resolution. It is particularly useful when the parties have reached an impasse or find it difficult to be in the same room together. The mediator needs to bear in mind, however, that if one party does not have a solicitor present, he or she will be left sitting alone while the mediator is with the other party. Each 'caucus' should therefore be kept to a certain time limit.

It may not always be necessary for the solicitors to participate in a mediation session. However, it can sometimes be helpful and it can aid finality; with lawyers present an immediate binding settlement can be achieved, and this may be attractive to both parties. This model, however, can create concerns for the parties and it does move away from the notion of parties dealing directly with one another and improving communications and should therefore be used with care. For example, where issues relating to children or finances are presented by either party in such a way as to create an imbalance, it may be sufficient for the parties to be invited to take separate legal advice between sessions.

This may help vulnerable parties to gain a better perspective on their rights, and this may be empowering for the following mediation session. The Resolution model encourages the parties to go back to their respective solicitors after each session so that they have suitable guidance the whole way through the process, and in particular at the financial disclosure stage and at the stage where options are being discussed. Notes of mediation sessions can be shared with the parties' solicitors too so that the solicitors know exactly what has been discussed and explored.

13.4.9 Option development

The development of options is an essential element of mediation. It can be used in relation to all aspects, for example the future of the relationship, arrangements for the children and financial issues.

Options offer the couple ways of moving forward and may arise initially from the couple or the mediator. When exploring financial options it is often helpful to start with the issue of housing as both parties will need to be rehoused, and the remainder of the possible settlement terms will often flow from any decisions on housing.

13.4.10 Use of language

The choice of language is important in mediation. It is always necessary to think whether or not the language is:

- appropriate for the mediation?
- appropriate for the couple?
- too legalistic or formal?
- too colloquial or relaxed?
- too compassionate?

13.4.11 Questioning

A skilled mediator will be able to use questions quite cleverly. Questions are used:

- to gather information, get a better understanding of the issues and to probe aspects which are unclear;
- to get a party to test reality by confronting perceptions or positions with alternative ways of viewing the situation (this may be essential for understanding and movement);
- to promote reflection on any situation or proposal and to help a party to become more fully aware of the issues;
- to encourage a party to review a position or to focus on specific issues;
- to redirect the way in which discussions are moving;
- as a form of intervention in conflict management, to divert parties from a heated discussion into a more productive area.

A question may be strategic, where for instance the mediator knows the answer but wishes the party to arrive at the answer himself or herself. Rather than expressing a personal view on a situation, the mediator can raise questions which allow parties to consider the issues needing to be examined without compromising the mediator's neutrality.

13.4.12 Impasse strategies

What does the mediator do when, as is often the case, both parties seem 'stuck' and neither can shift from their perspectives?

There are various strategies which mediators use in such situations. For example, the mediator may:

- arrange for the parties to pause and consider;
- allow the couple time to absorb the progress;
- help underlying concerns or issues to surface;
- discuss unresolved emotional blocks;
- use caucusing – going between parties, perhaps with solicitors;

- address different perceptions of fairness;
- suggest short-term experiments to test different options;
- deal with conflicting advice from respective lawyers;
- prepare a summary of the position;
- examine the best and worst alternatives to an agreement;
- help the couple prepare for adjudication – including a discussion of what it will cost;
- obtain an opinion from counsel on joint instructions.

13.4.13 Summaries

It is often helpful to provide detailed summaries for the parties which they can each take back to their respective solicitors. Such summaries can then be used to help the solicitors to finalise the proposals and to draft the consent order. Summaries can:

- set out financial information with copies of supporting documentation;
- set out proposals made and the nature of without prejudice communications; and
- set out interim arrangements which are made without prejudice to further adjustment in the context of an overall resolution.

13.4.14 Terminating the mediation

The mediation can be terminated if:

- the couple reach consensus on all issues;
- the couple reach consensus on some issues and take the others to a different forum;
- the couple jointly decide to end the mediation without resolving the issues; or
- either party unilaterally decides to end the mediation.

Mediation can be suspended for a period for counselling, therapy or for solicitors to deal with certain interim issues.

Mediators can of course decide to end the mediation themselves where continuing the mediation is inappropriate, or where there is an abuse of process by either party, or where the conduct of either party is such that the mediation must be terminated.

13.4.15 Co-mediation

The Resolution model is based on mediators being sole mediators. That is the method of working which prevails in family mediation in the US and in commercial mediation in the UK and elsewhere. However, some UK family models work with two mediators and the Resolution training is structured so that co-mediation is also taught. Co-mediation means simply that two mediators work together, either side by side throughout the whole process or dividing their functions. There is no rigidity in the way in which co-mediation is undertaken. It is useful to balance genders if the co-mediators are male and female, and both mediators can provide complementary functions – perhaps one writing up information on a flipchart while the other engages the couple. The costs need to be considered as it can be more costly to have two mediators present as opposed to one, and it can be more difficult to arrange meetings as another diary is involved. Also, if the mediators are not used to working together, they may be less efficient than one mediator working competently. Co-mediation can be particularly helpful, however, in difficult children cases, where a mediator from a counselling background can join forces with, say, a lawyer mediator, or in cases where the couple have not yet properly addressed the issues between themselves in either counselling or therapy.

13.4.16 Costs

Each mediation session normally lasts approximately one and a half hours. The number of sessions will depend on the issues but five or six sessions are not uncommon. More or fewer sessions may, however, be needed. The sessions may take place at approximately fortnightly intervals or as otherwise agreed.

Some parties may be entitled to public funding for mediation but where this is not available, the parties will have to pay private rates. Solicitors normally charge their traditional hourly charging rate for sessions and interim work (for example the preparation of summaries, etc.) and the costs are usually shared equally between the couple or as otherwise agreed. The fees are payable at the end of each session.

13.4.17 Training and accreditation

Resolution mediators attend and complete Resolution's eight-day training course which includes role plays and assessment throughout and submission of written work after the conclusion of the course itself.

Subsequently, Resolution trained mediators are encouraged to apply to become accredited mediators which involves:

- submitting a number of written summaries in relation to mediations actually conducted;
- attending peer group discussions;
- meeting with their consultant for supervision and to discuss cases;
- attending various seminars and workshops relating to mediation skills and practice;

- reading recommended books and journals; and
- writing published articles, books or other material.

Resolution accredited mediators are also required to apply for reaccreditation after a period of five years.

13.5 COLLABORATIVE LAW

13.5.1 Collaborative law principles

This is a relatively new model of resolving family disputes outside litigation. Essentially, each client is represented by separate, independent solicitors and both clients and solicitors attend meetings together ('four-way meetings') to try to resolve matters. The fundamental principle is that no court proceedings are permitted while the collaborative process is ongoing.

Both clients sign a binding agreement which precludes the solicitors or any experts (who may be retained jointly as neutrals within the process) from participating in litigation between the parties. There is a commitment to early and full disclosure and a commitment to good faith bargaining and respect for the other party. All the professionals agree to withdraw if either party issues an application with the court and thereafter new solicitors and new experts have to be instructed by both parties. This is to keep everyone at the negotiating table in the face of an apparent impasse.

The collaborative process is family centred and about achieving what is best for that particular family rather than trying to achieve the best financial outcome for a client. All successful collaborative lawyers have recognised the need for a second profession (the family consultant) which will provide a support service that will help the clients to address the non-legal agenda (i.e. all the practical issues regarding children and any emotional or relationship issues) and help them to be able to deal with the 'four-way' negotiations.

13.5.2 The collaborative lawyer

Collaborative lawyers (when acting in a collaborative capacity) can do everything that a conventional and traditional family lawyer does except initiate contested court proceedings. The collaborative model is also now being used in civil and commercial disputes.

The difference between mediation and the collaborative process is that in the collaborative model, each party has legal advice at all times during the process. Even if, for instance, one client lacks financial understanding, this power imbalance is rectified by the direct participation of the lawyers. If the clients are being unreasonable, it is the job of the lawyers to work with their own clients in order to ensure that the process remains productive. The participation/collaborative agreement also requires a lawyer to withdraw from the process on becoming aware that his or her client is not being frank or open or is participating in the process in bad faith. The same is true if the client fails to honour agreements made during the course of the negotiations.

Collaborative lawyers are specifically trained to help their clients achieve the best possible outcome for their families as opposed to achieving the largest possible financial award for a particular client. The collaborative lawyer encourages the highest good faith problem-solving behaviour from their own clients and from themselves. Collaborative lawyers are skilled in finding solutions that can be accepted by both clients.

Trust between the lawyers is essential for the collaborative process to work. In addition, collaborative practice demands specialist skills from the lawyers in guiding negotiations and managing conflict. It is critical therefore that both lawyers participating in the process are properly trained in collaborative law. It is not possible, for example, to work collaboratively with the other lawyer but still go to court if the process is not successful. It is felt that if the lawyers can still consider unilateral resort to the court as a fallback position, their thought processes are hampered. Only when everyone involved knows that it is down to the four of them to think up a solution (otherwise the process will fail and the lawyers will be disqualified from continuing to act), does the collaborative model actually work. All four need to take responsibility for finding an acceptable solution.

13.5.3 Other members of the collaborative team

Most family law practitioners, in their traditional work, will refer clients to counselling and mediation services wherever appropriate. The collaborative process recognises that other support (aside from the guidance from the lawyers) is often very helpful, if not crucial, if clients are to be able to deal with all the emotional and relationship issues involved in the breakdown of a relationship, as well as children issues. More generally, such support may be needed to help clients cope with the 'four-way' negotiations. This support can often be provided at a lower cost, notwithstanding the perceived extra cost of involving additional professionals such as the family consultant.

The family consultant is known as a 'coach' in the US. Typically, the family consultant will be a counsellor or therapist and often also a mediator and will be involved by a referral from one or both of the lawyers taking part in the collaborative process.

The family consultant might be supporting one party only (i.e. each party might have his or her own family consultant) or, alternatively, just one family consultant will be used to help both clients to deal with children arrangements and to facilitate better communication between them.

Family consultants are the professionals most commonly brought into the process but others may be involved including:

- accountants to assist with tax implications or with valuations of businesses and shares;

- independent financial advisers to provide information about mortgages and insurance policies, etc.;
- financial assistants to help with tasks such as preparing budgets, but at a lower cost to the clients than a lawyer; and
- actuaries to deal with pension issues.

13.5.4   The stages of the collaborative process

The initial stage – first meeting with the client

It is essential for all the options to be explained to the client, i.e. whether to mediate, negotiate in the traditional process or to deal with matters in the collaborative process. It is important to bear in mind that mediation and the collaborative process are not suitable for everyone and it is only right therefore that the clients know what to expect from each process so that they can gauge whether they can cope with them and make informed choices. Information on the various processes should be given to the client so that they can take it away to read at home, and Resolution produce a number of very useful pamphlets in this regard. Very often this leads to clients discussing the collaborative option with their spouse or partner and if both parties are interested, a second collaborative lawyer can be found through the collaborative family lawyers' website (**www.collabfamilylaw.org.uk**) or from the Resolution website. Alternatively, the client could ask the lawyer to provide a list of three to five names of suitable collaborative lawyers, from whom the spouse can choose.

The collaborative lawyers then make contact and preparations to proceed are put in place.

The first 'two-way' between lawyers

It is the lawyers' job to manage the process and this will include sharing information such as potential issues or stumbling blocks that are likely to be faced and whether or not the clients will benefit from family consultancy, the assistance of accountants, advice from independent financial advisers, etc. Usually this 'two-way' discussion will take place over the telephone and practical arrangements for the forthcoming 'four-way' meeting with clients will be made.

The client and lawyer 'two-way'

The lawyer will want the client to go into the 'four-way' meeting well prepared. There should be no real surprises for anyone at the first 'four-way' meeting, and family consultancy and the introduction of any financial experts will often be discussed with clients at this stage.

The first 'four-way' meeting

The aim of this first meeting is to ensure that the clients understand the process and appreciate their responsibilities within it. The participation agreement will be the main focus and this will be signed by the lawyers and the clients if everyone is satisfied that it is the best way forward for the clients given the issues involved.

As stated earlier, the participation agreement binds the clients to behave courteously and prevents them from beginning any contested proceedings during the course of the collaborative process. It also prevents the lawyers from ever acting on behalf of the clients in any contested proceedings. This typically makes everyone work harder to ensure that the negotiations work. Very few clients will want to start again on another process with fresh lawyers and all the costs that would be entailed.

The continuation of the process

Commonly, the collaborative lawyers are engaged primarily in trying to resolve the financial issues (whilst perhaps the children issues are dealt with through mediation) and so there may be a slight gap before the second meeting while each client prepares and collates their financial disclosure using Form E, although this is not always the case.

By the time the second 'four-way' begins, there will have been an exchange of financial information and the lawyers can then begin to explore and discuss various options with the clients within the 'four-way'.

The 'four-way' meetings will continue with the lawyers and clients preparing for each 'four-way' in advance. The two lawyers will also often have discussions in-between 'four-way' meetings to consider how best to manage the process so as to achieve an early resolution. When an agreement is reached, in due course, the lawyers can then turn it into a consent order in the usual way to be submitted to the court for approval and sealing.

13.5.5   Negotiating in the collaborative process

It is important for the negotiations to be interest based rather than position based, i.e. what would change for the better for the client if the client obtained what he or she is saying he or she must have.

13.5.6   Dealing with apparent impasse

It is inevitable that from time to time the collaborative lawyers and their respective clients will become 'stuck'. There are a number of ways to deal with these 'stuck' positions.

For instance, it can be helpful for the lawyers to be open as to their views on how a court might deal with the situation. If their views differ, this can only highlight the risk that the clients would take if they decide to litigate, as different judges will probably also have differing views, and in light of this compromises may be made. The costs of litigation (financial and personal) can be estimated and very often this will help to promote settlement.

Alternatively, the collaborative lawyers could bring in a mediator on a civil and commercial model basis, i.e. with the mediator caucusing between each collaborative lawyer and their respective client. Sometimes, a fresh approach is needed and an impartial mediator could be exactly the external influence needed to assist. (Conversely, the same applies when a mediation has become 'stuck'. The mediator could, and typically will, refer the couple to collaborative lawyers if they do not have lawyers already, to allow them to deal with the outstanding issues within the collaborative process.) Further alternatively, the collaborative lawyers and their clients could agree to seek an opinion from counsel on joint instructions to try to break the impasse.

13.5.7 Costs

The collaborative process is not a 'cheap' option although it is fair to say that the costs will not be as great as proceeding all the way to a final contested court hearing – assuming of course, everyone stays negotiating within the process.

The solicitors will charge their normal hourly rate and, clearly, each 'four-way' and preparation for it will be expensive. That said, if the process works and achieves a good outcome for the family as a whole, it will be money well spent. Also, the fact that the communication takes place mainly within the 'four-way' meetings, as opposed to communication within correspondence as in the traditional process, must mean that costs are minimised to an extent.

The Legal Services Commission has recently announced that public funding is to be available for collaborative matters, which is good news and follows Northern Ireland where a scheme has been up and running for some time.

13.5.8 Training and IACP

Resolution organises collaborative training, consisting of a two-day course with an additional two-day skills course for those collaborative practitioners who are not trained and practising mediators. The skills involved in both processes are similar and it is critical that the training covers both aspects.

Currently only members of Resolution with three years' post-qualification experience of family law can undertake the Resolution mediation and collaborative practice training. To be a mediator, the applicant needs to be a solicitor, a barrister, a Filex/Ilex or an experienced paralegal with five years' post-qualification experience. To be a collaborative practitioner, the applicant needs to be a solicitor, a barrister or a Filex/Ilex. Resolution has also set up some bespoke training for members of the Bar which is proving to be popular. Members of the Bar consider that it will be helpful for them to come in as another member of the team to help 'unstick' difficult matters.

The International Academy of Collaborative Professionals (IACP) is a very useful body and trained collaborative practitioners can apply to be members. IACP holds annual conferences with a huge variety of workshops which attract collaborative practitioners from around the world. IACP also produces a regular newsletter which contains helpful information and details of articles to assist practitioners.

13.6 COLLABORATIVE PRACTICE, MEDIATION AND THE TRADITIONAL PROCESS

The collaborative practice, mediation and the traditional process are all options and as stated above not all of them will be suitable for all clients. Mediation will work well for couples who do not consider that there are any power imbalances between them, and who are content to explore options without their lawyers at their side but with the knowledge that they can consult their solicitors in-between mediation meetings (although as explained above, in the mediation section, mediation can take place with lawyers present).

Where it is successful, mediation is also the cheaper option. However, even where all issues are not resolved, they are often very much narrowed, therefore containing the legal costs.

Mediation will also work alongside the traditional process where perhaps court proceedings have been issued as a backstop position but where the clients wish to reach an agreement outside the court process and before expensive brief fees and other significant costs are incurred. It is important to remember also that mediation can be entered into at any stage and not only at the outset of a case.

Collaborative practice, however, will probably be better suited to the clients who want to have the lawyers at their side but who wish to resolve matters outside the court process. The 'playing field' is levelled in the collaborative process by the direct participation of the lawyers. It is the job also of the lawyers to work with their own clients if they are being unreasonable, to make sure that the process stays positive and productive.

It is fair to say, however, that where there is little trust between the clients, particularly as far as financial aspects are concerned, neither mediation nor the collaborative process is likely to be appropriate.

For some clients, litigation or at least the traditional route to FDR appointment might be the only way forward, particularly where there is potentially new law to be made. It may also be the only way forward when it is difficult for meetings to be scheduled where, for instance, one or both clients work abroad a lot of the time.

For many couples, however, mediation or the collaborative process offers a better way forward than the traditional process, as it will allow them to consider all the issues relevant to their particular family as opposed to having a decision imposed upon them which cannot possibly take into account all the dynamics of the family. Mediation and the collaborative process will also be cheaper than litigation to a final hearing and again, this can only benefit the family as a whole, particularly when family finances are stretched, as they often are.

13.7   THE FUTURE OF ADR

With the increasing number of early intervention court schemes, the re-launch of the Court of Appeal Family Mediation scheme and the launch of a dedicated family mediation helpline, it is clear that the government and the judiciary increasingly see ADR as being helpful to clients and as such, it is becoming more widely encouraged.

The Court of Appeal Family Mediation scheme has been particularly successful, as can be seen from the relatively recent case of *Al-Khatib* v. *Masry* [2005] 1 FLR 381, which involved child abduction and ancillary relief. There was a long and troubled litigation history over four years in this case and although the court cannot force wholly unwilling parties to mediate, it can strongly encourage, it as it did in this case. In this particular case, the court retained an active role in the process in helping to make the practical arrangements for the mediation which involved the parties and their legal advisers as well as the children who were separately represented by their own solicitor. The matter settled and a consent order was presented to the Court of Appeal.

This case is particularly relevant as it shows that even where a dispute appears totally intractable, mediation can sometimes prove to be successful, and many more cases have also settled through the Court of Appeal Family Mediation scheme. As a result, and particularly when mediation and ADR are so common in civil and commercial matters, it is to be expected that we will see more judicial encouragement of ADR in family proceedings. Indeed, the courts are making more information available to court users about options open to them and it is to be hoped that ADR will be seen as more mainstream and 'normal' rather than 'alternative'.

The ideal would be to achieve that which is the system in Australia where, save in exceptional circumstances, court applications cannot proceed until such time as the various issues have been aired in mediation or some other alternative process and that process has failed/broken down.

13.8 CONCLUSION

Mediation and collaborative practice are by no means suitable for everyone, but they can work well for a large number of couples. It is increasingly important therefore for family lawyers to be aware of and train in these processes so as to be able to offer clients a range of options and a well-rounded service. Even where the processes are not used, the skills taught through the training stay with the practitioner and can be used in traditional practice, adding an extra special quality to the lawyer's practice and the service provided to clients and their families.

APPENDIX 1

Code of Practice for Resolution members

Membership of Resolution commits family lawyers to resolving disputes in a non-confrontational way.

We believe that family law disputes should be dealt with in a constructive way designed to preserve people's dignity and to encourage agreements.

Members of Resolution **are required to:**

- Conduct matters in a constructive and non-confrontational way
- Avoid use of inflammatory language both written and spoken
- Retain professional objectivity and respect for everyone involved
- Take into account the long term consequences of actions and communications as well as the short term implications
- Encourage clients to put the best interests of the children first
- Emphasise to clients the importance of being open and honest in all dealings
- Make clients aware of the benefits of behaving in a civilised way
- Keep financial and children issues separate
- Ensure that consideration is given to balancing the benefits of any steps against the likely costs – financial or emotional
- Inform clients of the options e.g. counselling, family therapy, round table negotiations, mediation, collaborative law and court proceedings
- Abide by the Resolution Guides to Good Practice

This Code should be read in conjunction with the Law Society's Family Law Protocol. All solicitors are subject to the Solicitors Practice Rules

Useful contacts

RESOLUTION

Resolution
PO Box 302
Orpington
Kent BR6 8QX
Tel: 01689 820272
Fax: 01689 896972
Press Office: 020 7357 9215
Email: info@resolution.org.uk
www.resolution.org.uk

Care Law
www.carelaw.org.uk (guide for young people)

ADVICE

Advicenow
Advice Services Alliance
63 St Mary Axe
London, EC3A 8AA
United Kingdom
www.advicenow.org.uk (information on rights and legal issues)

Advisory Centre for Education
Tel: 0808 800 5793 (advice line Mon to Fri 10am–5pm)
Tel: 020 7704 9822 (24-hour exclusion information line)
www.ace-ed.org.uk

Bullying UK
702 Windsor House
Cornwall Road
Harrogate
HG1 2PW
Email: help@bullying.co.uk
www.bullying.co.uk

Children's Legal Centre
Tel: 01206 877910
Tel: 0845 345 4345 (education law advice line)
Email: clc@essex.ac.uk
www.childrenslegalcentre.com

Family Rights Group
Tel: 0808 801 0366 (confidential advice and support for families whose children are involved with social services Mon to Fri 10am–3.30pm)
Email: advice@frg.org.uk
www.frg.org.uk

Grandparents' Association (formerly Grandparents' Federation)
Tel: 01279 428040 (office)
Helpline: 0845 434 9585 (information for grandparents, families and professionals on contact and residence issues)
Email: info@grandparents-association.org.uk
www.grandparents-association.org.uk

National Association of Citizens Advice Bureaux
www.citizensadvice.org.uk (nearest CAB)
www.adviceguide.org.uk (CAB information online)

National Youth Advocacy Service (NYAS)
Tel: 0151 649 8700 (general)
Young person's helpline: 0800 616101 (Mon to Fri 8am–8pm, Sat 10am–4pm)
Email: help@nyas.net
Legal advice: 0151 649 8700
Email:legal@nyas.net
www.nyas.net

Relate
Relationship Counselling
Tel: 0300 100 1234
Email: relateonline@relate.org.uk
www.relate.org.uk

Shelter
Tel: 0844 515 2000
Helpline: 0808 800 4444 (housing advice)
Email: info@shelter.org.uk
www.shelter.org.uk

ADOPTION AND FOSTERING

Adoption UK (support group)
Linden House
55 The Green, South Bar Street
Banbury
Oxon OX16 9AB
Tel: 01295 752240
Helpline: 0844 848 7900
Email: helpdesk@adoptionuk.org.uk
www.adoptionuk.org.uk

*British Agencies for Adoption and
Fostering (BAAF)*
Saffron House
6–10 Kirby Street
London EC1N 8TS
Tel: 020 7421 2600
Email: mail@baaf.org.uk
www.baaf.org.uk

The Fostering Network
87 Blackfriars Road
London SE1 8HA
Tel: 020 7620 6400 (London office)
Tel: 029 2044 0940 (Wales office)
Email: info@fostering.net
www.fostering.net

General Register Office
Information on registering adoptions.
http://www.gro.gov.uk/gro/content

Adults Affected by Adoption– NORCAP
112 Church Road
Wheatley
Oxford OX33 1LU
Tel: 01865 875000
Email: enquiries@norcap.org
www.norcap.org.uk

The Post Adoption Centre
5 Torriano Mews
Torriano Avenue
London NW5 2RZ
Tel: 020 7284 0555
Advice line: 020 7284 5879 (Mon–Fri,
10am–1pm)
Email: advice@postadoptioncentre.org.uk
www.postadoptioncentre.org.uk

ASYLUM AND IMMIGRATION

Asylum Aid
Tel: 020 7354 9264 (advice)
Email: info@asylumaid.org.uk
www.asylumaid.org.uk

Asylum and Immigration Tribunal
Tel: 0845 6000 877
Minicom: 0845 6060 766
Email: Customer.Service@tribunals.gsi.
gov.uk
www.ait.gov.uk

Immigration Advisory Service
3rd Floor, County House
190 Great Dover Street
London SE1 4YB
Tel: 0844 974 4000
Fax: 020 7378 0665
www.iasuk.org

Immigration and Nationality Directorate
www.ind.homeoffice.gov.uk

Joint Council for the Welfare of Immigrants
Tel: 020 7251 8708
Fax: 020 7251 8707
Email: info@jcwi.org.uk
www.jcwi.org.uk

Refugee Council
Tel: 020 7346 6700
www.refugeecouncil.org.uk

AUDITING AND PUBLIC FUNDING

Partnership Quality Systems
78 Murray Avenue
Bromley
Kent BR1 3DL
Tel: 020 8466 6677

Email: Vicky@pqsonline.co.uk
www.pqsonline.co.uk

COMMISSIONERS AND OMBUDSMAN

Care Quality Commission
Tel: 03000 616161
Email: enquiries@cqc.org.uk

*Children's Commissioner for England
(Sir Al Aynsley-Green)*
Tel: 0844 800 9113
Email: info.request@11million.org.uk
www.11million.org.uk

*Children's Commissioner for Wales
(Peter Clarke)*
Tel: 01792 765600
Email: post@childcomwales.org.uk
www.childcomwales.org.uk

*Children's Rights Director (CSCI)
(Dr Roger Morgan OBE)*
Tel: 0800 528 0731
www.rights4me.org.uk

Equality and Human Rights Commission
Tel: 0845 604 6610 (England)
Tel: 0845 604 8810 (Wales)
Email: info@equalityhumanrights.com
www.equalityhumanrights.com

*Parliamentary and Health Service
Ombudsman*
Tel: 0345 015 4033
Email: phso.enquiries@ombudsman.org.uk
www.ombudsman.org.uk

DOMESTIC VIOLENCE AND VICTIM SUPPORT

Rape Crisis England and Wales
Email: info@rapecrisis.org.uk
www.rapecrisis.org.uk

Refuge
Tel: 0808 200 0247 (24-hour helpline, run in partnership between Women's Aid and Refuge)
www.refuge.org.uk

Rights of Women
Advice line: 020 7251 6577 (Tues to Thurs 2–4pm and 7–9 pm, Fri 12–2pm)
Sexual violence legal advice line: 020 7251 8887 (Mon 11am–1pm, Tues 10am–12pm)
www.rightsofwomen.org.uk

Samaritans
Tel: 0845 790 9090
Email: jo@samaritans.org
www.samaritans.org

Victim Support National Office
Victim Support helpline: 0845 303 0900
Email: supportline@victimsupport.org.uk
www.victimsupport.org.uk

Welsh Women's Aid
Tel: 0808 801 0800 (domestic abuse helpline)
www.welshwomensaid.org

Women's Aid Federation of England
Head Office
PO Box 391
Bristol BS99 7WS
Tel: 0117 944 4411 (office)
Helpline: 0808 200 0247
Email: helpline@womensaid.org.uk
www.womensaid.org.uk

Worst Kept Secret
Tel: 0800 028 3398 (Merseyside domestic violence confidential helpline)
www.worstkeptsecret.co.uk

EMERGENCY POWERS

Family Division Lawyer
President's Chambers, Royal Courts of Justice
Strand
London WC2A 2LL
Tel: 020 7947 7965
Fax: 020 7947 7274

Police National Ports Office: Heathrow Airport
Tel: 020 7230 4800 (24-hour advice line)

FAMILIES AND CHILDREN

Childline
Tel: 0800 1111 (helpline for children and young people)
www.childline.org.uk

Gingerbread
Tel: 020 7428 5400
Helpline for single parents: 0808 802
0925 (Mon to Fri 9am–5pm; Weds
9am–8pm)
Email: info@gingerbread.org.uk
www.gingerbread.org.uk

*National Association of Child Contact
Centres*
Minerva House, Spaniel Row
Nottingham NG1 6EP
Tel: 0845 450 0280
Email: contact@naccc.org.uk
www.naccc.org.uk

National Council for One Parent Families
255 Kentish Town Road
London NW5 2LX
Tel: 020 7428 5400
Helpline: 0800 018 5026
Email: info@oneparentfamilies.org.uk
www.ncopf.org.uk

National Family and Parenting Institute
430 Highgate Studios
53–79 Highgate Road
London NW5 1TL
Tel: 020 7424 3460
Email: info@familyandparenting.org
www.familyandparenting.org/

*National Society for the Prevention of
Cruelty to Children (NSPCC)*
Helpline for adults: 0808 800 5000
Helpline for children: 0800 1111
Textphone: 0800 056 0566 (English only)
Email: help@nspcc.org.uk
www.nspcc.org.uk

Parentline Plus
Tel: 020 7284 5500
Helpline: 0808 800 2222
www.parentlineplus.org.uk

*Reunite International Child Abduction
Centre*
Tel: +44 (0) 116 2555 345
Advice Line: +44(0) 166 2556 234
Email: reunite@dircon.co.uk
www.reunite.org

GOVERNMENT DEPARTMENTS

*Department for Children, Schools and
Families*
www.dcsf.gov.uk
www.dfes.gov.uk/youngpeople/

Department of Health
www.dh.gov.uk

Ministry of Justice
www.justice.gov.uk

National Assembly for Wales
www.wales.gov.uk

LAW SOCIETY OF ENGLAND AND WALES

113 Chancery Lane
London WC2A 1PL
Tel: 020 7242 1222
DX 56 London/Chancery Lane
www.lawsociety.org.uk

Children Panel
Tel: 0870 606 2555
Email: accreditation@lawsociety.org.uk
www.panels.lawsociety.org.uk

Family Law Panel
Tel: 0870 606 2555
Email: accreditation@lawsociety.org.uk
www.panels.lawsociety.org.uk

Professional Ethics
Tel: 0870 606 2577
Email: professional.ethics@sra.org.uk
www.sra.org.uk

LEGAL

*Association of Child Abuse Lawyers
(ACAL)*
Tel: 0208 390 4701 (Tues–Thur
10am–1pm, 2pm–4pm)
Email: info@childabuselawyers.com
www.childabuselawyers.com

*Association of Lawyers for Children
(ALC)*
Tel: 020 8224 7071
Email: admin@alc.org.uk www.alc.org.uk

261

Children and Family Court Advisory
Service (CAFCASS)
Tel: 0844 353 3350
Email: webenquiries@cafcass.gov.uk
www.cafcass.gov.uk

Community Legal Service Direct
www.clsdirect.org.uk
Tel: 0845 345 4345 (referrals to local
specialist legal adviser/solicitor)

Crown Prosecution Service
www.cps.gov.uk

Education Law Association
Tel: 0118 966 9866
Email: secretary@educationlaw
association.org.uk
www.educationlawassociation.org.uk

Family Law Bar Association
Tel: 020 7242 1289
Fax: 020 7831 7144
www.flba.co.uk

Legal Aid Practitioners Group
Tel: 020 7183 2269
www.lapg.co.uk

Legal Services Commission
Legal helpline: 0845 345 4345
www.communitylegaladvice.org.uk

Liberty (formerly National Council for
Civil Liberties)
21 Tabard Street
London SE1 4LA
Tel: 020 7403 3888
Public advice line: 0845 123 2307
(Mon and Thurs 6.30–8.30pm, Wed
12.30–2.30pm)
Email: info@liberty-human-rights.org.uk
www.liberty-human-rights.org.uk

National Association of Guardians
ad Litem and Reporting Officers
(NAGALRO)
Tel: 01372 818504
Email: nagalro@globalnet.co.uk
www.nagalro.com

Office of the Official Solicitor
Tel: 020 7911 7127
Email: enquiries@offsol.gsi.gov.uk
www.officialsolicitor.gov.uk

MARRIAGE AND DIVORCE

Family Mediator's Association
Grove House, Grove Road
Redland
Bristol BS6 6UN
Tel: 0117 946 7062/0808 200 0033
www.thefma.co.uk

Forced Marriage
Tel: 0207 008 0151 / 0207 008 0230
(9am–5pm)
0207 008 0135 / 0207 270 1500 (out of
hours only)
Email: clu@fco.org.uk
www.forcedmarriage.nhs.uk/localsup-
port.asp
www.fco.gov.uk

Jewish Divorce
www.gettingyourget.co.uk

POLICY AND SERVICES

Barnardo's
www.barnardos.org.uk

Children in Wales
Tel: 029 2034 2434
Email: info@childreninwales.org.uk
www.childreninwales.org.uk

Joseph Rowntree Foundation
Tel: (0)1904 629241
Email: info@jrf.org.uk
www.jrf.org.uk

National Association for the Care and
Resettlement of Offenders (NACRO)
Tel: 020 7840 7200
Resettlement Helpline: 020 7840 6464
Email: helpline@nacro.org.uk
www.nacro.org.uk

National Children's Bureau
Tel: 020 7843 6000
Email: enquiries@ncb.org.uk

www.ncb.org.uk
www.childpolicy.org.uk (information on policy and legislation)

National Society for the Prevention of Cruelty to Children (NSPCC)
Helpline: 0808 800 5000
Email: help@ nspcc.org.uk
www.nspcc.org.uk

Voice for the Child in Care (VCC)
Tel: 020 7833 5792
Young person's freefone: 0808 800 5792
Email: info@voiceyp.org
www.voiceyp.org

Who Cares Trust
Tel: 020 7251 3117
Email: mailbox@thewhocarestrust.org.uk
www.thewhocarestrust.org.uk

REFERENCE

The Stationery Office
Tel: 0870 600 5522
www.tso.co.uk

British and Irish Legal Information Institute (BAILII)
www.bailii.org

Casetrack (transcripts of judgments)
www.casetrack.com

European Court of Human Rights portal (HUDOC)
www.echr.coe.int/echr

Family Law Journal
www.familylaw.co.uk

House of Lords judgments
www.publications.parliament.uk/pa/ld/ldjudgmt.htm

HM Courts Service
www.hmcourts-service.gov.uk

Lawtel
www.lawtel.co.uk

Legislation
www.opsi.gov.uk

Index